D-DAY
NEW GUINEA

ALSO BY PHILLIP BRADLEY

On Shaggy Ridge
The Battle for Wau
To Salamaua
Wau 1942–43
Hell's Battlefield
Charles Bean's Gallipoli Illustrated
Australian Light Horse

PHILLIP BRADLEY

D-DAY
NEW GUINEA

The extraordinary story of the battle for Lae
and the greatest combined airborne and
amphibious operation of the Pacific War

ALLEN&UNWIN
SYDNEY・MELBOURNE・AUCKLAND・LONDON

First published in 2019

Copyright © Phillip Bradley 2019

All rights reserved. No part of this book may be reproduced or transmitted in any form or by any means, electronic or mechanical, including photocopying, recording or by any information storage and retrieval system, without prior permission in writing from the publisher. The Australian *Copyright Act 1968* (the Act) allows a maximum of one chapter or 10 per cent of this book, whichever is the greater, to be photocopied by any educational institution for its educational purposes provided that the educational institution (or body that administers it) has given a remuneration notice to the Copyright Agency (Australia) under the Act.

Allen & Unwin
83 Alexander Street
Crows Nest NSW 2065
Australia
Phone: (61 2) 8425 0100
Email: info@allenandunwin.com
Web: www.allenandunwin.com

A catalogue record for this book is available from the National Library of Australia

ISBN 978 1 76063 258 8

Maps by Keith Mitchell, unless otherwise attributed
Set in 12.75/17.5 pt Adobe Garamond Pro by Midland Typesetters, Australia
Printed and bound in Australia by Griffin Press

10 9 8 7 6 5 4 3

The paper in this book is FSC® certified. FSC® promotes environmentally responsible, socially beneficial and economically viable management of the world's forests.

Dedicated to NX101723 John Aloysius Bradley

CONTENTS

List of maps and sketches ix
Abbreviations x
Prologue xiii

Chapter 1   The observation game   1
Chapter 2   'Such a dangerous looking mob'   19
Chapter 3   'We will die fighting'   35
Chapter 4   Mountains to climb   54
Chapter 5   The secret airbase   81
Chapter 6   MacArthur's navy   101
Chapter 7   Airborne infantry   123
Chapter 8   D-Day dawns   143
Chapter 9   'The wolf at the back gate'   165
Chapter 10 'A terrifying but magnificent spectacle' 187
Chapter 11 'Fix bayonets'   209
Chapter 12 'A precarious retreat'   229
Chapter 13 'Like beggars in a procession'   249
Chapter 14 Beyond Lae   271

Acknowledgements	281
Notes	283
Bibliography	307
Index	315

LIST OF MAPS AND SKETCHES

1. Papua and New Guinea, 1942–45 — xii
2. Lae–Salamaua area, 1942–43 — 3
3. West of Lae, 1942–43 — 13
4. Japanese supply lines to Lae and Salamaua, 1942–43 — 40
5. Japanese 51st Division dispositions, April 1943 — 47
6. Huon Peninsula–Ramu Valley area, 1942–43 — 55
7. Kitamoto and Ryan patrols across Saruwaged Range, 1943 — 63
8. Kitamoto patrol to Kaiapit, 26 May–13 June 1943 — 71
9. Lae area of operations, September 1943 — 145
10. Japanese air attack at Red Beach, 4 September 1943 — 151
11. Lae operations, September 1943 — 166
12. Markham Point, 4 September 1943 — 181
13. The road to Lae, September 1943 — 210
14. Whittaker's Plantation, 13 September 1943 — 213
15. Edwards' Plantation, 15 September 1943 — 220
16. Japanese evacuation route from Lae, September 1943 — 251
17. Sketch of the upper Yanam (Sanem) River valley — 258
18. Sketch of Japanese evacuation route, September–October 1943 — 263
19. Huon Peninsula–Ramu Valley operations, September 1943 — 274

ABBREVIATIONS

AAR	After Action Report
ABC	Australian Broadcasting Commission
AIF	Australian Imperial Force
AJRP	Australian Japanese Research Project
ANGAU	Australian New Guinea Administrative Unit
APD	auxiliary personnel destroyer
ATIS	Allied Translator and Interpreter Section
AWM	Australian War Memorial
Bde	Brigade
Bn	Battalion
Coy	Company
Div	Division
DUKW	amphibious wheeled vehicle
EBSR	Engineer Boat and Shore Regiment
EP	enemy publication
ESB	Engineer Special Brigade
GOC	General Officer Commanding
HQ	headquarters
Ind Coy	Independent Company
Intel	intelligence
IR	interrogation report

LCI	landing craft, infantry
LCM	landing craft, mechanised
LCT	landing craft, tank
LCVP	landing craft, vehicle personnel
LSD	landing ship, dock
LST	landing ship, tank
MG	machine gun
MLC	motorised landing craft
MLO	Military Landing Officer
mm	millimetre
MMLA	MacArthur Memorial Library and Archives
MSA	Murdoch Sound Archive
NAA	National Archives of Australia
NARA	National Archives and Records Administration
NGF	New Guinea Force
NGVR	New Guinea Volunteer Rifles
NLA	National Library of Australia
ONR	Office of Naval Records
OP	observation post
PIB	Papuan Infantry Battalion
PT boat	patrol torpedo boat
RAAF	Royal Australian Air Force
RAN	Royal Australian Navy
Regt	Regiment
Rfn	Rifleman
RPC	Royal Papuan Constabulary
SNLP	Special Naval Landing Party
Sqn	Squadron
SWPA	South West Pacific Area
US	United States
USAAF	United States Army Air Force
WD	War Diary

Map 1: Papua and New Guinea, 1942–45

PROLOGUE

The top of the mountain range loomed, a tenuous makeshift ladder ascending the sheer cliff to whatever lay beyond. 'Regardless of night or day' men climbed, forced forward by those jamming in behind. The men waiting to climb took turns to sit on the narrow one-man path, their legs dangling over the precipice, their backs to the wall of rock behind. As they had approached this final obstacle, these men had made every shuffling step in the hope that the track would hold. 'Using the dead bodies as stepping stones', shivering with cold in their tattered rags, the line of Japanese troops looked like 'beggars in a procession'. This was a ghost army, fighting for its very existence by crossing one of the most treacherous mountain routes in New Guinea in the wake of the defeat of their garrison at Lae.[1]

The Australian Army had already moved on from Lae after a stunning victory, striking east along the coast to Finschhafen and west into the Markham and Ramu valleys. However, many of the Australian troops at Finschhafen would never forget Lae and the raging river they had entered 'as though on parade until the current hit them' when the torrent determined their fate. Some of the men now in the Markham and Ramu valleys would forever carry another vision, that of a deadly fireball engulfing their loaded trucks at the end of a Port Moresby airfield as they waited for their flight to Lae. One young Australian warrant officer would look up at the imposing mountain range to the north that the Japanese now struggled to traverse and remember when fear had driven his feet across that range.

•

Operation Postern, the plan to capture Lae in September 1943, was one of the most complex undertaken by the Allied forces in the Pacific in the Second World War. It involved coordinated land, sea and air operations that included the amphibious landing of a division, a regimental parachute drop and the air landing of two infantry brigades. Yet it succeeded beyond all expectations, leading to the fall of the most important Japanese base on mainland New Guinea and turning the tide against the Japanese. The complexity of Operation Postern had much in common with Operation Overlord, the invasion of France on 6 June 1944. In a number of ways it was a blueprint for that later plan, incorporating an amphibious landing combined with an airborne assault, all carried out under the guise of a number of strategic diversions. For those troops who would make the D-Day landings east of Lae on 4 September 1943, it would be the first Australian amphibious landing on a hostile shore since that at Gallipoli on 25 April 1915. In that there hangs a tale, one that began when the New Guinea town of Lae was still in Australian hands as the battle for New Guinea unfolded in early 1942.

Chapter 1

THE OBSERVATION GAME

War came to Lae on 21 January 1942. The German settlement of Lae, assigned to Australian control with the rest of German New Guinea after the First World War, would now be a key objective in the Second World War. Just before midday Lloyd Pursehouse, a Coastwatcher at Finschhafen on the north-eastern coast of New Guinea, reported that about 60 enemy aircraft were flying west along the coast towards Lae. As the air raid siren rang out across Lae the Japanese fighters came in from the sea and strafed the township and adjoining airfield. A large formation of bombers followed, dropping their loads across the town, after which the fighters continued their strafing. The raid left the Guinea Airways hangars, workshops and stores as well as the power plant completely destroyed and many other buildings damaged. Before the war Lae airfield had been the supply hub for extensive gold mining operations and the valuable runway was deliberately left intact though five aircraft were destroyed. Fortunately Pursehouse's timely warning had prevented any casualties.[1]

One Junkers transport piloted by Bertie Heath managed to take off before the raid and reach Bulolo carrying a load of beer. He was initially waved off while obstructions were cleared from the airfield so that he could land. However, it was only a temporary reprieve for Heath as 'five Japanese Zeros arrived hedge hopping with the sound of angry bees'. The Zeros began flying back and forth, strafing the three Junkers transports on the airfield. The seven New Guinea Volunteer Rifles (NGVR) guards at the airfield soon depleted their few Lewis gun magazines to no effect and could only watch on as the three Junkers aircraft burned.[2]

Other raids hit Salamaua, on the coast 40 kilometres south of Lae, and Wau which was 50 kilometres inland from Salamaua (see Map 2). Lloyd Pursehouse and the airfield guards at Bulolo typified Australia's role in the opening months of the war in New Guinea. Given the almost total neglect of the responsibility for defending the islands to the north of Australia, the Australian government and people were reduced to the role of hapless observers as the Japanese moved south.

•

After the air attacks of 21 January a Japanese landing was considered imminent and it was decided that the government and civilian population should immediately be evacuated from Lae to a hidden position further inland. Under NGVR supervision, all available motor transport was assembled to move foodstuffs and other goods from the Burns Philp store and the airfield, and this work continued throughout the night. The stores were

The observation game

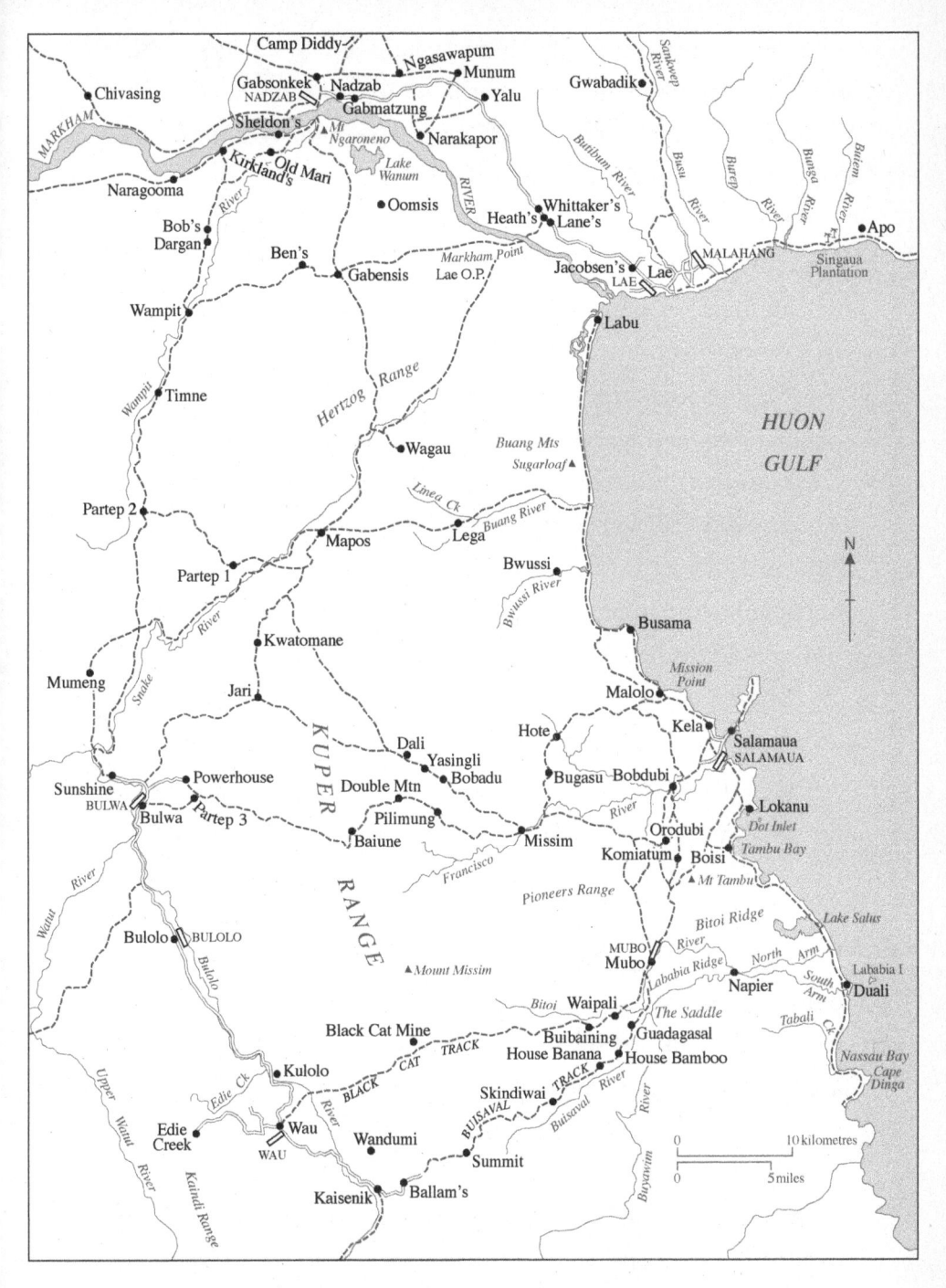

Map 2: Lae–Salamaua area, 1942–43

temporarily distributed along the Markham Road west of Lae in various houses and under tarpaulins in the bush. The work was hampered by heavy rain, which rendered the road practically impassable beyond 8 kilometres from Lae.[3]

At this stage the total strength of the NGVR and attached personnel in the Lae area was twelve officers and 327 other ranks under the command of Captain Hugh Lyon. On 27 January authority was granted to compulsorily call up all males of European origin between eighteen and 45 years of age for military service unless required for essential services. Within three days 87 new recruits were enrolled and fifteen men of Chinese and Malay origin were also enrolled for transport and medical duties. The men added 2000 to their enlistment numbers so the Japanese would later overestimate the unit's strength.[4]

Instructions had been received from Port Moresby to prepare Lae, Salamaua and Madang aerodromes for demolition and a former miner was sent to each centre to prepare the explosives. However, all aerodromes were to remain open until the evacuation of civilians was completed while Salamaua airfield was still required by the Royal Australian Air Force (RAAF) for operational purposes. Once the expected Japanese landing at Lae occurred, the intention was to hold a line from Gabensis to Wampit and to prevent the Japanese from entering the foothills behind Lae. If the Japanese entered the Markham Valley west of Lae, harassing tactics were to be adopted. On 2 February the NGVR detachment at Lae was instructed to transfer all stores to the south side of the Markham River near Nadzab at the earliest opportunity.[5]

Meanwhile the observation game continued. On 5 February the Lae detachment was instructed that the radio transmitter was not to leave the coastal area under any circumstances, as it was the only means to inform Port Moresby of an enemy landing. A section including three signallers was to proceed immediately with a radio transmitter to a point in the ranges south of Lae to establish an observation post overlooking the Huon Gulf from Lae to Salamaua. Sergeant Stan Burton was one of the NGVR signallers taken by boat from Lae to a point south of the Markham River below the Buang Ranges to set up the observation post on a prominent position known as Sugarloaf. The Amalgamated Wireless Australasia 3A radio was designed to be used from a static location and it took twelve men to move the radio, batteries, charger and fuel to the new site. From a lookout point in one of the trees on the coastal side of the mountain, both Lae and Salamaua could be easily observed and any information radioed back to Port Moresby.[6]

On 13 February the NGVR strength in the Lae and Buang areas was five officers and 89 other ranks, mainly equipped with rifles and grenades, but also with two Vickers machine guns, five Lewis light machine guns and eight Thompson sub-machine guns. In the Salamaua area there were four officers and 74 other ranks similarly equipped. Units in both areas were widely separated and communications were difficult. In the Wau, Bulolo and Bulwa areas there were another 230 NGVR troops although less than half were considered adequately trained and about 10 per cent were ill.[7]

•

Despite the expectation that the Japanese would follow up the capture of Rabaul with an immediate landing on mainland New Guinea, that was not their plan. The first concern for the Japanese command in Rabaul was to capture the airfield at Gasmata on the southern coast of New Britain. An invasion force and support group left Rabaul at dawn on 8 February under heavy rain cover and made an unopposed landing early on the following day at Gasmata. The airfield was long enough to service carrier-based fighters and the first Japanese aircraft landed there on 11 February. The airfield would have great value for future operations against mainland New Guinea.[8]

On 16 February the chief of staff of the Japanese South Seas Force, Lieutenant Colonel Toyonari Tanaka, travelled to the Japanese naval base at Truk to meet with the commander of the Fourth Fleet to finalise the invasion plans for Lae and Salamaua.[9] The Fourth Fleet would provide an invasion force with a strong naval escort and air cover. A special naval landing force battalion, the 8th Base Force of about 620 men, would be landed from five transport vessels at Lae while Major Masao Horie's 2/144th Infantry Battalion from the South Seas Force would make the Salamaua landing from two transports. The entire force would depart Rabaul three days before the landing date, tentatively scheduled for 3 March.[10] However, on 20 February a US aircraft carrier task force approximately 740 kilometres northeast of Rabaul launched aircraft against the Fourth Fleet, delaying the planned landing until 8 March.[11] Despite the presence of the US Navy, the wretched lack of Australian military preparation in New Guinea meant both Lae and Salamaua were there for the taking and the Japanese knew it.

The invasion force left Rabaul at 1300 on 5 March, and at 1255 on 6 March the convoy was spotted by Allied aircraft off the southern New Britain coast west of Gasmata heading towards mainland New Guinea. Early on the morning of 7 March the

The observation game

convoy, made up of one cruiser, four destroyers and six transports, was again sighted east of Lae but that night the naval and army components of the force divided, bound for Lae and Salamaua respectively. The army transport fleet encountered a violent storm when it entered the anchorage area to the east of Salamaua but the landing barges were lowered at 2300, with boarding completed by midnight. Major Horie's battalion landed unopposed at 0055 on 8 March and two hours later Salamaua airfield had been successfully occupied.[12]

On that morning of 8 March the men at the Sugarloaf observation post reported that four vessels were approaching Lae and five others were heading for Salamaua. Without access to codes, the message to Port Moresby had to be sent in clear English. 'We were disappointed to sit and watch their unloading of cargo etc. without them being attacked by our planes,' Stan Burton noted.[13] Marines of the 3rd Kure Special Naval Landing Force landed south of Lae at 0230 and occupied the airfield and township unopposed. Work on repairing Lae airfield commenced later that same morning, with preparations for its use as a fighter base completed by 1300 the following day, 9 March. Three RAAF Hudson bombers were sent to attack the Japanese landings but were only able to damage the destroyer *Asanagi*.

•

It would be left to the United States Navy to do more than just observe the relentless drive of the Japanese south towards Australian shores. Early on 10 March, aircraft from the two US aircraft carriers *Yorktown* and *Lexington* made more serious attacks against the Japanese anchorages at Lae and Salamaua.

Vice-Admiral Wilson Brown launched his attack from 70 kilometres off the southern Papuan coast, across the imposing cloud-shrouded Owen Stanley Range. This ensured the safety of the carriers from Rabaul-based strike aircraft but set a daunting task for the heavily laden aircraft to cross the mountains.[14] There were 104 aircraft in the strike force, 25 Devastator bombers, twelve of them carrying torpedos, 61 Douglas Dauntless dive bombers and eighteen Grumman Wildcat fighters. The fully laden aircraft struggled to cross the Owen Stanley Range but were helped by Commander William Ault, from the *Lexington*'s air group, who positioned his scout plane over the pass in the range to guide them through. Commander Jimmy Brett, the *Lexington* torpedo squadron chief and a former glider pilot, found an area clear of jungle and, circling above it, found a thermal updraft that gave him enough altitude to get through the pass. His squadron followed.[15]

At Lae the Dauntless bombers hit three ships, sinking the 8600-tonne armed merchant cruiser *Kongo Maru* and forcing the 5400-tonne converted minelayer *Tenyo Maru* aground off the end of Lae airfield. Seven other vessels were damaged. One Dauntless was shot down over the Huon Gulf, the only aircraft lost in the raid. The converted minesweeper *Tama Maru No. 2* was also sunk at Lae and the transport *Yokohama Maru* was sent to the depths off Salamaua.[16] Three other vessels, the *Yûnagi*, *Kôkai Maru* and *Kiyokawa Maru*, were significantly damaged. The Japanese lost 132 men killed and another 257 wounded during these air raids.[17]

A few days after the landing, Japanese aircraft circled the NGVR observation post at Sugarloaf, apparently now aware of its existence. The observers therefore decided to move the post some 5 kilometres further up the mountain to the west. This move came none too soon as Japanese troops reached the camp the next morning, destroying everything including the food supplies. The men then had to walk out to the west via a sago swamp before contacting some natives who led them out to Sunshine camp in the Bulolo Valley. On arrival, one of the men at the camp exclaimed 'Hey fellows! Have a look! Jesus Christ and some of his disciples have just walked in.'[18]

•

The first aircraft from the Japanese 4th Naval Air Corps landed at Lae on the afternoon of 10 March, too late to have any impact on the devastating American air attacks. About half the strength of this air corps had moved to Lae, tasked with patrolling the Coral Sea area and attacking Port Moresby. On 14 March, nine bombers attacked Port Moresby, while eight bombers escorted by twelve Zeros made their first attacks on Australian soil, targeting Horn Island. Although six bombs hit the Horn Island runway, none of the Hudson bombers based there were hit.[19]

The Royal Australian Air Force was also busy. On 21 March seventeen P-40 Kittyhawks of RAAF No. 75 Squadron landed at Port Moresby despite 'friendly' fire from Australian machine-gun posts. The following day Squadron Leader John Jackson led nine of the Kittyhawks in a surprise dawn attack on Lae, catching the Japanese aircraft lined up wingtip to wingtip along the runway.[20] Five Kittyhawks made two passes each over the airfield while four others provided top cover. Virtually the entire contingent of Japanese planes at Lae, nine Zeros and one bomber, were strafed on the ground and caught fire, while two other Zeros were shot down.[21] One of the Kittyhawks was downed by anti-aircraft fire, and the pilot, Flying Officer Bruce Anderson, was killed. Three

Zeros attacked the top cover, and one of the Kittyhawks, piloted by Flying Officer Wilbur Wackett, son of the Australian aviation pioneer Lawrence Wackett, was shot down over the Huon Gulf. Wackett managed to swim to shore near Busama on the coast between Lae and Salamaua and, with the aid of two selfless local guides, made it to the Bulolo Valley four days later. He then trekked to the south coast along the Bulldog Track, and ultimately made it back to his squadron. The Japanese riposte came on 23 March when nineteen bombers escorted by three Zeros attacked Port Moresby.[22]

More aircraft were moved to Lae in early April when most of the 45 fighters and six reconnaissance planes of the Tainan Air Group arrived. The 30 Japanese naval fighter pilots at Lae under the command of Captain Masahisa Saito were the cream of the crop, among them the 'Devil', Lieutenant Hiroyoshi Nishizawa, who would become the war's leading Japanese air ace.[23] Meanwhile the Kittyhawks of No. 75 Squadron kept up the attacks on Lae, destroying two and damaging eight Zeros and nine bombers on 4 April. Over the following days the Japanese hit back with attacks on Port Moresby but heavy losses caused the bombers at Lae to evacuate to Rabaul on 11 April. Commander Sadayoshi Yamada of the 25th Air Flotilla lamented that 'The number of serviceable aircraft for attacks on Port Moresby on 14 April did not exceed three fighters and three attack planes.' Meanwhile low-level United States Army Air Force (USAAF) bomber raids on Rabaul took a toll. On 9 April Rear Admiral Masao Kanazawa, commander of the 8th Base Force, wrote in his diary: 'Suffered a severe raid . . . Conspicuous signs of defeat in the air war.'[24]

On 10 April, as John Jackson carried out an early morning reconnaissance flight over Lae and Salamaua, the Japanese airmen

The observation game

were waiting for him. The Japanese maintenance crews at Lae had begun preparing the Zeros at 0230, and by 0330 the pilots were awake. Following a sparse breakfast, six pilots waited by the warmed-up planes, ready to scramble.[25] When Jackson's aircraft was spotted, three Zeros were scrambled, forcing him to jettison his extra fuel tank and try to use his speed to get away. He soon realised he would not be able to outrun the Zeros, but when he turned to fight he found his guns had been hit and would not work. Outnumbered and defenceless, Jackson's plane was soon riddled with gunfire and he had no alternative but to ditch the plane into the sea, about 1 kilometre from shore. The Kittyhawk quickly sunk and, with the three Zeros circling, Jackson lay in the water, feigning death. Like Wilbur Wackett he was fortunate enough to be helped by local natives who alerted NGVR troops at Wau, from where he was flown back to Port Moresby on 23 April.

•

By 1 April the NGVR troops at Lae had moved to the comparative safety of the south side of the Markham River. Supply dumps and staging posts had been established at Sunshine, Mumeng and Partep leading from the Bulolo Valley down to the Markham River. These posts enabled the NGVR to maintain a detachment at Gabensis and an observation post at Sheldon's camp opposite Nadzab. The Partep post had the secondary advantage of being on a dominant hill position from which any Japanese move across the river and up the Bulolo Valley could be countered. A native swam the Markham River and reported that the obstacles that had been placed on Nadzab airfield were still in place and Gabsonkek village was unoccupied.[26]

Rifleman George Wharton made a canoe trip down to the mouth of the Markham to confirm the Japanese had not crossed the river to Labu. He also observed smoke which indicated that a line of Japanese outposts had been set up at Jacobsen's and Emery's plantations about 3 kilometres out along the road from Lae. Native scouts also told Wharton that Malahang airfield, on the eastern outskirts of Lae, was not being used and that three barracks buildings had been constructed in Lae. In late April Wharton found an ideal observation point above Labu village which provided an excellent view over Lae, Salamaua and the Huon Gulf. All aircraft take-offs and landings from Lae could be clearly seen, though the airfield itself was blocked by tree growth.[27]

Major Bill Edwards, who had worked as a doctor with Guinea Airways before the war, was the NGVR area commander at Lae. On 9 April he crossed the Markham and set up his headquarters at Nadzab before moving to the edge of the valley flats on the track to Boana. This new camp, some 18 kilometres north-west of Lae, was code-named Diddy (see Map 3) and had a milking cow, cattle and sheep as well as stoves for baking bread.[28] Stan Burton moved to Diddy camp as a radio operator, passing on information about the Japanese base at Lae.[29] That information would come from small patrols to observation posts set up around the outskirts of Lae. Lieutenant Phil Tuckey and six men established such a post on a ridge overlooking Heath's Plantation, approximately 10 kilometres west of Lae on the Markham Road.[30] The Japanese had established a small outpost there.

The most important observations involved the movements of Japanese aircraft at Lae. Following the earlier Allied air attacks on Lae the Japanese now started up their fighters before dawn and maintained a constant watch all day with at least two fighters at

The observation game

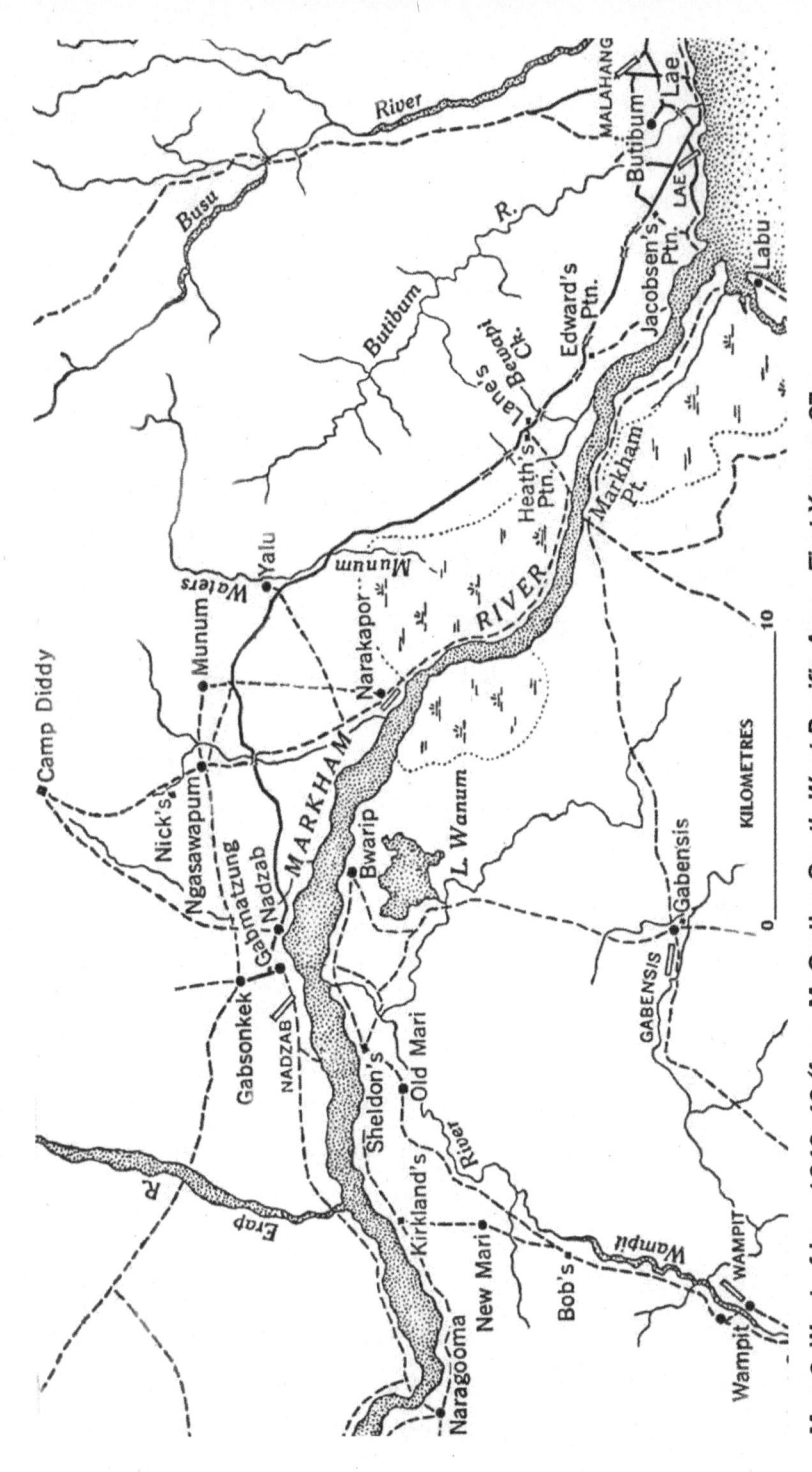

Map 3: West of Lae, 1942–43 (from McCarthy, *South-West Pacific Area—First Year*, p. 87, Copyright Australian War Memorial)

high altitude patrolling a radius of some 8 kilometres out from the airfield. Lieutenant Bob Phillips and two other men boldly scouted right up to Lae airfield where they observed the exact location and identification numbers of 27 fighters and four large two-engine bombers, a number of which had been camouflaged with foliage. There were 100 men working on the airfield and their arrival and departure times for the workday were also noted. Buildings, storage tanks and bomb dumps were also spotted along with a bulldozer and five large trucks, one doubling as a petrol tanker. Meanwhile local natives provided information on the location of anti-aircraft guns at Lae airfield, Jacobsen's Plantation, Mount Lunamun and the Busu River.[31] Back in Port Moresby, the commander of New Guinea Force, Major General Basil Morris, expressed his delight with the valuable intelligence from Bob Phillips' patrol.

•

On 12 April Lieutenant Roy Howard from the 1st Independent Company had arrived at Bulwa after travelling overland from the head of the Lakekamu River on the south coast to Wau via the daunting Bulldog Track. Howard brought a platoon of some 50 men with him. On 19 April it was suggested that no action be taken against the enemy in the Salamaua area until the forces in the Lae area were ready to undertake a similar action, thus ensuring surprise.

Sergeant Bob Emery had been in Lae since 1934, first working at Carl Jacobsen's plantation and then taking up his own allotment between Jacobsen's and the Butibum River. By 1941 he was running the local dairy, using cattle he had brought

The observation game

up from Australia. A number of Lae men had joined the AIF (Australian Imperial Force) and went off to fight, but Emery was loath to abandon his farm so had joined the local NGVR militia. As war came closer, Major Edwards asked Emery if he would go to Madang with two other soldiers, Dick Vernon and Peter Monfries, and a dozen native policemen to help guard the airfield there.[32] Emery was still at Madang when the Japanese captured Lae but was soon ordered back, arriving at Diddy camp around 1 May.

The NGVR troops at Diddy camp were brazenly using a truck by day to bring supplies from Nadzab to Ngasawapum from where the cargo could be carried up to Diddy camp by native carrier. However, it did not take long for one of the Zeros circling high over Lae to spot something and the Japanese soon responded in force.[33] On 1 May a strong enemy patrol moved up from Lae to Yalu where it was delayed by the brave native man Alisipi, who had also sent other men to warn the NGVR posts at Munum and Ngasawapum of the patrol. A telephone at Ngasawapum was used to warn Diddy camp and at 1030 another call from Corporal Frank Purcell at the observation post near Munum village reported 300 enemy troops moving up the road from Yalu. Half an hour later he was back on the line to report that the Japanese patrol was now only 200 metres away. 'I'm off, they're here,' he said and hung up.[34] As he finished his report two shots were fired at Purcell but he managed to get away.

In the late afternoon the supply truck was returning to Diddy camp from Nadzab with a load of supplies. As the truck reached the Ngasawapum turnoff the driver could see a native up ahead waving his cloth wrap in obvious warning. It was a brave thing to do as Japanese troops were lying in ambush in the dense head-high kunai grass between him and the truck. The truck was hastily abandoned as the occupants went bush. The Japanese removed the stores from the truck and burned them before some got aboard, turned the truck around and headed back towards Nadzab.[35]

Further along the road, 4 kilometres east of Nadzab, a party of four men were also making their way towards Diddy camp. Unaware that the truck had been captured, the two leading men, Signaller Len McBarron and Sergeant Robert Mayne, let it drive up to them. They were captured and never seen again. Riflemen John Rouse and George Cochrane were further back but when they came around a corner on the Markham Road they were confronted by a Japanese soldier. Rouse fired his rifle and the two got away into the scrub.[36]

Back at Diddy camp, after receiving the warning from Frank Purcell at Munum, Captain Lyon told Bob Emery, 'Now, I want you to take a small party down to Ngasawapum and see what they're up to.' Emery got halfway to Ngasawapum when he saw a native policeman approach along the track. 'The Japs, big Japanese patrol just captured the truck,' he told Emery. Emery and Bill Murtagh continued down to the road and, as night fell, followed the path of the captured truck until they found it bogged up to its axles and abandoned. 'It's like going to a football match,' Emery observed, 'and then they all go home.'[37]

Meanwhile, on the day before the truck incident, a strong patrol had left Diddy camp for Lae. It was led by Captain Roy Howard, accompanied by Lieutenants Colin Anthony and Bob Phillips with fourteen native carriers and a native policeman. The patrol reached Munum at midday and then spent the first night at Tuckey's camp which was located past Yalu village. On reaching Lae the men set up an observation post about 2 kilometres from Lae airfield. Early

The observation game

on the morning of 3 May the observers watched as two flights, each of seven bombers, passed over Lae heading south escorted by thirteen fighters from Lae. Soon thereafter the patrol was fired on by a stronger Japanese patrol which was only some 75 metres away. Five men, including Howard and Phillips, managed to flee into thick scrub, though they had to abandon their equipment.[38] The men had been surprised in a tent on the outskirts of Jacobsen's Plantation while drying their clothes in the sun and they turned up at Diddy camp the next day, 'bare-footed and in their pyjamas'.[39]

On 21 May Bob Emery, his younger brother John, Lieutenant Keith Noblett, Frank Anderson, John Clark and James Savage went back to the observation post above Whittaker's Plantation, on the high ground across the road from Heath's.[40] 'When we did get there everything was exactly as it had been left,' Bob Emery later said. The lookout was up a hill behind the camp and from there one could look directly down onto the house at Heath's Plantation where the Japanese had an outpost and field gun.[41] At dawn the next day, John Emery took Anderson up to the post, but soon after heading back he heard a rifle shot so returned to investigate. As he got close he could hear Japanese chatter so he once again headed back down to the camp. 'The Japs are up there and they've got Frank Anderson and they're coming over the hill now,' he told his brother. Bob Emery headed up the hill to look for Anderson but soon realised the Japanese were indeed on the way down using a spotlight to light the way. Emery got down on the ground and shot the leading enemy soldier at 50 metres. 'This poor old Jap folded up, and another bloke stepped over him,' Emery said. But by firing in the dark, Emery had betrayed his position and he soon attracted considerable fire. 'God, spare me days,' he thought, 'the whole bloody army's shooting at me,' and he headed off. There was more shooting, some shelling from the field gun at Heath's and some aircraft circled overhead but the NGVR patrol managed to get out. Frank Anderson was likely ambushed and shot dead by that first rifle shot and his body was never found.[42]

With the Japanese now awake to the Australian presence and Japanese air patrols now keeping a close eye on the river and the area around Diddy camp, Captain Lyon pulled most of his men back across to the south bank of the Markham.[43]

•

With the observation posts on the outskirts of Lae now compromised, an alternative site was set up in the ranges south of the Markham River, about 150 metres above Markham Point. Known as the Tojo observation post, any movement on Lae airfield could be observed through a powerful telescope. As Stan Burton noted, it was not so difficult to find good observation posts but the concern was ensuring that the smoke the generator produced when charging the radio batteries was not apparent from the air.[44] Tojo was staffed by two RAAF signallers who radioed details of any air movements to Port Moresby. However, as Bernie 'Buster' Mills observed, 'the results of our bombing did little to prevent the Zeros taking off as they only needed a short runway'.[45]

Lae had been garrisoned since March by the 82nd Naval Garrison and since 2 April the 2nd Maizuru Special Naval Landing Party had augmented the garrison.[46] By 21 May it was estimated that there were 600 to 800 Japanese personnel in Lae with another 150 to 200 at Salamaua. It seemed clear that the Japanese would soon contest the NGVR presence in the Lae area but Australian reinforcements were also on the way.

Chapter 2

'SUCH A DANGEROUS LOOKING MOB'

Following his dramatic escape from the Philippines and arrival in Australia on 17 March 1942, General Douglas MacArthur had been appointed the Supreme Commander of Allied Forces in the South West Pacific Area on 18 April 1942. When the official historian Gavin Long met the famous general in June 1944 he wrote of him, 'This is a man of mind and feeling rather than a man of iron,' who was 'convinced that he was born to command'.[1] In May 1942, just two months after the fall of Lae and Salamaua, General MacArthur urged General Thomas Blamey, the Allied ground forces commander, to raid or even retake the two towns. The latter option was unrealistic at this stage but reality was not MacArthur's strong suit in mid-1942.

With the threat to Port Moresby eased following the turning back of the Japanese invasion force at the Battle of the Coral Sea,

Major Paul Kneen's 2/5th Independent Company, which had been in Moresby since 17 April, was flown across the Owen Stanley Range to the Wau area. Most of Kneen's company plus an attached mortar unit was flown to Wau on 23 May. Six transport planes were used, a mix of former civilian DC3s and USAAF C-47s, escorted by about a dozen P-39 Airacobras. The six aircraft made two flights into Wau that day and five of them made a third flight. A further two flights of the five airworthy transports flew to Bulolo on 26 May with the final platoon. Stephen Murray-Smith wrote that 'the planes were only down a few minutes and were then off again'.[2] Earlier that month Captain Hugh Lyon had called Bob Emery aside and told him, 'I don't want everybody to know, the AIF are landing in Wau, our reinforcements are coming.' When Emery finally saw them he noted, 'Oh God, were we pleased to see them, all these young men with the latest killing equipment . . . you never seen such a dangerous looking mob in all your life.'[3]

On 5 June some of the commandos were trucked from Bulwa to Sunshine and the next day Lieutenant Bill Doberer's 8 Section and Lieutenant Keith Stringfellow's 9 Section began the trek down to the Markham River. Three nights later Doberer's section, accompanied by Major Kneen and some NGVR troops, moved down to the river bank by night and crossed at dawn in native canoes. That afternoon the commandos arrived at Diddy camp, the NGVR base west of Lae.

Lieutenant Mal Wylie's 4 Section, all but one of them West Australians, arrived in mid-June. 'The quarters at Diddi were in fairly open country, and the subsection left at camp had to man the lookout,' Jack Boxall noted. 'This was situated in a tree, on a knoll overlooking open, flat country, with trees covering the hilly outcrops.'[4] Keith Stringfellow's section reached Diddy camp on 26 June and four men were used to bring Doberer's and Wylie's sections up to strength for a proposed commando raid on Lae.[5] General MacArthur would get his wish.

•

The raid was planned for the night of 30 June and would target Heath's Plantation, about 10 kilometres north-west of Lae. This was the former home of Bertie Heath, the pilot who had flown out of Lae to Bulolo during the first Japanese air raid in January only to have his Junkers aircraft shot up on the ground. The Japanese had set up an early warning station at Heath's at the end of April and a field gun, believed to be of 75 mm calibre, had been installed there.[6] A sand-table model was made up at Diddy camp showing the area around Heath's in small scale to help with planning and, while inspecting it, 'each soldier was invited to have a small Scotch and a smoke' laid on by Major Kneen who believed 'what is good enough for the officers is good enough for the men'.[7]

There were thought to be 30 to 50 enemy troops at Heath's with two sentries posted at the junction of the road to Heath's with the Markham Road. A wireless aerial at the house meant that the garrison may be able to call on reinforcements if required. Accompanied by his intelligence sergeant Bob Booth, Kneen made a reconnaissance of Heath's Plantation and then drew up his plans for the raid. The objectives were to blow up the bridge across the Bewapi Creek east of Heath's, destroy the nearby field gun and any wireless equipment, gather any papers or articles of intelligence value and to cause general mayhem.

It was also the intention to destroy all Japanese personnel in the area. Four officers and 54 men would take part in the raid, split into three sections, one section made up of NGVR troops under Lieutenant Bob Phillips with the two commando sections under Doberer and Wylie.[8] The attack would follow what would be a very successful commando raid on Salamaua by other members of Kneen's company under Captain Norm Winning in the early morning hours of 29 June.[9]

The three sections departed Diddy camp at 1410 on 29 June, arriving at Narakapor three and a half hours later and spending the night in the teeming rain hounded by mosquitoes and dodging snakes.[10] However, dinner was good as some sheep had been brought along and roasted, the cooks heading back to Diddy camp the next morning. The raiders departed Narakapor the next morning and made their way along the northern bank of the Markham River to the form-up point at Bewapi Creek, twenty minutes from the Markham Road. At 1630 two scouting parties, one led by Major Kneen and the other by Bob Booth, set out to make a final reconnaissance of the target. Kneen's party returned two hours later. Though Booth confirmed that two enemy sentries had been posted at the road and that there was no barbed wire around the house, he did not return until 2230. The two sentries had come and sat on the log behind which Booth had been sheltering and he had been unable to move until the sentries had left. As Jim Hamilton noted, Booth 'was late back which upset our plans'.[11]

The three sections moved off in single file up Bewapi Creek east of Heath's. The moon was up 'but in the creek it was too dim to see more than five yards,' Stephen Murray-Smith noted. Murray-Smith and his mate Rob Hamilton had been given the bridge job as both had been well-trained in the use of explosives. The two men had earlier waded up the creek with Kneen and Bob Booth to inspect the bridge, a sturdy log construction built over the ruins of the original crossing about 10 metres long and 3 metres wide and unguarded. Murray-Smith and Rob Hamilton were dropped off at the bridge with Bob Booth to cover them. By then 'the rest of the party had already vanished into the gloom of the bush flanking the road'.[12]

The three sections moved along the south side of the Markham Road until they reached the grove of kapok trees at the junction of the drive to Heath's. Doberer's section was then to move diagonally across the paddock to a clump of trees east of the house where a sentry was to be knifed. Meanwhile Lieutenant Wylie's section was to move off along the line of kapok trees and be responsible for killing the guards at the top of the drive. Wylie's men would then move down to the front of the house and open fire. In the event, the section was held up 200 metres from the house because of a lack of cover due to the cleared grass in front of the house. Doberer's section was also held up, choosing to stay back from the house after a dog started barking. Doberer's task was to move his men up to the east side of the house and prevent any enemy troops escaping out the back while the NGVR section was to move to the north-east corner of the house with Doberer's men on their left covering the eastern side. Meanwhile, after destroying the bridge, the bridge demolition party was to move to Heath's and destroy the Japanese field gun.[13]

Up at the road junction Wal Strickland and Ted Solin silently stalked the sentries, who were manning a machine-gun pit. However, any hope of a silent killing was stymied by a barking dog which came from the house then ran up and down the drive, waking some of the Japanese in the house. Twice a voice told the dog to be quiet but the barking continued and prevented Strickland and Solin getting close enough to the sentries on the other side of the brightly lit driveway. At 0215 Solin realised he would have to use his rifle and fired two shots followed by a grenade to deal with the first sentry. Two more grenades were then thrown into the adjacent machine-gun pit. Then, as Stephen Murray-Smith wrote, 'all hell was let loose in the calm of that tropical night'.[14]

Hearing the gunfire, Major Kneen gave the order to attack the house. Fred Wilsher was with Doberer's section as the men dashed forward to the Japanese slit-trenches along the driveway. 'Prepare to throw,' Wilsher heard Kneen order, and then 'Throw grenades. Dive!' Heath's was a timber house, built on stilts with steps up to the door and, as Jack Boxall wrote, the men from Wylie's section 'sprinted to the front of the house and each man threw grenades into and around the house'. Major Kneen had ordered them to throw their two grenades before opening fire. He then told Mick Dennis to throw a grenade onto the roof, but despite Dennis holding it a few extra seconds, the grenade rolled back off the sloping roof before exploding. Jack Boxall watched as 'Japanese trying to escape were still in their pyjamas, and were picked off'. However, a group of about fifteen Japanese were allowed to escape as it was unsure if they were men from Doberer's late-arriving section.[15]

A light mist had now settled across Heath's and, despite the bright moonlight, Doberer's section was out of view of Kneen by the time they were halfway across the paddock heading for the driveway. Dick Vernon, a NGVR man, had led Doberer's section to the tree clump but the two men tasked with dealing with the sentries were still not in position. Then unexpected firing broke out on the far right of Doberer's section and the men returned to the driveway where Wylie told them to head down the drive to the house. Jim Hamilton later said, 'Well, I might as well tell the truth about it. The firing started right beside us, and we all ran back to the road.' Once at the road, Doberer's men found most of the rest of the commandos in a trench along the left-hand side of the drive while Wally Hulcup had been sent to deal with the field gun. Meanwhile Kneen stood up out of the trench with Lieutenant Phillips, giving orders. The men would come out of the trench, throw their grenades and then return to the trench. 'That will do, we will go through the house now,' Kneen told his men.[16]

The Tommy-gunners moved in and riddled the house before throwing their grenades inside. Firing and grenade explosions continued for about twenty minutes and, in the intervals between explosions, 'a considerable amount of groaning and bumping noises came from the house,' Wylie wrote. Wylie also thought that a number of attempts by the field-gun crew to get to their gun were stopped but at least one gunner made it and managed to fire off some rounds.[17]

Back at the bridge Murray-Smith and Rob Hamilton had set the charges and waited for the attack on the house to begin before they lit the fuse. The first three of only seven dry matches would not light before the fourth caused the fuse to splutter into life, blowing the bridge away in a huge explosion. When the smoke had cleared Stephen Murray-Smith saw that 'the bridge was virtually matchwood: a heap of splintered wood smoking in the bed of the creek'. Murray-Smith, Rob Hamilton and Bob Booth then headed for the house but as they moved through the kapok grove there 'was suddenly a violent explosion ahead and a great crackling rushing sound immediately above our heads'. The sound came from the Japanese field gun firing three or four shells which impacted near the bridge.[18]

Meanwhile a Japanese machine gun fired from a hill on the Lae side of Heath's as Major Kneen called 'cease fire Australia' and moved up to the house with Jack Boxall, Les Matthews and Fred Howe alongside him. Kneen was standing beside a banana tree wiping his glasses when there was a 'terrific flash' and the tree toppled over. Kneen, who had been blown into the air by the blast, was killed while Matthews and Howe were wounded. As Kneen had suffered a severe wound to his midriff, Fred Wilsher thought that one of the grenades on Kneen's belt may have gone off, though Wylie later said that the explosion had come from the second round fired from the field gun. Jim Hamilton agreed with Wilsher. 'I think he was hit by one of our own grenades,' he later said.[19] Whatever the cause, Kneen's decision to be at the forefront of the attack was a poor one given he was responsible for directing the entire operation, and the plan fell apart with his death.

Wylie, who had been called for by Kneen just before the fatal explosion, found his commander dead and, not surprisingly, it 'had an upsetting effect' on him.[20] There was an argument about who would take over command and a shaken Wylie finally did so. When a cool head was required Wylie panicked and ordered the raiding party to withdraw west along the Markham Road. Bob Emery and the other experienced NGVR men were 'astounded by this order'.[21] With Wylie's order, the attack broke down and the house was not even entered, let alone searched. The men who had been on the house steps, about to enter, hesitated then turned back and withdrew. Doberer's section never even got into position for the attack and the men now withdrew without firing a shot. All the men's packs and belongings, which had been deposited at the kapok grove prior to the attack, were abandoned. This was despite Wylie's later report clearly stating that 'In the event of anything unforseen [sic] happening every man was to report back to where the packs were dumped.'[22]

Wylie's section followed Doberer's section out. Showing some modicum of calm, the more experienced Bob Phillips, 'the only one who kept his head' and whose NGVR section came under his own command once Kneen was killed, formed his men into a rearguard. As Stephen Murray-Smith moved back past the house 'there was not a sound, neither groans from the Japanese nor calls from our men'.[23] No one went inside to look for intelligence, one of the key objectives of the operation. The field gun was also left undamaged despite Kneen's plan to use it to fire on Lae before removing the breech block and destroying the barrel with some of Murray-Smith's explosives.[24] Murray-Smith carried those explosives all the way back to Diddy camp. By the time Wylie caught up with Murray-Smith at 0420 it was considered too late to go back and destroy the gun. Shortly after this the field gun started firing again, this time in the direction of the withdrawing raiders who were fortunately now out of range.[25] As the sections withdrew down the track towards Nadzab, Captain Eric Shepherd and Lieutenant Stringfellow met them at Munum with a truck which was used to evacuate the two wounded men from Wylie's section.[26]

Wylie's report on the raid stated that 21 Japanese were definitely killed, presumably outside of the house. Another twenty defenders were estimated to have been killed or wounded in the house. At least twelve Japanese had escaped.[27] The Japanese only admitted to ten casualties from the raid on Heath's. The more important effect was that two companies of marines from the 5th Sasebo Special Naval Landing Party were rushed from Rabaul to Lae on 1 July and then on to Salamaua, where the commando raid had been much more successful.[28] Having to deploy these crack troops to Lae and Salamaua meant they could not be used during the crucial operations at Milne Bay or Guadalcanal.

At midday on the next day two Japanese bombers appeared and circled the area, obviously looking for the raiders. Crossing the kunai grass, the commandos tried to hide from view but, as Stephen Murray-Smith wrote, the kunai grass 'cut us and stifled us but did not hide us . . . like hiding from heavy rain under a handkerchief'.[29] Gabmatzung village, which was adjacent to Nadzab, was bombed, badly shaking up some of the commandos though there were no casualties. Most of the men then crossed the Markham River but Wylie's section was sent back to Heath's to finish the botched job. This time a raid by US B-25 Mitchell bombers had been laid on to precede the attack. The Mitchells hit Lae but none bombed Heath's so Wylie aborted the plan and once again withdrew his men.[30]

•

One thing that neither the Lae or Salamaua raids produced was an enemy prisoner. Major Norman Fleay, the commander of Kanga Force which included the 2/5th Independent Company, now directed Captain Shepherd to send out a platoon to capture one. Shepherd did not have many fit men and to send out a platoon on such a task would invite discovery by the Japanese, so he sent out two four-man parties instead. The two parties, one led by

Sergeant Bill Chaffey and the other by Sergeant Paul Beal, set off down the Markham Road and divided at Narakapor.[31]

Skirting previous tracks, Chaffey's party reached the Markham Road east of Heath's and set up an ambush. A Japanese truck approached but got bogged about 30 metres away, and when the Australians broke cover two guards with a machine gun opened up from the back of the truck. Chaffey shot one with his Tommy gun but the other kept firing, hitting Dick Vernon in the chest. Jack Gregson tried to drag the badly wounded Vernon out until Vernon said he was done for and pleaded for Gregson to get to safety himself. Meanwhile Chaffey had also killed two of the three men in the front seat of the truck before running out of ammunition. With more Japanese troops coming up the road from Lae, Chaffey and the other two men then withdrew, leaving the badly wounded Vernon behind. A single revolver shot and a burst of fire signalled the end for the brave rifleman. Meanwhile Beal's group had reached Jacobsen's Plantation near the airfield but the noise from Chaffey's ambush alerted the Japanese and the men were fortunate to escape.[32]

On 21 July the Japanese responded by carrying out a mopping-up operation at Ngasawapum. There were two Japanese parties one hour apart, the first of 81 men, the second of 53 men. Twenty of the Australians were preparing to leave camp when the Japanese opened fire, hurrying their exit. Bill Underwood was wounded in the arm and remained behind under cover. George Whittaker went out that night, and after a six-hour search found Underwood and then brought him back to Nadzab and across the Markham in a canoe.[33] Following this incident, all fixed camps north of the Markham River were abandoned by the Australians and it would be over 13 months before the Australian army returned to the area.

The commandos of the 2/5th Independent Company would remain in the front line in New Guinea for twelve months, engaged in critical battles at Lae, Salamaua, Mubo and Wau. By April 1943 only 104 men remained out of 340, including reinforcements, and 30 of these men were barely fit for action. The rest were sick and exhausted. As Jack Boxall later wrote, in early 1942 the men were 'Physically as hard as stone, eagerly on to New Guinea—the next year glad to be back on the mainland.'[34]

•

Lae stood out as a vital objective for the Allies in order to take the fight for New Guinea to the next stage and beyond. The abandoned airfield site at Nadzab, 30 kilometres north-west of Lae, provided a great opportunity to land troops close to the town. In August 1942 Major General George Kenney, the Allied air commander, had discussed a similar bold air-landing operation in Papua with Brigadier General Ennis Whitehead, his forward air commander in New Guinea. This involved using a bush strip well behind Japanese lines on the northern Papuan coast at Wanigela to get troops and supplies into Buna.[35] However, Kenney found it difficult to get Lieutenant General Richard Sutherland, MacArthur's chief of staff, to take such an operation seriously. Sutherland had an aversion to any risk and he was proving difficult for the Australian commanders to work with. 'There is no use talking to him about Wanigela let alone Nadzab if the Aussies are to be depended on to do the job,' Kenney wrote on 8 September.[36] On 18 September Kenney went over Sutherland's head and conferred with General MacArthur about sending troops by air to Wanigela in order to capture Buna. As part of that conversation he told MacArthur that 'after Buna comes Nadzab and Lae'. 'We'll see,' MacArthur replied.[37] On 23 September Kenney was at it again. He wanted to begin planning the Nadzab operation but MacArthur told him 'no decision would be made until Buna was occupied'.[38]

On 18 October 1942, after two regiments of US troops had been successfully flown across the Owen Stanley Range from Port Moresby to the rough landing ground at Wanigela, General Blamey had told General MacArthur of his desire to follow up the expected defeat of the Japanese in Papua with operations against Lae and Salamaua. At that stage intelligence showed that there was a Japanese regiment at Lae and Blamey thought that an air operation to retake the town was feasible. Blamey considered that it was possible to land troops at the former airfield site at Nadzab and wanted two Australian brigades under Major General George Vasey's command deployed for the task. One of the brigades would be Brigadier Murray Moten's 17th Brigade, at that point uncommitted to the Kokoda campaign. Brigadier Ron Hopkins flew to Wau on 18 October to discuss the plan with the commander of Kanga Force, Lieutenant Colonel Norman Fleay.[39]

Two days later MacArthur, understandably concerned about the threat of Japanese naval and air strength, replied to General Blamey's proposal. 'Operations against the north coast of New Guinea must be approached with great caution and implemented by carefully drawn plans,' he advised. He was also against moving the 17th Brigade from Milne Bay due to intelligence that the Japanese may make another landing there in November. He rightly stressed that the 7th Division would be needed to reduce the Japanese-held Papuan beachheads first and it had not yet even retaken Kokoda. However, MacArthur did send a staff officer to look at Blamey's Nadzab proposal.[40]

On 24 October General Kenney was informed that the Australian army had adopted the Nadzab plan and he was to allocate all available transport aircraft including Australian civilian models to the operation, 70 transport planes in all. 'We want to pour troops into Nadzab fast,' Kenney was told. An experienced transport pilot had flown in to Wampit and trekked overland to Nadzab to confirm whether the airfield site was suitable for such a sustained operation.[41]

At a conference in Brisbane on 27 October Blamey again pressed his Lae plan onto MacArthur, the intention now being to land both the 17th and 21st Brigades at Nadzab. Three weeks later on 18 November an outline plan, code-named Haggis, was put forward for implementation once the Papuan beachheads at Gona, Buna and Sanananda had fallen. The plan anticipated flying the Australian 7th Cavalry Regiment to Wau and then moving it down the Bulolo Valley and across the Markham River to capture and repair Nadzab airfield. Brigadier Moten's 17th Brigade would then be flown in to make the assault on Lae. At the same time Kanga Force would carry out diversionary actions against Salamaua before a second infantry brigade was flown in to Wau, Salamaua or Nadzab as appropriate. Artillery, anti-aircraft, engineer, medical, signal and service corps troops would also be required. It was expected that the ground forces would be available by 14 December.[42]

At that stage the Australians were still on their way back across the Kokoda Track and well short of winning that battle let alone retaking Buna and the other Papuan beachheads.

It would be over three months before Papua was secure and the cost would be great, severely limiting the ability of the Allies to carry out other offensive operations in the short to mid-term. The 7th Cavalry Regiment ended up being sent to Sanananda in December 1942 where it was all but destroyed in the fighting while the 17th Brigade was flown to Wau in January 1943 to counter the Japanese threat against that area. The 21st Brigade would also be unavailable for some time as it needed to be totally rebuilt after the Papuan campaigns.

•

Meanwhile the transport of troops and supplies over the Owen Stanley Range was stretching General Kenney's air transport planes to the limit. Even if the troops were available to land at Nadzab, Kenney just did not have the transport aircraft available to support the operation. In early December 1942 he only had three transport squadrons available in New Guinea. The newest of these, the thirteen C-47s of Captain John Lackey's 6th Troop Carrier Squadron, had left San Francisco on 2 October. Due to the fuel required for the first leg to Hawaii, eight extra fuel tanks were installed in the aircraft cabin in addition to the four wing tanks. Each aircraft took off with twice the normal maximum payload which meant it would not be able to stay in the air if one of the two engines failed within the first ten hours of the flight.[43]

Staff Sergeant Ernie Ford was one of the pilots in Lackey's squadron. 'The bird was straining and groaning for all she was worth to break ground', he wrote of the take off from San Francisco.[44] When Captain Lackey's C-47 touched down at Hickam Field on Hawaii after a 14-hour flight, it was the first such aircraft to have flown directly from the US mainland. Ernie Ford's aircraft was the second one down. From Hawaii the squadron flew via Christmas Island and Canton Island to Fiji and New Caledonia before touching down at Amberley airfield west of Brisbane on 9 October, one week after leaving the US mainland.[45] The aircraft then flew to Townsville where they loaded maintenance personnel and equipment and headed for Port Moresby, reaching there on 13 October. Lackey's squadron joined the 21st and 22nd Troop Carrier Squadrons. The 33rd Troop Carrier Squadron, delayed on New Caledonia, would not reach New Guinea until late December.

Chapter 3

'WE WILL DIE FIGHTING'

Japanese plans were also evolving. On 1 November 1942 there had been 2133 Japanese troops in Lae but by 6 January 1943 this had increased to about 3000. Most of these men were part of 7th Base Force supported by the 82nd Naval Garrison comprising three Special Naval Landing Parties (SNLP): the 5th Yokosuka, the 2nd Maizuru and the 5th Sasebo, the latter two units based at Salamaua. These troops came under the command of Rear Admiral Ruitaro Fujita.[1]

The change of year brought a change in Japanese strategy in New Guinea. With the imminent loss of the Papuan beachheads, the revised defensive perimeter in New Guinea would be centred on Salamaua and Lae. 'The Army and Navy agreed that the security of the Lae–Salamaua sector was vital in determining the outcome of the New Guinea Campaign.' To secure that area from direct land attack the Japanese command decided to commit army troops to capture Wau, 50 kilometres inland from Salamaua as it 'posed a constant menace to the Lae–Salamaua area'.[2] The Okabe Detachment, comprising the 102nd Regiment of the 51st Division, with attached artillery and engineer units, was shipped from Rabaul to Lae on five merchant ships from 5 to 7 January 1943. Despite the loss of one of the transports, the *Nichiryu Maru*, sunk by an RAAF Catalina, most of the troops reached Lae. The resultant offensive by the Okabe Detachment against Wau was unsuccessful and by the end of February the front line had coalesced at Mubo, some 15 kilometres south of Salamaua.[3] One of the Australian commandos who fought at Mubo called it 'some of the toughest country in the world'.[4]

Determined to try again and buoyed by the relative success of the January convoy when a 50 per cent loss had been expected, another convoy was sent from Rabaul to Lae in March 1943. This convoy carried infantry reinforcements from the 115th Regiment as well as anti-aircraft units and substantial supplies that would enable Lae to continue to operate as a front-line Japanese airbase. However, the Allied air forces had refined the tactics required to sink such a convoy, perfecting low-level mast-height bombing and strafing techniques. The convoy, made up of eight transports escorted by eight destroyers, left Rabaul on 1 March 1943 but, when it was attacked by long-range bombers on 2 March, the transport *Kyokusei Maru* was sunk. Then on the morning of 3 March, in the Bismarck Sea east of Lae, Allied attack squadrons sank all remaining seven merchant ships and four of the eight destroyers.

One of the Australian Beaufighter crewmen later told Burton Graham, 'On most of the transports and cargo ships, you could see the troops packed on the decks . . . think of the trouble and loss of life that would result if this convoy should ever succeed in landing at Lae.'[5] One of the Beaufighter pilots, Bob Brazenor, watched as the high- and low-level bombers and fighters 'all hit the target together'. It was 'amazing that everything clicked', he said. Brazenor's navigator Fred Anderson saw the bombs hit the water like torpedos before skimming into the ships.[6]

Down below on the transport *Oigawa Maru* Lieutenant Kiyoshi Nishio watched as 'a cloud of aircraft appeared'. Two bombs soon struck the ship amidships, stopping the engines before fire took hold.[7] Reiji Masuda was on the destroyer *Arashio* and remembered how the Allied bombers 'would come in on you at low altitude, and they would skip bombs across the water like you'd throw a stone'. He also observed the demise of the transports. 'Their masts tumbled down, their bridges flew to pieces, the ammunition they were carrying was hit, and whole ships blew up,' he wrote. *Arashio* was one of the ships sunk and Masuda was fortunate to survive.[8]

At Lae, the waiting Japanese were tense, praying that the convoy would arrive and land safely. Japanese observers at the Lae lookout tower had spotted the convoy that morning. 'Convoy sighted in the direction of Finschhafen!' they reported. Then came another report that a 'large formation of enemy planes heading for the convoy!' More reports followed: 'the escorting destroyers are fighting back', 'bombs are falling . . . a black cloud is rising in the air'. It soon became apparent that 'it had become a disastrous defeat'.[9] Of the 8740 men on the transports and destroyers, 2890 were lost, 2450 of them army and marine troops.[10] Also lost were 40 landing barges, 36 artillery pieces, 500 tonnes of ammunition, 2000 drums of aviation fuel and 8800 cubic metres of provisions.[11] Rokuzo Komatsu was based at Tuluvu where many of the survivors came ashore after the battle. On 7 March he wrote, 'The sea must have been like a mountain of dead.'[12]

The four surviving Japanese destroyers did an extraordinary job rescuing many men from the sea. Despite the loss of the eight merchant ships, some 1300 surviving troops were brought ashore at Lae and Finschhafen by the escorting destroyers following the debacle.[13] With the loss of the aviation gasoline, it spelt the death knell for Lae as a front-line airbase. 'Our intention to carry out lively air operations at the strategic moment by sending our air force for a time to the Lae and Saramoa areas had to be discarded owing to the sinking of *Kembu Maru* with her cargo of airplane fuel and materials,' Captain Toshikazu Ohmae later stated.[14]

Having survived the attack on the convoy, Private Shotaro Tamura found that his lifeboat was a target for the Allied fighters. 'They came in to strafe again and again,' he said, 'their guns like a great rake collecting leaves.' Tamura's regimental commander, Lieutenant Colonel Torahei Endo, was one of nine men killed in Tamura's lifeboat. Only thirteen of the 40 original survivors from that boat were able to drag themselves ashore on New Britain in early April after being adrift for 31 days.[15]

Despite this Allied success at sea, the Japanese would still need to be defeated on the ground. A week after the battle, leaflets showing news and pictures of the convoy's destruction were dropped over the Japanese base at Wewak. One recipient noted how the troops, though inclined to believe what had happened, only wanted to take revenge for the defeat.[16]

One of the survivors of the Bismarck Sea convoy was 53-year-old Lieutenant General Hidemitsu Nakano, the commander of the 51st Division and now in charge of the defence of Lae and Salamaua. He had been commissioned in 1912, had extensive service in China and had held his divisional command since November 1941. Nakano 'had a soft laughing face with a white beard' and 'though he was short, measuring only five foot and several inches, he was a brave soldier, a man of quick decision and action,' one of his officers wrote of him.[17] All these qualities would be tested as he held the fate of Lae in his hands over the coming months.

By 17 March 1943 there were 3115 Japanese troops in the Salamaua area and 3141 at Lae.[18] Most of the troops at Lae were naval shipping engineers and men from labour and anti-aircraft units. The main army infantry component in Lae was a company from the 115th Regiment, survivors from the Bismarck Sea convoy. Further reinforcements arrived over the following months but most were destined for the ridges that shielded Salamaua.

Unable to reinforce and supply Lae by means of merchant ship convoys, the Japanese command looked for alternatives (see Map 4). Fast destroyers were initially used, the first one landing 480 troops via collapsible boats at Finschhafen on the night of 30 March in the face of Allied air attacks made under the light of parachute flares. 'The landing point area was like daylight,' one of the Japanese engineers observed.[19] Due to the air threat, the Japanese destroyers then switched to landing troops at Tuluvu at the western edge of New Britain from where they moved down the coast to Cape Bushing and then across the Vitiaz Strait by motorised landing craft. However, after the loss of the two destroyers *Mikazuki* and *Ariake* to low-level US bombers after the *Mikazuki*

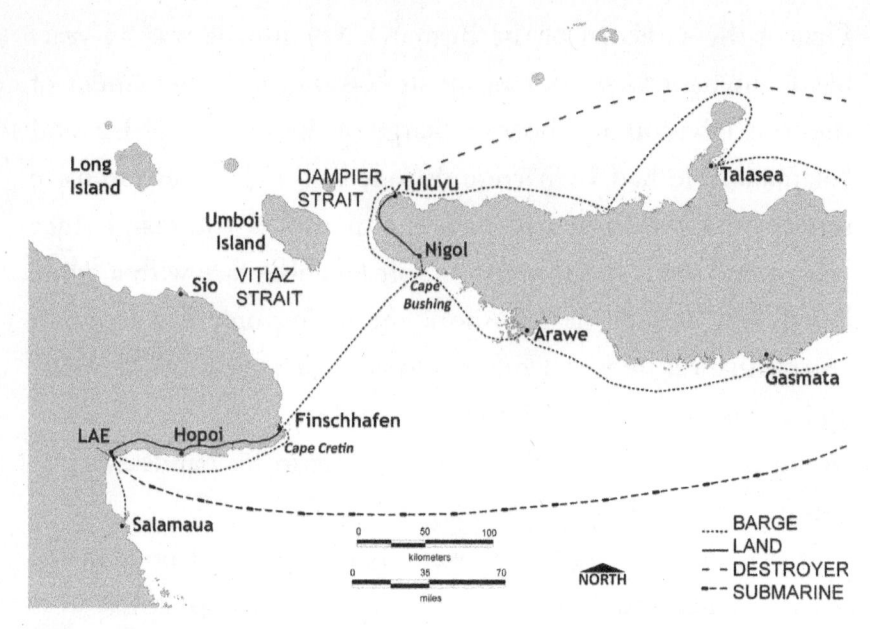

Map 4: Japanese supply lines to Lae and Salamaua, 1942–43 (Rohan Bola)

had grounded on a reef off Tuluvu on 27 July 1943, destroyers were withdrawn from the transport role.

Motorised landing craft (MLCs) augmented by some fishing vessels (*Gyosen*) were then more widely used to supply Lae, initially from Rabaul and later from the new supply base at Wewak along the northern New Guinea coast.[20] These landing craft were called Daihatsu, from the Japanese *Dai-Hatsudokitei* or large motorboat. Most of the MLCs used in New Guinea were single-engine boats, 14 metres long and 4.5 metres wide with a crew of seven and a carrying capacity of 70 men. There was a complete disregard for any comfort, with the men having to stand the entire time and small tins passed around for toilet use. The craft would only travel by night, operating in columns some 300 metres offshore, on the lookout for reefs, enemy patrol boats and aircraft.[21] As Lieutenant

General Kane Yoshihara wrote, 'In the daytime, lying hidden in small inlets, river mouths, etc., and in the gloom of night advancing from hiding place to hiding place.'[22]

Lieutenant Masuo Shinoda left Rabaul with the 2nd Battalion of the 66th Regiment on the night of 4 May. Two battalions were carried aboard the cruiser *Yūbari* and the destroyers *Nagatsuki*, *Satsuki* and *Minazuki*. Travelling close to the north coast of New Britain, the warships safely landed the troops at Tuluvu before dawn on 5 May. Shinoda's unit dispersed and camped in the jungle to avoid detection by enemy aircraft before leaving for Cape Bushing on the south coast of the island on 7 May. From there the unit was progressively transported across the Dampier Strait to Lae in MLCs. Company-sized groups crossed by night to Finschhafen in two or three MLCs, with the engines cut when any Allied planes flew over to avoid possible detection. In order to avoid contact with US PT (patrol torpedo) boats, the journey from Finschhafen to Lae was made through dangerous waters close to shore that were filled with numerous coral reefs. The Japanese marine engineers did an amazing job, working during the day to repair and prepare the boats for their nightly journey.[23]

Twelve coastal hideouts were set up along the coast from Madang to Lae. By May 1943, the Japanese were operating 50 MLCs along this route bringing units from the newly arrived 20th and 41st Divisions to Sio, Finschhafen and Lae. The route became particularly difficult between Sio and Finschhafen, where there were very few opportunities for hiding the craft by day while at night the PT boats operating out of the forward base at Morobe hunted them down remorselessly.[24] With a shallower draft than the PT boats, the MLCs would travel as close inshore as possible and 'watch for the spray in the waves in order to locate the torpedo boat before they attacked'. If a PT boat was sighted, the MLC would turn its stern to the enemy to minimise its target area.[25] Travelling with a group of four MLCs from Wewak to Lae, a 238th Regiment private noted that travel was always by night and, when suitable lying-up areas were unavailable, the boats were 'beached and camouflaged with leaves and grass'. On occasions the troops would remain under cover of the jungle for a week at a time.[26]

As time went by the Allied air force became more familiar with the Japanese MLC routes. Tuluvu was a key location on the route between Rabaul and the New Guinea mainland. Only the larger oceangoing MLCs could be used between the mainland and Tuluvu and, although 70 were available in March, by mid-May this number was down to 40, with ten fishing boats also in use. From 13 to 30 May five to eight large MLCs left Rabaul every second day for Tuluvu to maintain the supply line.[27] Allied air attacks hit Tuluvu hard. On the morning of 3 August, sixteen aircraft attacked the anchorage and hit five MLCs loaded with prime movers and twelve MLCs loaded with rations, ammunition and fuel, destroying most of them. 'Black smoke from the exploding fuel and ammunition filled the sky . . . the material was reduced to ashes,' a Japanese field diary related.[28] A new term now entered the lexicon of the American airman: when a target was hit as hard as Tuluvu had been, it was considered 'Gloucesterized', taken from the Allied name for the location, Cape Gloucester.[29]

Between 24 July and 3 August, Allied air force intelligence estimated that 94 Japanese MLCs had been destroyed and 60 damaged around the coasts of New Guinea and New Britain.[30] Even given the tendency for such claims to be inflated, it was

'We will die fighting'

clear that the Japanese coastal transport capacity had been severely reduced in the lead-up to the planned Allied operation against Lae. Japanese records show that, in early August, 30 MLCs were destroyed over a ten-day period, severely affecting supply to Lae.[31] American PT boats operating out of Morobe also had a significant effect as they carried out night patrols of the Vitiaz Strait between Tuluvu and Finschhafen. As Japanese commanders later noted, 'Enemy torpedo boats dominated this strait.'[32]

•

In order to keep Lae reliably supplied, 'There was no method of doing so other than by submarines,' Lieutenant General Kane Yoshihara wrote. However, the lack of submarines and their limited capacity meant the force at Lae and Salamaua would have a ceiling of 10,000 men.[33] As Japanese 18th Army staff officers later noted, 'we had to be satisfied with getting just a handful of supplies through to our forces'.[34] The Japanese submarine commanders were not happy with this new role but it was the emperor's wish that the isolated garrisons be supported and there was no alternative but to obey an imperial order.[35]

In the early evening twilight of 19 March 1943 submarine *I-176* was unloading supplies into four MLCs about 400 metres offshore from Lae when Lieutenant Asakichi Araki 'saw red rockets rise above the beach and burst', a danger warning. Captain Yahachi Tanabe called for an emergency dive as five Mitchell bombers led by Captain John Henebry came in low, strafing and bombing his vessel. After the submarine's presence had been detected earlier in the day, the five Mitchells had flown from Port Moresby to Dobodura before taking off for a surprise attack by night to catch the submarine on the surface. Henebry's bombers came in from the west flying low along the Markham River with the enemy submarine 'silhouetted against a rising full moon'. The Mitchells opened fire with their machine guns before each dropped four 500-pound bombs. Two submarine crewmen were killed and another two, including Captain Tanabe, were badly wounded.[36]

The heavy strafing and a bomb that had exploded near the stern of *I-176* had pierced the pressure hull, fractured pipes and damaged the fuel and ballast tanks. Lieutenant Araki 'felt a concussion which seemed to send the boat lunging upward, and she started to heel over to port'. The stricken vessel crash-dived and, with water already up to his knees, Araki took over command and ran the submarine aground at the mouth of the Markham River to prevent its loss. Araki then told his engineering officer 'that we would repair *I-176* or die trying'. After ripping up the decking on the outside of the hull, the crew were able to find and seal the holes using wooden plugs and cloth. The MLCs returned to unload the rest of the supplies plus the dead and wounded crewmen except Captain Tanabe, who refused to go. Moving the crew from side to side, Araki managed to free the submarine then took it into deeper water. Tanabe advised Araki to spend the day submerged on the bottom to avoid detection. 'We dived at dawn,' Araki wrote, 'but the dive proved to be full of anxiety.' Down on the seabed at a depth of 36 metres, the crew watched anxiously for any leaks but the repairs held despite one of the trimming tanks leaking due to bullet holes below the waterline. When the submarine surfaced at sunset, the hull was heavy but the *I-176* was able to set off on the surface for Rabaul at 18 knots (33 km/h).[37]

'We will die fighting'

Diving again at dawn on 21 March, another day was spent submerged and despite problems with the holed trimming tank, the submarine managed to remain down until sunset. 'It was a clear starlit night and the sea was calm' as the *I-176* surfaced and headed for Rabaul but about halfway along the south coast of New Britain an RAAF Catalina flying boat spotted it from above. Coming under machine-gun fire, Araki decided to fight it out on the surface and the *I-176* returned fire with its 13 mm twin-barrel machine gun. The Catalina was flying at 1350 metres and the pilot, Flight Lieutenant Percy Shields, maintained that height as he thought that the target was a destroyer because it remained on the surface. The Catalina dropped four 250-pound bombs, two of which were near misses. In reply, the Japanese gunners hit the Catalina's wing and, after a final ineffective pass, the seaplane headed for its base at Cairns and a few days later to Rathmines in New South Wales for repair. The *I-176* also headed for home and reached Rabaul the next morning, 22 March.[38]

In the three months from the start of April to the end of June 1943 there were 32 submarine supply runs to Lae using six I Class submarines at any one time. The submarines carried artillery, ammunition, provisions, spare parts and at times up to 40 troops from Rabaul to Lae or Salamaua.[39] Troops could be transported in the forward torpedo room in place of the spare torpedos with twenty men being crammed for three days into a space 3.6 by 2.3 metres and only 1.7 metres high. Fresh air was only available when the submarine surfaced at night. Twenty 220-litre drums of rice were also lashed to the deck of the submarine which submerged by day and travelled on the surface by night using its diesel engine.[40]

Each supply submarine would usually leave Rabaul at 0700 and travel on the surface at 15 knots (28 km/h) until 0500 the next day when it would be off the south coast of New Britain between Gasmata and Arawe. It would then proceed submerged at 8 knots (15 km/h) until 1900 when the submarine would be entering the Huon Gulf approximately 90 kilometres east of Lae. It would then surface and proceed by night at 15 knots (28 km/h) to Lae or Salamaua, arriving some three hours later at about 2200. This would allow unloading to take place by night and the submarine would be on its way again before dawn.[41] When the submarine reached Lae it would anchor offshore and usually be unloaded within three hours using three small MLCs, faster, sampan-like craft known as *yammasen*, with each making three trips.[42]

The transport submarines also employed two unique attachments. The *unpoto* comprised two hollow cylinders with a platform on top to which artillery pieces could be lashed. It displaced 37 tonnes when loaded and was strapped to the afterdeck of a submarine. It was detached when it arrived off the coast and then used two attached torpedo propellers to reach the shore. A number of field guns were taken to Lae and Salamaua using the *unpoto*. As night fell on 11 June, submarine *I-38* unloaded one 155 mm gun and three 105 mm howitzers from an *unpoto* at Salamaua.[43] The *unkato* was a 45-metre long, 5-metre diameter sealed cylinder with ballast tanks at either end and in the centre of the cylinder. The cylinder was towed submerged behind the submarine and could carry 377 tonnes of cargo. However, it proved too unstable for use on the Lae and Salamaua supply runs.[44]

There were six supply submarines available up until June 1943 before the number was cut back to three, leaving most of the

'We will die fighting'

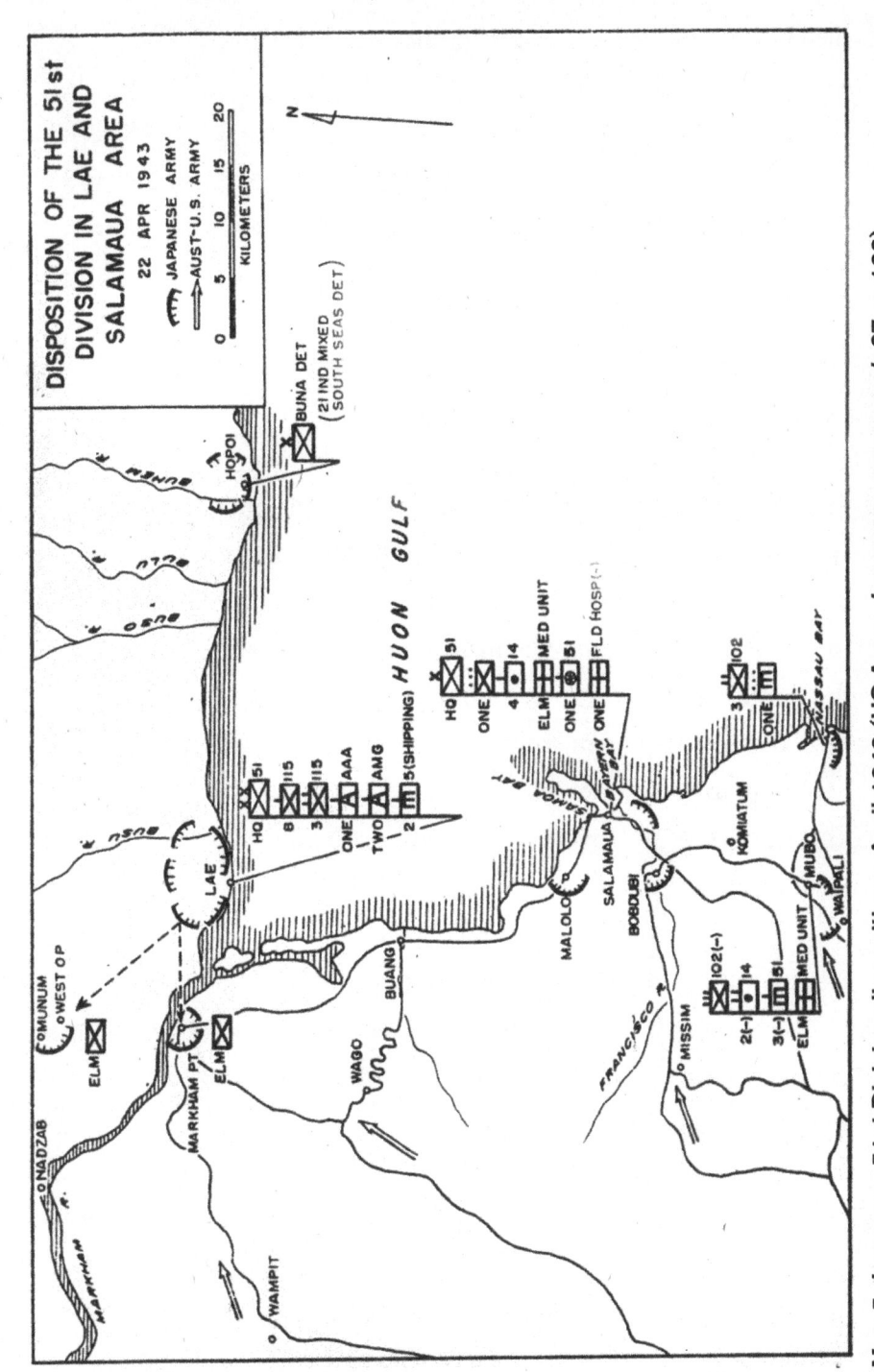

Map 5: Japanese 51st Division dispositions, April 1943 (US Army, *Japanese monograph 37*, p. 133)

supply work to be carried out by the MLC convoys.[45] The *I-177* was the last submarine to reach Lae before the Allied attack, arriving on the night of 3–4 September 1943 carrying eighteen reinforcements for the 102nd Regiment plus ammunition and provisions. The reinforcements were exchanged for eighteen seriously wounded men and, after eluding torpedo boats and destroyers, the submarine returned to Rabaul.[46]

•

On 22 April 1943 General Nakano set out his operational plan. 'The Division is to form a strong key position against the enemy from land, sea and air in the Lae and Salamaua areas,' he ordered (see Map 5). At Lae, Lieutenant Colonel Keiji Matsui commanded the under-strength 115th Infantry Regiment and a battalion from the 21st Regiment while two companies from the 115th were deployed to Markham Point under Major Tokuzo Nishikawa. These infantry units were supported by a field artillery regiment, an anti-aircraft battalion and two field machine-cannon companies. Naval units were responsible for the defence of Lae and the area east of the Busu River including Hopoi.[47]

Able Seaman Kiichi Wada had reached Lae on the evening of 22 February 1943 aboard the Japanese submarine *I-36*. 'Like ants swarming around their prey,' about a dozen MLCs unloaded the submarine. Supplies were also carried in drums attached to the submarine's deck by ropes which were cut upon arrival and attached to buoys so that when the submarine submerged the drums would float free to be gathered and taken to shore. 'Each of these drums contained two and a half sacks of rice,' Wada

'We will die fighting'

wrote, 'but about a quarter of each was waterlogged because of the pressure on the drums.'[48]

Wada was assigned to the 1st Company of the 50th Anti-Aircraft Battalion, on duty at the Higashiyama (Eastern Mountain) camp. The effect of the Allied air attacks on Lae were immediately apparent to Wada. There were 'countless large mortar-shaped holes, filled with water and glowing', he wrote. Having lost all his belongings when his transport ship had been sunk near Truk some months earlier, Wada was given a 'new' uniform at Lae. 'They were little more than rags!' he wrote, 'filthy and covered with patches.'[49] This reflected the dire straits of the Japanese supply system in Lae even before the loss of the Bismarck Sea convoy.

The lack of a normal supply pipeline to Lae badly affected air operations at Lae airfield. Following the withdrawal of the Tainan Naval Air Group from Lae in November 1942, Japanese army air units took over the airfield in January 1943. The 11th Hiko Sentai (Air Squadron), an Oscar fighter squadron based at Rabaul, received regular supply from Lae airbase up until 21 March but from then on there were only two further supply issues to the unit at Lae, on 16 May and 11 July. At the end of March 1943, the 24th Hiko Sentai, flying Oscar fighters based at Wewak, and the 83rd Hiko Dokuritsu Sentai (Air Reconnaissance Squadron), which flew Sonias based at Madang, had detachments at Lae. However, from mid-May onwards there were never more than four serviceable aircraft sighted on Lae airfield. On 11 July substantial issues of aviation fuel were made at Lae, the last such issue recorded. Lae airfield had been abandoned as a front-line operational base.[50]

•

Back at Imperial General Headquarters in Japan there had been considerable debate about the overextension of Japan's armed forces in trying to hold an outer defence perimeter that in New Guinea now rested on Lae and Salamaua. The army put forward the case that a much tighter main line of resistance needed to be established which, in the case of New Guinea, would be much further west, resting on the cornerstones of Hollandia and Biak Island. However, there was a perceived wisdom, confirmed during a series of studies on 5 and 6 June 1943, that the outlying garrisons such as Lae and Salamaua needed to be held and even sacrificed to buy time for the main defence line to be established. This aligned with the Imperial Japanese Navy's desire that all forward positions be held to enable its 'forward decisive battle' strategy to continue.[51]

It was against that background that Lieutenant General Hatazo Adachi, the commander of the 18th Army and responsible for the defence of mainland New Guinea, visited Salamaua from 3 to 7 July. He agreed with General Nakano's assessment that the combat strength of the 51st Division was now only equivalent to a battalion and that there were 'critical shortages in personnel and munitions'. Nonetheless Adachi requested that Nakano hold the positions around Lae and Salamaua as long as possible but 'to avoid annihilation'.[52] Lae had strong defences, 'probably more complex and intricate than any others in the SWPA [South West Pacific Area]' with the strongest positions overlooking the most likely approaches as dictated by the difficult terrain.[53] However, no defences were evident east of the Busu River or at Nadzab, the two initial objectives of the proposed Allied operation against Lae.

Adachi had long realised that Lae and Salamaua needed to be reinforced if they were to be held. Two infantry divisions, the

'We will die fighting'

20th and 41st, had been transferred to Adachi's 18th Army from Korea and China respectively and had reached Wewak in January and February 1943. Since arrival both divisions had been involved in building the new airfields around Wewak. In mid-May it was decided that a battalion from the 80th Regiment (20th Division) and two battalions from the 238th Regiment (41st Division) would be moved to Lae and on to Salamaua, a move scheduled to be completed by mid-July. Major Otoichi Jinno's 1/80th Battalion reached Lae around 22 July, Lieutenant Colonel Toshio Sakata's 3/238th Battalion arrived around 5 August and Major Shigeru Tashiro's 2/238th Battalion arrived around 18 August. All three battalions immediately deployed to the front lines at Salamaua.

Second Lieutenant Shinji Sonohara was a platoon leader with 11 Company of the 238th Regiment, which had reached Wewak in February 1943. After working for nearly five months on building a series of new airfields, Sonohara's company had left Wewak late on 7 July on a 30-tonne fishing boat. 'Wewak gradually melted into the darkness and finally disappeared into the waves,' Sonohara wrote. After considerable delays along the journey, Sonohara finally reached Lae by MLC on 3 August. 'The morale of the 51st Division is very low,' Sonohara observed. 'I realised the condition and doubted if this was the Japanese army... The scene at Lae aerodrome is also disastrous. About two to three score of our fighter planes were destroyed on ground and they are a sorry sight.' Sonohara went on to the Salamaua front lines and on 10 August he wrote, 'I will defend to my death.' Three days later he was killed in action.[54]

On 17 July General Nakano wrote, 'The whole fate of the Japanese empire depends upon the decision of the struggle for

Lae–Salamaua. These strongholds must be defended to death.'[55] A month later on 24 August his attitude to defending Salamaua had not changed. He told his troops that 'If we are unable to hold we will die fighting. I will burn our Divisional flag and even the patients will rise to fight in close combat.'[56]

The Japanese command was aware of the amphibious threat to Lae. A 51st Division intelligence report on 25 July stated that there was 'some excitement amongst the natives due to the enemy propaganda which said the attack on Lae was near'. Intelligence reports showed that 'The enemy plans to land in the vicinity of Busching, Cape Cretin, Hopoi and, of course, Lae and Salamaua. It is necessary to keep strict watch.'[57] Another intelligence report on 21 August covered information received from native sources regarding Allied operations south of the Markham River. Attention was finally drawn to Tsili Tsili, the new Allied airfield being constructed north of Marilinan. 'There is a considerable number of men, and they appear to be gradually increasing in number, their plan being to attack the Nadzab and Chivasing areas.' The information was classified as level B for reliability, so it may not have been taken as seriously as it should have, particularly given that the Tsili Tsili base had been spotted by Japanese air reconnaissance on 11 August.[58]

There was little Japanese activity at Nadzab, with the closest troops north of the Markham River at Boana and Heath's Plantation, both locations about 20 kilometres away. There were 200 troops reported at both locations although there was also a machine-gun platoon, two 75 mm field guns and three 37 mm anti-aircraft guns at Heath's. In addition, a patrol of 100 troops from Lae had been visiting the Nadzab area every two weeks up until mid-August.[59] There were also 100 troops, possibly with one 75 mm field gun, at Markham Point on the south side of the Markham River.[60]

By 15 August the Allied intelligence estimate of Japanese strength in the Lae and Markham Valley area was 4620 field troops with 44 field artillery pieces, 730 anti-aircraft troops with 38 anti-aircraft guns and 910 base troops, a total of 6260 troops in all.[61] It was estimated there were another 2695 base troops and 4346 field troops, 7041 in all, at Salamaua.[62] The Japanese field artillery at Lae included twenty-eight 75 mm, four 105 mm and two 155 mm guns.[63] What the Allied intelligence didn't know was that the key coastal defence weapons, those that precluded any direct amphibious assault on Lae, had a limited ammunition supply. Each of the two 155 mm guns only had 30 shells available while the four 105 mm guns only had 50 rounds apiece.[64]

On 4 September 1943, the day the Allied operation against Lae would commence, there were actually 2650 Japanese field troops at Lae (57 per cent of the estimate) and 5000 (115 per cent of the estimate) at Salamaua.[65]

Chapter 4

MOUNTAINS TO CLIMB

Up until 1943 the Japanese had been satisfied to occupy the coastal towns in New Guinea north of the Owen Stanley Range and not move too far inland. This policy changed with the loss of the Papuan beachheads and led to the unsuccessful operation to capture Wau. Further afield the New Guinea highlands area remained under Allied control and became increasingly important as the war moved north from Papua into New Guinea. In early April 1943 New Guinea Force headquarters stated that Bena Bena in the highlands was assuming increased importance as a possible base for operations against Madang, Lae and Wewak. From Bena Bena, patrols could also harass any Japanese moves into the Ramu Valley (see Map 6).[1] The highlands also served as a major source of native labour while at the same time denying the Japanese that same resource. To protect Bena Bena airfield, Major Fergus MacAdie's 2/7th Independent Company was flown

Mountains to climb

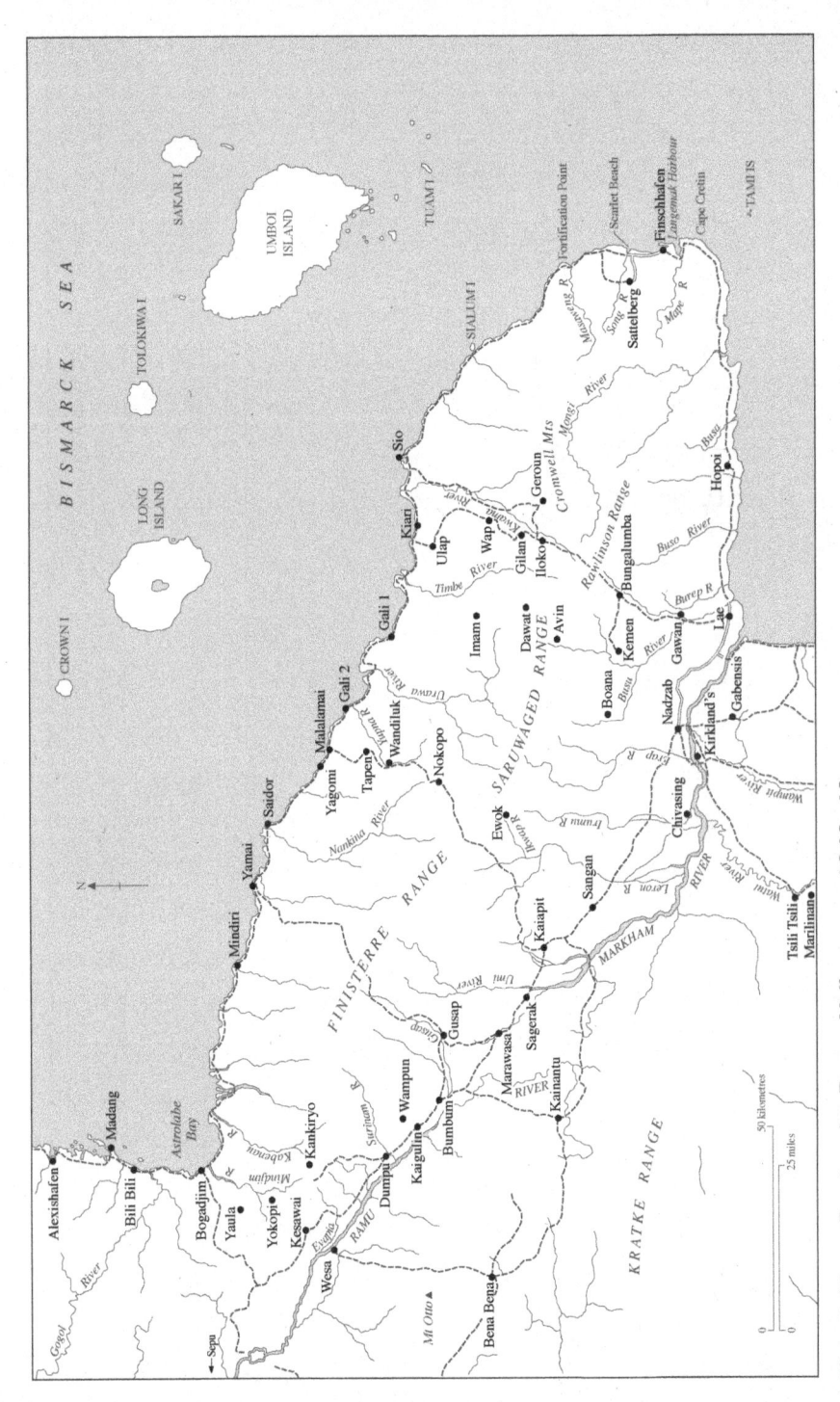

Map 6: Huon Peninsula–Ramu Valley area, 1942–43

in from Wau on 27 May 1943.[2] Known as Bena Force, MacAdie's company came under the direct command of New Guinea Force.

Lieutenant General Kenney's 5th USAAF had used Bena Bena airstrip as early as August 1942 when a C-47 transport had landed with aircraft engineers to salvage much-needed wheel bearings from a crashed B-25 Mitchell. They also found a P-40 Kittyhawk wreck, which was stripped for parts and, with the help of a hundred local natives, brought back to the airstrip. After three days the C-47, piloted by Captain Edgar Hampton, who Kenney said could 'land and take-off a C-47 from a good sized well', returned and flew the engineers and the recovered parts out.[3]

Desperate for forward fighter bases, Major General Ennis Whitehead wanted to develop Bena Bena. After a meeting on 29 May 1943, his commander, General Kenney, wrote, 'Whitey wants to build up Bena Bena but we have only enough troop carrier effort to do some deceptive stuff. I'm going to pretend to build an airfield there to prevent the Japs from looking at Marilinan . . . The Nip is worried about Bena Bena . . . I'm going to keep baiting him to keep him interested in that area.' Therefore Bena Bena played the part of a dummy airbase to divert attention from the airfield complex being developed further east at Marilinan, also known as Tsili Tsili. On 8 June Kenney wrote of Bena Bena, 'tomorrow we will start raising a lot of dust . . . in about a week the Nip should get worried and start attacking'.[4]

On 3 June the Deputy Chief of the Australian General Staff, Major General Frank Berryman, flew to Port Moresby and met with Brigadier General Paul 'Squeeze' Wurtsmith, the commander of the 5th USAAF fighter units. Wurtsmith wanted another infantry battalion plus a light anti-aircraft unit to protect

Mountains to climb

Bena Bena. However, due to other commitments, the 5th USAAF could only maintain 1000 men at Bena Bena so Berryman got agreement from General Blamey for a second Australian independent company being sent there. On 7 June it was agreed that the 2/2nd Independent Company would be sent to reinforce the 2/7th provided that 5th USAAF could maintain it.[5] 'Real tough babies,' Kenney said, impressed by the Australian commandos.[6]

In line with General Kenney's prediction, there were twelve Japanese air attacks on the Bena Bena area from 4 to 19 June, though damage was negligible.[7] The Japanese command estimated that the equivalent of three Australian battalions was operating in the New Guinea highlands and that there were seven large airfields in the region. They were concerned that a road could be built to link the area with Wau and the south coast which would 'convert these airfields into very powerful airbases' directly threatening the Japanese hold on New Guinea. The Japanese therefore planned to move troops into the highlands to attack Kainantu, Bena Bena and Mount Hagen from the ground. It was planned to use the main force of the 20th Division against Bena Bena and elements of the 41st Division to occupy Mount Hagen. The operation, scheduled to commence in early September 1943, required 3000 men for the attack on Bena Bena and another 1000 to hold a base at Marawasa in the Markham Valley. However, because 26,000 men would be required to carry supplies to the Marawasa base and beyond, it was doubtful that the operation could commence before a planned road across the Finisterre Range to the Ramu Valley was complete in April 1944. In preparation for the operation, Japanese forces had occupied Kaiapit and patrols had moved further up the Ramu Valley and occupied Dumpu and Wesa. However, with the increasing Allied threat to Salamaua and Lae, on 1 August 1943 General Adachi decided to postpone the Bena Bena operation.[8]

The impact of two Australian independent companies at Bena Bena on Japanese strategy in New Guinea was astonishing, diverting Japanese attention away from the main game at Lae. After the war it was stated that 'the 18th Army commander and his staff decided to execute the above mentioned plan at all cost although it might mean the sacrifice of Lae and Salamaua'.[9]

•

In February 1943 Captain John Murphy, who was working with the Australia New Guinea Administrative Unit (ANGAU), reported that between 50 and 100 Japanese troops were moving overland from Madang to Lae, a clear indication that the Japanese were intent on exerting control over the Ramu and Markham valleys. The Japanese party, from the 21st Regiment and led by Major Takahashi, had set off from Madang on 31 December 1942 with 200 troops using pack mules to carry supplies and machine guns. However, once the party reached the Gogol River, only 14 kilometres south of Madang, it had to proceed without the mules and heavy weapons. Despite losing four men to a strafing attack by Allied aircraft while trying to bridge a river in the Markham Valley, Takahashi's men reached Chivasing on 1 February. For the final part of the journey to Lae the Japanese party used native guides and carriers recruited from the Markham Valley, 39 of them from Chivasing and another 28 from Sangan. Takahashi considered that, apart from those around Marawasa, 'the natives in the area were gentle'. Now averaging 20 kilometres a day, and despite a 90 per cent incidence of malaria, Takahashi's party reached Lae on 7 February. These Japanese troops had generally got on well with the native population of the Ramu and Markham valleys and this would have major ramifications for the Australian commandos and ANGAU operatives trying to maintain native loyalty and recruit native labour in the coming months.[10]

At the Australian 3rd Division headquarters in Wau there were also concerns about the Japanese threat to the Bulolo Valley, so any more enemy moves along the old trade route from Madang to Lae needed to be closely monitored. It was considered that an ANGAU officer based at Chivasing, employing native intelligence sources, would give ample warning of such a move from the Markham Valley along the Wampit Valley towards Wau.[11] Captain John Murphy was already engaged in convincing the villagers of the Markham and Ramu valleys that the Japanese were losing the war. Photographs of Japanese prisoners and Japanese dead, the more graphic the better, proved to be a very powerful tool to convince the native population that the Australians were still in control. Murphy also requested badges taken from Japanese troops to add to the effect.[12]

Also serving with ANGAU, Warrant Officer Peter Ryan used a similar approach to convince hostile natives closer to Lae that they needed to back the Allies and not the Japanese by pointing out the size of the bomb craters left by Allied bombing. Ryan explained that bombs of that power could devastate any native village that refused to cooperate with the Allied cause.[13]

Ryan, who had originally been serving with a searchlight company in Port Moresby, had transferred to ANGAU in the hope of seeing some front-line action. After trekking from the south coast along the Bulldog Track the 19-year-old Ryan had arrived in Wau in July 1942. Some months later he volunteered to undertake his first mission across the Markham River, to contact Jock McLeod, who had been operating in the Wain mountain district north of the Markham Valley for some time. Accompanied by two native police constables, Ryan crossed the Markham River and headed up the Erap River into the mountains to Boana, within two days walk of Japanese-held Lae. Hearing that McLeod was at Samanzing, but misled as to the shortest route to get there, Ryan headed off east via mountain tracks to Kasenobe and Bungalumba before contacting McLeod near Samanzing. McLeod told Ryan of the increased Japanese presence around Lae and shared his plan to cross the Saruwaged Range to the north coast. Using a shorter return route to Boana via Kemen, Ryan then headed back across the Markham River to report and arrange supplies for McLeod.[14]

Once resupplied, Ryan returned to Boana and on 22 January 1943, accompanied by his police constable, Watute, he travelled via Kemen to Gawan in the foothills west of Lae. After seeing the improvement in the tracks between some of the villages it was quite clear to Ryan that the Japanese had been in the area and were exerting considerable influence. 'Only the fact that my constable and myself kept cocked rifles continually in hand prevented our being attacked,' he wrote. On 24 January Ryan and Watute moved by moonlight from Gawan to the junction of the Busu and Sankwep rivers. From there Watute adopted local dress and manner and went into the nearby village of Gwabadik where he arranged for three villagers to cross the unbridged Busu River and go into Chinatown on the outskirts of Lae. They were to bring out one of the Chinese civilians who may be able to provide intelligence on Japanese operations in Lae.[15]

Holding onto a log with one hand, and paddling with the other, the three Gwabadik natives crossed the Busu and soon returned with Peter Ah Tun. 'He was of medium height, with gold-brown skin, and a face that looked as much European as Chinese,' Ryan wrote. Ah Tun had been in charge of the freezing plant in Lae pre-war, and along with a number of other Chinese mechanics and carpenters he was now being used by the Japanese to maintain services in Lae. Having only recently been released after spending three days shackled in handcuffs and leg irons in a Japanese gaol, Ah Tun had no qualms about talking to Ryan. He provided critical intelligence about the Japanese troops that had landed at Lae earlier in January. 'They are infantry, and they boast that they have been brought here to capture Wau,' Ryan wrote. Ah Tun was also able to pinpoint where the Japanese defences and supply dumps were in Lae and relate how conditions had steadily deteriorated for those residents who remained, with only a meagre rice ration available to them.[16]

Ryan played a dangerous game patrolling to the edge of Lae but the information he gained from Peter Ah Tun was vital intelligence. However, without a radio he had to write out the report and have it sent by messenger back to Bob's camp on the other side of the Markham River (see Map 2). By then the information had been superseded by events at Wau. The Japanese soon found out Ryan was in the area, but with the Busu River proving a formidable barrier to pursuit, he was able to leave the area unmolested.[17]

•

The loss of the Bismarck Sea supply convoy highlighted just how isolated the Japanese garrison in Lae was. The Japanese command was forced to look inland for a solution including a way across the fearsome Saruwaged Range from the north coast to Lae. As part of those preparations, a detachment from the 30th Independent Engineer Regiment under Lieutenant Masamichi Kitamoto was given the task of crossing the range to Lae from the north. Kitamoto, who had been a long-distance runner for his country at the 1932 Olympic Games in Los Angeles, had decided to 'use those legs of yours and go out to fight' when he volunteered to lead the detachment.[18]

The engineer regiment, in reality 'a group of middle-aged men who led [an] easy life as civilians and never carried a gun in our lives', had shipped out of Hiroshima's port of Ujina in Japan around 23 February 1943, stopping at Palau from 13 to 15 March before disembarking at Rabaul on 24 March. On 7 April the regiment boarded three destroyers at Rabaul and was taken to Tuluvu, on the western tip of New Britain. As the men disembarked they had watched some of the survivors of the Bismarck Sea convoy also come ashore. 'They were all worn out and their tired water soaked bodies could be seen from beneath their torn and tattered uniforms,' Kitamoto wrote. His previously confident men 'became clouded with uneasiness and fear and finally they all looked down at their feet, trying to avoid looking directly at the pitiful scene before them'.[19]

On 24 April Lieutenant Colonel Murai issued the order for Kitamoto's detachment to carry out the reconnaissance of an overland route from Kiari to Lae (see Map 7). According to Murai, the detachment was made up of Kitamoto and 22 men plus a wireless section and a code man, around 30 men in all. However, Kitamoto is quite adamant in his post-war writings that the detachment strength was 50 men.[20] Kitamoto's engineers embarked on three landing craft at Tuluvu on the evening of 24 April and crossed the Dampier Strait to Umboi Island by night,

Mountains to climb

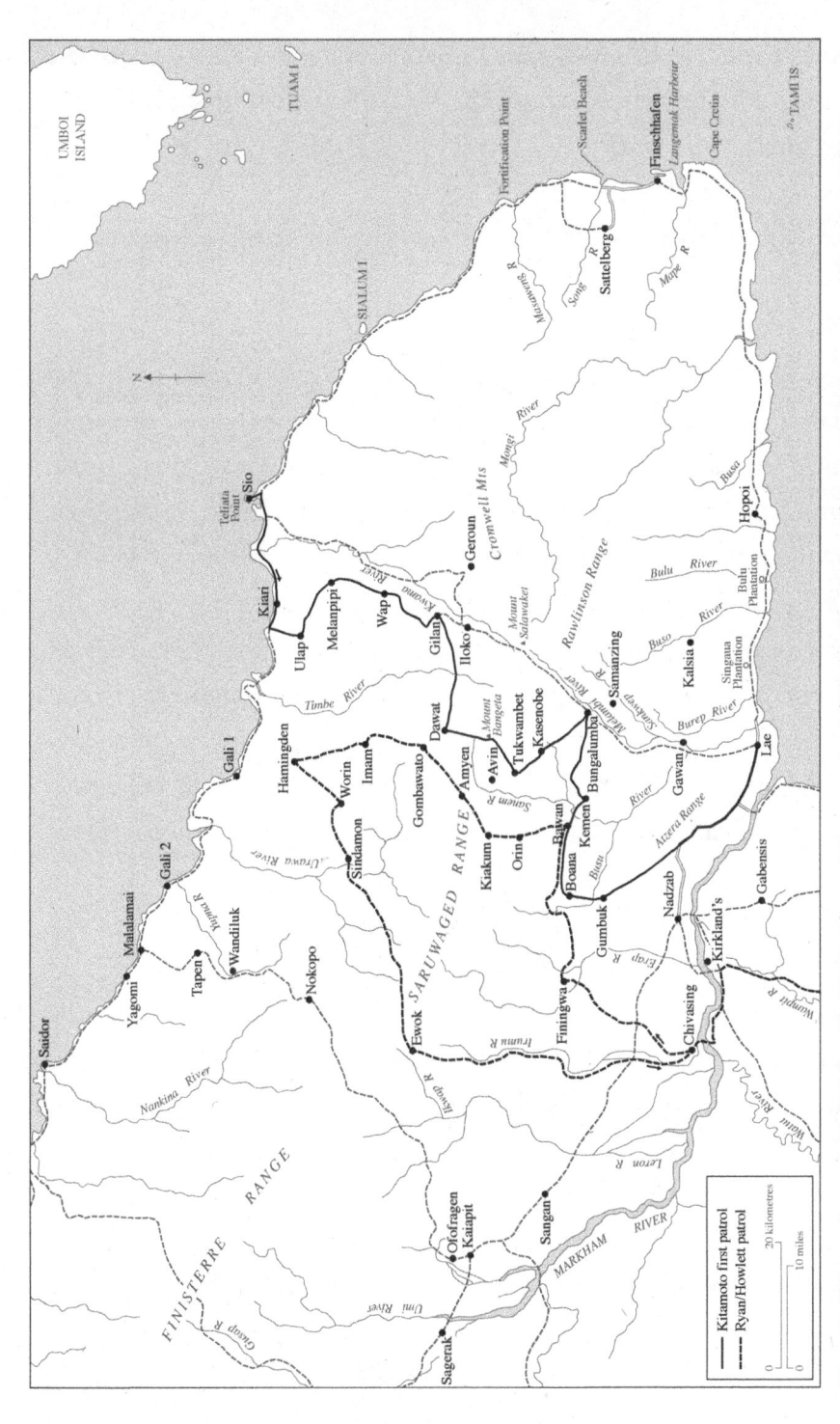

Map 7: Kitamoto patrol (27 April–18 May) and Ryan patrol (25 April–23 June) across Saruwaged Range, 1943

sheltering the three boats under overhanging trees throughout the next day. They then crossed the Vitiaz Strait to the New Guinea mainland and landed at Teliata Point (see Map 7) on the northern coast of the Huon Peninsula.[21]

Kitamoto was fortunate to soon come across a local native named Rabo who agreed to guide the detachment across the Saruwaged Range and organise 100 native carriers, to be replaced on reaching new tribal areas. 'We had stepped into an unknown land,' Kitamoto thought as his detachment began the long trek south to Lae. Further help came after the first night's stop at Ulap, where a Lutheran missionary sympathetic to the Axis cause provided much-needed tents and new ropes for the journey ahead. However, the most important gift was a map of the Saruwaged region with a red line indicating the route to Lae. 'I became filled with confidence as if I had gained a million allies for I had prepared to cross the mountains relying only on stars and a compass,' Kitamoto wrote. Changing porters at each village, using salt and cloth as payment, Kitamoto's expedition moved south, steadily gaining height. The track soon disappeared and Private Yoshizo Kitaide, a master carpenter from Kainan City, showed exceptional skill as he 'built bridges over the marshes and wove ladders from the vines for climbing the cliffs . . . the natives were astonished'. At night Kitaide would also build hammocks in the trees to keep the men off the damp ground. As Kitamoto observed, 'Kitaide had no time to rest.' At the village of Dawat, at the base of the towering Mount Bangeta, half the native carriers refused to go further, afraid of cannibals on the other side.[22]

To reach Dawat, Kitamoto's detachment had followed an east–west ridge line for some 15 kilometres from Gilan, gaining no distance to the south. As Kitamoto wrote, 'In New Guinea, the only way to climb the mountains was to follow the ridges', even if you went the wrong way. Battling rain, cold and sharp inclines, the detachment, now down to 50 native carriers, struggled up the Saruwaged Range. 'It was just like climbing a slide from the bottom to the top . . . We continued our climb looking for a piece of flat ground but the incline kept going up and up into the skies.' As the men climbed higher, 'It was so cold that it seemed that our hands which grasped the rocks to pull us up would become frozen . . . A single hemp rope was the only lifeline for 100 men.' The summit of Mount Bangeta 'was a world of snowy white', incompatible with the tropical world below. For Kitamoto, reaching the summit 'was the same feeling of victory when one cuts the tape in a race'. With his men gathered around the Japanese flag crying tears of joy, Kitamoto experienced 'the most dramatic and impressive sight that I have ever experienced in my life'. From the summit he could look down into the Markham Valley and the Markham River beyond, flowing to the sea at Lae. Kitamoto's wireless operator Tsutsui sent out a message that his men had reached the summit and the 'Successful achievement of mission is near.'[23]

As the detachment approached the first village on the southern side of the range, the 50 carriers were loath to continue, afraid of cannibals. 'Trembling with fear we entered the village of Tukaget,' Kitamoto wrote, but 'It appeared that they did not have the strength of eating people, let alone killing them.' From Tukaget the detachment trekked through Kasenobe and 'spent hours making detours of ravines and valleys that obstructed our course'. Using the same route from Kasenobe as Peter Ryan had taken three months previously, the detachment crossed two steep ridges and was reported as reaching Bungalumba on 10 May. Kitamoto's men 'were completely worn out and about half of them came down with fever'.[24]

Kitamoto then turned west for Bawan, where two Australian soldiers with about 30 accompanying natives had been reported.[25] He selected at least ten of his best men and they moved fast, reaching Bawan at dawn on 15 May. However, the two Australians had seen him coming. 'After engaging in gun battle, they escaped into the hills,' Kitamoto noted of the incident. 'It was very regretful that we could not catch them.'[26]

Having split his detachment, it is probable that the remainder of Kitamoto's men followed him from Bungalumba to Lae via Boana once they had recovered their health, although some may have taken the shorter route through Gawan, crossing the Busu River at the Kunda (cane) bridge (if it had already been built) or else at the river mouth. Kitamoto took his fit group of men on to Boana and then back to Lae via Yalu and the Markham Valley road.[27] On 18 May, three weeks after landing on the north coast, he marched into Lae with nineteen of his men, their 'torn and soiled uniforms all pointed to the difficulties experienced in crossing the mountains' and he was able to tell General Nakano that a route across the Saruwaged Range, although difficult, was feasible. At this stage Kitamoto's path across the Saruwaged Range was looked upon as a possible route to bring units from the 20th and 41st Divisions, currently at Madang and Wewak, across from the north coast to Lae.[28]

Nakano had also sent out a reconnaissance party from Lae on 13 April to investigate the easiest routes to Gawan and Kalsia from Lae. Both villages were in the foothills of the Saruwaged Range north of Lae. The party returned to Lae on 24 April and confirmed a route through to Bungalumba via Gawan.[29] Another party, the Arai Tai, made up of ten engineers and fifteen infantrymen, left Lae on 18 April to check tracks in the Boana area.[30]

Three days after he had reached Lae, Kitamoto was sheltering from Allied bombing when a bomb hit a nearby shelter killing a number of fellow officers. 'It was horrible to look at and the severity and merciless nature of war struck me strongly,' he wrote. 'If I stay in this place any longer, I may have to die an unnecessary death.'[31] He would have other work to do soon enough.

•

Meanwhile the Australians continued their own patrols of the Huon Peninsula. After his successful patrol to Lae in January, Peter Ryan was back for more, this time accompanied by Captain Les Howlett, eight native police constables and five native carriers. Their patrol crossed the Markham River on rafts near Chivasing on 25 April 1943 tasked with obtaining further intelligence on Japanese operations around Lae and the Huon Peninsula or, to put it more simply, 'keep an eye on the Japs' and 'keep in touch with the native situation'. The patrol would be the first Australian presence in the Lae region since Ryan had gone to Lae in January but, due to rumours of Japanese patrols along the Erap River, he had crossed the Markham further west than on his previous trip. 'Each time I crossed the Markham on my way to the mountains,' Ryan wrote, 'I felt I had passed through a door into another life.'[32]

After crossing the flat country of the Markham Valley the patrol moved into the cover of the foothills and made its way east towards Lae. After being told that a fifteen-man Japanese patrol had been at Boana on 17 April, Ryan and Howlett decided to take an alternative route to Bawan. There were signs the track had seen recent heavy use, and Singin, the head man from a village near Boana, also told Ryan and Howlett that a Japanese party, Kitamoto's engineers, had recently crossed the Saruwaged Range from the north coast to Bungalumba and then gone on to Lae.[33] Such information went both ways as Ryan's presence in the area had also been reported by other natives to the Japanese.[34]

Ryan headed off to Boana where he found indications that the Japanese had indeed recently been there. He then sent his most trusted native policeman, Watute, and one of his carriers, Pato, who understood the local dialect, to investigate. They heard of a food cache left by the Japanese at Samanzing and surmised it may be there 'for Japanese troops being evacuated from Lae'. Once Ryan and Howlett reached Bawan on 8 May, Ryan was laid up for four days with malaria. On 12 May Ryan heard that Japanese troops were at Kasenobe and was concerned that they were headed to Bawan so it was decided to look for a new camp.[35]

As Ryan and Howlett scouted for a new location near Orin on 15 May, they were fired on by a patrol of seventeen Japanese troops from the track far below. Kitamoto's patrol had found Ryan and Howlett. 'The machine guns opened fire,' Kitamoto wrote. 'The noise was amplified to three times the sound heard in open country as the cracks of the guns vibrated among the cliffs.'[36] 'Buzzing bullets seemed to fill the air round us, clipping through the grass and ricocheting,' Ryan wrote. Unable to give chase, Kitamoto's detachment proceeded through to Bawan and Boana. 'After perhaps ten minutes the leader put his pistol back in its holster,' Ryan observed, 'and we heard him shouting to the natives to pick up their loads.'[37]

'The enemy showed his back once and disappeared into the jungle,' a frustrated Kitamoto wrote. 'It was impossible to locate them in the maze of vegetation . . . That night we spent at the enemy camp and next morning burned it to the ground.' Aware of the danger they were now in, Ryan and Howlett moved higher up into the Saruwaged Range.[38] After the author showed Kitamoto's account of the incident to Ryan in 2006, Ryan referred to Kitamoto as 'a foeman, a chap that didn't kill me, but he tried'.[39]

•

Even before the loss of the Bismarck Sea convoy, the Japanese had decided to try to open an overland supply route from Madang to Lae via the Ramu and Markham valleys. A road would be constructed from Madang to Bogadjim and up to Kankiryo in the Finisterre Mountains to join with a supply track into the Ramu Valley. On 9 February 1943 a detachment from the 20th Division under the infantry group commander, Major General Shinichi Yanagawa, left Wewak by landing craft for Madang to commence the work. The Yanagawa Detachment was made up of two infantry battalions and most of the 20th Engineering Regiment.[40] The importance of the project was stressed during a visit to Madang by the Japanese emperor's aide-de-camp on 27 March. 'His majesty's enquiries and anxieties were conveyed,' one officer wrote.[41]

By mid-April the detachment had been reinforced with two further regiments of engineers and three road construction units. The course of the road was also changed to continue through the mountains via Yaula and Yokopi towards Kaiapit as this route was considered 'less vulnerable to air attacks' than the shorter route via Kesawai into the Ramu Valley. Battling steep grades, cliff faces, waterfalls, ravines and dense jungle as well as malnutrition and malaria, Yanagawa's men pushed the road forward. Due to the terrain challenges and supply difficulties, 'troops were compelled to attack the virgin forest with shovels, picks and explosives'. Horses and trucks were sent to help but both soon became useless, the former from lack of suitable fodder and the latter from constant breakdowns under such harsh conditions.[42]

Soon after he had returned from his Saruwaged crossing, Masamichi Kitamoto was given a new task. He was ordered to lead a force up the Markham Valley from Lae to report on the progress of the Yanagawa Detachment as well as investigating Australian activities at Kaiapit and further west (see Map 8). Kitamoto put together a detachment comprising 19 infantrymen under Sergeant Sogabe, ten of his own engineers, a five-man communications squad and a doctor. The native guide Rabo, Kitamoto's constant companion since they had met in Kiari, would again travel with the detachment.[43]

Kitamoto's group left Lae by night on 26 May, travelling on trucks as far west as possible before daylight so as not to alert any Lae natives who may report the departure to the Australians. When the patrol arrived at Boana the next evening, Kitamoto came down with a bad case of malaria and, when his men left for Kaiapit on 31 May, Kitamoto was carried.[44] His detachment was travelling through the foothills north of the Markham Valley and would approach Kaiapit out of the hills to the north. As he approached Kaiapit, his native guide Rabo went out and discovered that there were supposedly six Australians at Ofofragen, a small village 2 kilometres north-west of Kaiapit.[45] Kitamoto's unit

Mountains to climb

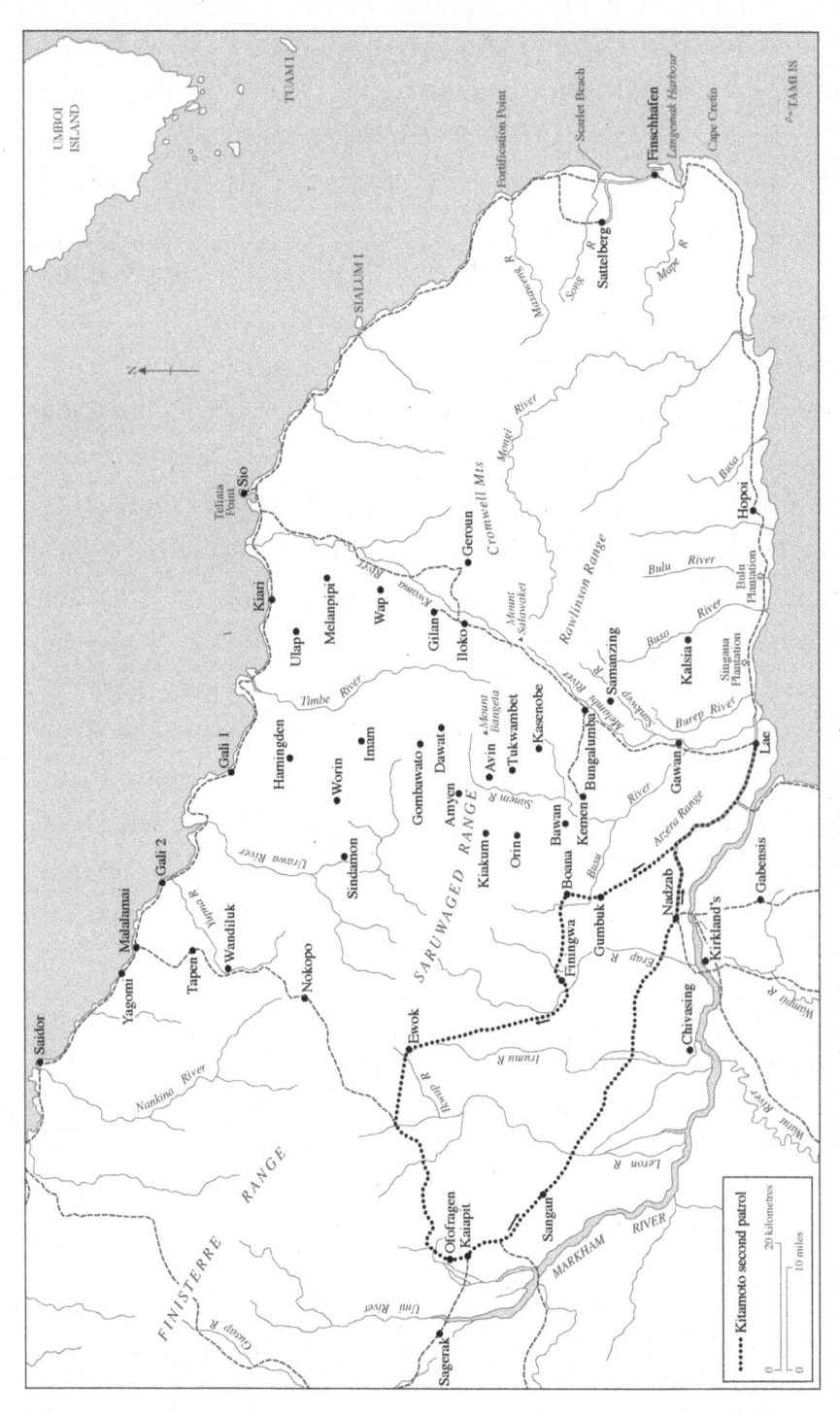

Map 8: Kitamoto patrol to Kaiapit (26 May–13 June 1943)

had come across Warrant Officer Harry Lumb who, accompanied by five native policemen, was recruiting native carriers around Sangan and Kaiapit to work on the Kaiapit airstrip. It was later thought that the Ofofragen village leader had betrayed Lumb to Kitamoto's party.

According to Kitamoto, his men moved to the village on the night of 6 June and were in position before dawn. Two squads of Sogabe's infantrymen covered any escape to the rear or flanks while Kitamoto led his engineers in from the front. 'Stifling the noise of our footsteps we gradually closed the net,' he wrote. Early on the morning of 7 June his engineers opened fire but Lumb and his native police fought back. 'The bullets of automatic rifles came flying from the hut,' Kitamoto wrote, 'we concentrated our fire on the hut. The outcome was obvious.' The six men were killed.[46] An alternative account by one of the native policemen, Arwesor, says the attack took place at about 1600 in the afternoon while he was away from the village. When he returned an hour later the Japanese had arrived and were accompanied by an interpreter, a Chinese man from Lae. Arwesor was captured and bound but later escaped, reaching safety at Marilinan on 12 June.[47]

Documents found on Lumb identified him and his mission, which was to recruit native carriers and obtain information on the enemy as he moved west along the Markham and Ramu valleys. One of the letters dated 12 October 1942 stated that 'I do not trust Chivashings.' 'Even the information they give about the Japanese Army is half trustworthy and half doubtful,' Lumb had written.[48] He had been proved correct at the cost of his life.

On 13 June the Japanese patrol returned to Lae with one of the officers wearing Lumb's clothing and spectacles while Kitamoto rode the captured donkey like 'Don Quixote leading the soldiers through enemy territory'. Other soldiers carried Lumb's Owen sub-machine gun and the rifles taken from the native police.[49] Kitamoto later returned to Boana with a platoon of Taiwanese infantry known as the Takasago Volunteers and trained the local natives in ancillary tasks. By August the military police unit at Ngasawapum and Kitamoto's unit at Boana had together trained some 100 native soldiers.[50]

•

Meanwhile, on 25 May Peter Ryan had returned to Boana for supplies, contending with leeches, landslides, biting cold and violent headaches brought on by the altitude. When Watute rejoined him he told Ryan that they had been betrayed and a Japanese patrol was now searching for them. Ryan headed back north into the mountain range, crossing a landslide via a vine ladder which was then cut away to make it very difficult for anyone to follow. Like Kitamoto two months before him, Ryan and Howlett were now faced with crossing the Saruwaged Range but this time from the southern side. They would also cross further to the west of Kitamoto's route. When the party reached Amyen, at the base of the range, Pato was able to advise the best way to make the crossing and he assembled fifteen carriers to assist.[51]

On 5 June the party left Amyen and commenced to climb along a narrowing ridge up into the Saruwaged Range. 'Remote, cold, incredibly high and distant seeming, they frightened us,' Ryan wrote of the daunting mountains. The cliffs were sheer, 'just like that bloody wardrobe door,' Ryan later told me. The party faced 'bare rock-faces, smooth and polished by the water'.

Knowing what lay ahead, the guides cut vines for the climb as they went along the track, wrapping them around their bodies to carry them. They were 'tremendous, looking like a bloody Michelin man,' Ryan said. The guides would somehow traverse the cliffs and then secure the vines to enable the loads to be carried forward. 'Hardly daring to breath, we crept over,' Ryan wrote.[52]

The rain and freezing cold on the first night led to five carriers dropping out which resulted in one-third of the stores having to be abandoned. On 6 June the party set off at dawn knowing that it would be their longest day. 'No more depressing sight can be imagined than this moss forest in the half light.' They crossed the crest of the range and began an at times vertical descent before reaching Gombawato on the northern side after thirteen hours of punishing toil (see Map 7). Corporal Kari had been invaluable, relieving carriers of their loads at crucial moments to allow them to recover and continue. 'His enormous strength of both physique and character were an inspiration to all of us,' Ryan wrote. Still carrying the vital radio, Ryan and Howlett now received a message to withdraw from the Huon Peninsula and head either to Bena Bena or back across the Markham to Wampit. They decided on the latter course. The next day they were advised to move rapidly as the Japanese had moved deep into the Markham Valley and Harry Lumb had been betrayed and killed.[53]

Negotiating a series of rough and steep tracks, Ryan and Howlett's party moved west along the northern side of the Saruwaged Range. The natives on this side of the range were not helpful and it was difficult to obtain carriers. Nonetheless on 12 June the party trekked for over nineteen hours straight before reaching Worin village. Here they were fortunate to meet a friendly village chief who fed the party well and offered to guide them back across the Saruwaged Range via an easier route than had been planned. At Sindamon, after they had asked to sleep in one of the huts, the villagers 'politely removed a decomposed corpse, and motioned us to enter'. After recrossing the range by a much easier route, Ryan's party reached Ewok on 17 June only to discover that Japanese patrols had already been there twice. On 20 June, carrying only their packs and weapons, the men set out to follow the Irumu River down to the Markham Valley, but after getting lost in 'tangled belts of pit pit and sago swamp' they headed back onto the main track and made their way to Chivasing.[54]

At about 1450 on 21 June Ryan's party warily approached Chivasing. An accompanying native guide, Arong, was then sent ahead to check all was clear while Ryan and Howlett remained at a coconut grove on the edge of the village. Local natives told Arong that no Japanese were present in the area and that rafts and canoes were available for the trip down the Markham River to Kirkland's camp, an Australian commando outpost. Arong returned to Ryan to confirm the absence of enemy troops and, with most of the native police left in the coconut grove, he led Howlett and Ryan into Chivasing where an obvious air of unease permeated the demeanour of the inhabitants. Suddenly rifle shots and machine-gun fire opened up from a row of houses and the two Australians dashed through the village, making for the creek. Another volley of fire broke out and Les Howlett cried out and fell face down, fatally hit in the head and chest.[55]

The quicker Ryan had jumped into the creek before the second volley of fire but had then lost his Owen gun and shirt climbing out through the thick undergrowth on the other side. Fear drove his feet as he scrambled away with small-arms fire lancing through the undergrowth around him. He then hid in the mud of a pig wallow as his pursuers continued the search. After about half an hour he heard the villagers calling out that the Japanese soldiers had gone but, having being deceived once, Ryan stayed hidden. Then as night fell he made his way southwest towards the Markham River, spending the night in a mud pool to escape the mosquitos. Next day he reached the Markham at a point opposite the Watut River and swam across from island to island. He then forced two local villagers to take him downriver by canoe to Kirkland's camp and safety. On arrival he was 'too spent, emotionally, to feel or think or care'.[56] 'I lost everything at Chivasing,' Ryan later said, 'My trousers, I looked like Malcolm Fraser!'[57]

The Japanese intelligence report on the incident stated that two Australians and fifteen native troops were ambushed by a military police unit at Chivasing with one Australian soldier and one or two native soldiers killed. The Japanese patrol consisted of ten men led by Lieutenant Tomita, who was the commander of the Lae Military Police and had left Lae on 10 June to reconnoitre the Markham Valley.[58]

•

Further west the Japanese were also contesting the presence of the Australians in the Ramu Valley. Much of the increased activity was related to the military road which was being constructed from Bogadjim on the north coast up the valley of the Mindjim River to Yaula and Yokopi with the intention of crossing the Finisterre Range into the Ramu Valley.[59] The stretch from Erima to Yaula was 29 kilometres long and required 45 bridges to be built. After that it was still another 25 kilometres to Yokopi.[60] On 6 June the astute General Kenney wrote, 'I don't think he [the Japanese] will ever finish it. If he does, air attack will keep him from using it.'[61]

Keen to know more about the road, a native police constable, Corporal Merire, who had good knowledge of the Madang area, was sent out to do a reconnaissance of the road with another native policeman, Constable Kominiwan. The two men left the Bena Bena area on 18 June and after wading across the Ramu River reached Kesawai village. They then headed north across the Finisterre Range to the headwaters of the Mindjim River. From here the two men heard the sound of dynamite explosions and discarded their rifles as they approached the Japanese controlled area. Entering a valley carrying baskets of food, the two disguised constables 'saw hundreds of houses and tents, and what appeared to be thousands of enemy troops', as Merire later recalled. The head man at the village next to the Japanese camp kept the men safe and they were able to observe the Japanese at work building a road 5 metres wide. The Japanese were using three groups for the work: one to clear a wide path through the undergrowth, a second to cut down any trees in their path and a third using dynamite to clear any rock obstacles. All the work was being done by manual labour using picks, mattocks, shovels, crowbars and hoes to clear the blasted rock. Only Japanese workers, most of them front-line troops, were used and they worked from dawn to dusk and into the night if the moon was out. After the two native policemen had moved nearer to the coast, some hostile locals betrayed them but both managed to escape capture and were able to return with their valuable information about the Japanese road.[62]

Good use was made of this intelligence. On 18 July an F-5 Lightning photo-reconnaissance aircraft took excellent photos of the road from Bogadjim to Yaula. 'The size and scope of this construction project amazed all of us . . . the target appears lucrative,' General Whitehead wrote in a report to General Kenney. On 20 July three medium-bomber squadrons, taking part in the deepest penetration by attack bombers into enemy territory to date, attacked supply dumps and three bridges on the Madang to Bogadjim section of the road. The next day the medium-bomber squadrons were back in a major air attack on the road itself.[63] 'At noon their airplanes strafed and bombed us with terrific firepower,' one Japanese officer wrote. The raid killed 114 Japanese officers and men.[64]

On 1 August New Guinea Force headquarters estimated that the road could reach the Ramu Valley within six to eight weeks and there was concern at the threat that posed. In response the 2/2nd Independent Company had flown to Bena Bena to join the 2/7th. On 8 August a patrol under Lieutenant Bill Hawker reached Wesa, about 3 kilometres south of the Ramu River, from where it was planned to carry out a reconnaissance patrol across the valley to investigate the road. Lieutenant Pat Dunshea went with Hawker on the patrol. Dunshea, who had been decorated for his long-range patrol work during the Wau campaign, had recently been appointed as the 2/7th Independent Company's intelligence officer.

Apart from Hawker and Dunshea, Merire also took part in this patrol as well as Kalamsei, a native police constable from the Ramu Valley. Lieutenant Ted Byrne later said that Kalamsei 'was the best shot I ever saw. Brilliant young man.' Pat Dunshea added that Kalamsei 'knew everybody and knew where the trails were'.[65] The patrol left Wesa on 9 August with Merire and Kalamsei scouting out in front. The two native police constables would play a key role as some of the villages in the area around Bogadjim were in the pay of the Japanese. When Merire ran into some hostile locals who thought he was unarmed, he brought out a revolver from beneath his lap-lap and killed them.[66] Pat Dunshea later said that he 'didn't do much myself, but verified what Kalamsei and Merire had said'.[67] Merire, the 'warrior', was later awarded the British Empire Medal for his service. Kalamsei, who Lieutenant Colonel Fergus MacAdie referred to as 'the most willing and most courageous member of the RPC [Royal Papuan Constabulary] that I have ever encountered', was awarded the same medal but did not survive to receive it, killed by friendly artillery fire on 21 December 1943 in the Ramu Valley. On 29 August 1944 the medal was presented to Kalamsei's wife, Kumisi, before some 500 proud locals at Atsunas village in the upper Markham Valley.[68]

•

Even at Wesa, on the south side of the Ramu, the Australians never felt safe among the locals due to the earlier Japanese influence. Ted Byrne was told 'it's a different warfare down there. At Wesa they have always hated us, they are antagonistic.'[69] On the night of 11–12 August a Japanese patrol cut the Australian phone lines and tried to get into the commando camp at Wesa. Ken Monk let them get to within a metre of his post before opening fire, wounding a Japanese officer in the upper leg. The officer dragged himself into the scrub where he was later found dead by Captain David Dexter, his demise 'indicated by automatic pistol in hand and beautiful hole between the eyes'. After further patrolling found no more signs of the Japanese, most of the commandos returned to Wesa camp.[70]

Next morning at 1115 the call 'come and get it' came from the cookhouse at the commando camp. But as the men headed over to get their lunch a Japanese patrol opened fire on the camp, catching most of the Australians without their weapons. Tom Foster managed to grab his Owen gun from the hut, jumped into a nearby slit trench and opened up on the enemy troops, who were no more than 20 metres away. The Japanese moved away but then came back, attacking Foster and Tom Giles in the slit trench. Throwing seventeen grenades and firing eleven magazines from their Owen guns, the two men held their ground. Other commandos had by then grabbed their weapons and helped repel three further Japanese attacks. Captain Dexter fired his Owen gun from the hip, bowling over about half of the twelve enemy soldiers he could see gathered and putting the rest to flight. Then another attack came, led by an officer waving his sword. Dexter fired off three magazines and threw some grenades and by 1150 the Japanese had had enough and withdrew, dragging their dead and wounded with them.[71]

The Australians also had their casualties. Lieutenants Bill Hawker and Andrew Beveridge along with three other men who were at the nearby observation post heard the firing and headed for the camp. They soon came across Japanese troops and, after Hawker's weapon misfired, he was shot in the back, although not seriously wounded. Merire 'just about did for himself helping to carry me out', Hawker later wrote. Another commando, John Maley, who had been cut off from the camp, was killed during this action.[72]

Whatever clashes took place on the ground, the prerequisite for any Allied operation against Lae would be control of the air over New Guinea.

Chapter 5

THE SECRET AIRBASE

The Papuan campaigns had seen some of the fiercest infantry fighting of the Pacific war. To minimise such losses of ground troops, the New Guinea campaigns that followed would concentrate on securing airfield sites to extend Allied air power. 'There are three enemies out here from the air point of view and the Jap is the least of the three,' the Allied air commander Lieutenant General Kenney told the ABC journalist Dudley Leggett. 'There's the tropical climate and the diseases associated with it, and the weather, and these two things are worse than the Jap.'[1]

As 1942 progressed, Allied air attacks on Lae had ramped up. A good example of their effectiveness came on 31 August 1942 when nine B-26 Marauders bombed Lae airfield before ten A-20 Havocs flying at minimum altitude strafed everything in sight on and around it. Living up to their name, two of the Havocs shot up a house overlooking the airfield apparently crowded with enemy troops relaxing over lunch, leaving the house burning. 'That night Tokyo Rose called us murderers,' General Kenney wrote.[2]

On 25 November 1942 the new P-38 Lightning fighters were over Lae and, with a lot of rivalry among the pilots over who would get the first victory, the pilots boldly announced their presence to the Japanese over a common radio frequency. 'We are the P-38s. We are taking over patrol of the Lae airdrome,' the radio squawked, 'come on up and we'll accommodate you.' One Japanese pilot was sufficiently insulted to take off, but did so as two 500-pound bombs from Captain Robert Faurot's Lightning hit the water off the end of the runway. The resultant water splash brought the Japanese plane down, prompting General Kenney to later tell Faurot, 'I want you to shoot them down, not splash water on them.'[3]

For the Japanese, Lae airfield became unusable until early February 1943 when repairs were made in order to concentrate planes for an air attack on Wau. On 4 February, after A-20 Havocs and B-25 Mitchells had again bombed the airfield, Kenney wrote, 'Japs had been working on it for several days. Now they can start over again.' But the Japanese persisted and managed to stage air attacks on Wau on 6 February using Lae as a refuelling base. When Kenney's bombers next returned to Lae a lone B-24 Liberator left two massive 2000-pound bomb craters on the runway.[4]

The Japanese command also understood that air power was the vital factor in the battle to hold onto New Guinea. In January 1943, even before the loss of Lae as a forward airbase, it was decided to build three new airfields on the north-western coast of New Guinea at But, Dagua and Boram Plantation and upgrade the current airfield at Wewak. On 14 February Kenney noted that aerial photos over Wewak 'show 77 aircraft dispersal bays

The secret airbase

built or building'.[5] The two Japanese infantry divisions that had landed at Wewak in February 1943 provided most of the labour to construct the new airfields.

As Lieutenant General Kane Yoshihara observed, the airfield work was not without its difficulties for the Japanese. 'As we were about to land at Madang airfield the first thing that met my eyes was the sight of officers and men scattered all over the airfield, backs bent, doing something incessantly,' he wrote. 'When I looked closer, it seemed that they were plucking grass with their hands.' Deprived of all their equipment after an Allied air raid just after it had been landed, the Japanese airfield engineers had been reduced to maintaining the airfield by hand. The contrast with the capabilities of the Allied airborne engineers was stark. 'This was the special characteristic of the New Guinea fighting,' Yoshihara observed. 'The enemy had the latest equipment and fighting methods, while we had primitive equipment and fighting methods.'[6]

With the advent of the new airfields around Wewak, the responsibility for Japanese air operations on the New Guinea mainland now switched from the navy to the army with aircraft flown in from Dutch New Guinea and Rabaul and also directly from Japan via the islands to the north. The navy would retain responsibility for air operations in the Solomon Islands and at Rabaul. The Japanese 4th Air Army, comprising the 6th and 7th Air Divisions, was ordered to Wewak on 27 July. This had a major impact on Allied plans to carry out any air landing or amphibious operations at Lae and beyond. Japanese air power would have to be neutralised before any such operation could take place.

•

At this stage the main Allied forward airbase was at Dobodura on the coastal plain behind the Papuan beachheads on the northern side of the Owen Stanley Range. The heavy bombers still operated from Port Moresby while most of the shorter-ranged medium bombers and fighters were based at Dobodura. However, the new Japanese airbases at Wewak were out of range for most of Kenney's air arm. 'It will become our primary target as soon as we can get close enough to hit it,' Kenney wrote on 14 February.[7] He desperately wanted an airfield closer to Wewak.

Salamaua was Kenney's first choice for a forward airfield. On 23 February he had asked Lieutenant General Iven Mackay, who was to temporarily take over New Guinea Force from Lieutenant General Edmund Herring, whether the Australians could capture Salamaua. 'He said he would need a lot more troops to even start that campaign,' Kenney wrote.[8] Kenney got the same response from General Blamey, who preferred to leave Salamaua in Japanese hands as its seizure would be a definite signal for the assembly of additional enemy strength at Lae.[9] Four months later, on 20 June, Kenney approached General Herring about capturing Salamaua and 'offered to slug the place to death and lay a carpet of bombs all the way to the place . . . I believe the Aussies could do the job in about three days and that would squeeze the Japs out of Lae way ahead of schedule.'[10] But General Blamey had already told Herring that 'Salamaua should not be seized; it should be bypassed.'[11] Right up to the start of the Lae operation Kenney was still 'arguing with Blamey about taking Salamaua and giving me a fighter field there'.[12]

It was clear that General Kenney would have to look elsewhere for an airbase closer to Wewak. In early May 1943 a reconnaissance party went searching for suitable airfield sites south of

The secret airbase

the Markham River, and an overgrown 600-metre runway at Marilinan, a pre-war supply strip, was chosen as a likely location. A patrol led by Lieutenant Edward Robinson from the 24th Battalion, with Major Charles Duchatel from ANGAU as the guide, reconnoitred the area in mid-May. Photos taken from ground level by Sergeant Donald Langford confirmed that the Marilinan area was a suitable location and Robinson estimated that 30 men could make the overgrown strip suitable for transport aircraft within a week.[13]

On 29 May Kenney wrote that 'Marilinan is the place for the advanced base to cover the assault on Lae and the preliminary take-out of the Jap air at Wewak. I don't dare mention it to Gen MacA's staff yet. They would throw a fit at the idea of building a field by air 40 miles in behind the Jap front.' Yet how else would Kenney get a base that would give his fighters and medium bombers the range to strike the enemy airbases at Wewak, a prerequisite for any attack on Lae? On 1 June he wrote, 'As soon as I can get a forward airdrome at Marilinan or somewhere we can take care of Wewak. That place will have to be knocked out and kept out if we are to capture Lae and develop the Nadzab area for airdromes.'[14]

When Lieutenant Robinson returned to the area with the US engineer Lieutenant Everette 'Tex' Frazier in late May, it was confirmed that the strip at Marilinan could be used.[15] Peter Ryan wrote of Frazier that 'He was about thirty, with red hair, and a face brick-red from sunburn. Blue eyes smiled a little nervously from behind gold rimless glasses.'[16] Frazier flew into Bulolo and then trekked into the Watut Valley to Marilinan where native labour was used to carry out some initial clearance under his direction, ensuring the edges of the landing strip were cut unevenly so the airfield would not be obvious from the air. Trees on the runway approaches also had to be lopped or cleared. 'This was a better airfield location than could possibly be hoped for in such rugged country,' Frazier declared.[17] From then on, in answer to queries regarding the suitability of the Marilinan area for a major airbase, Kenney would reply conclusively, 'Well, Lieutenant Frazier has been there.'[18]

Frazier returned to Port Moresby on 13 June to meet with General Kenney and General Wurtsmith. 'Hell, Tex, if it is as good as you say it is, I'll fly a P-40 there myself tomorrow,' Wurtsmith told him.[19] Wurtsmith did fly a Kittyhawk in the next day, following Frazier who had been flown back in an A-24 Dauntless. The two men then selected a better airfield site at Tsili Tsili, 6 kilometres along the Watut River directly north of Marilinan. The new site had enough space to build a double 2100-metre runway with dispersal areas. Kenney had already given orders to go ahead and develop Tsili Tsili as an advanced fighter base and refuelling point.[20] Knowing that heavy rains starting in September would flood the area, it was important to have the airfield ready for the planned attack on Lae, at that stage scheduled for late August 1943.

On 7 June Kenney commented in relation to Japanese attempts to build a route from Wewak to Lae, 'If I can build Marilinan up soon enough I can stop this business but right now I can't afford unsupported day bomber attacks.'[21] The following day General Blamey added his support for Kenney's airfield at Tsili Tsili by allocating ground troops to protect it. Major General Frank Berryman was at the meeting. 'GOC decided to put Bn into Watut to assist Kenney to develop a fighter airfield,' he wrote. On 12 June, Berryman met with Kenney to discuss the forward airfields at Bena Bena and Marilinan and later wrote in his diary, 'Kenney going full steam ahead with the latter.'[22]

The secret airbase

On 17 June Kenney briefed General MacArthur on Marilinan and how he planned to base a fighter group and some strafer squadrons there rather than just use it as a refuelling base. MacArthur asked him, 'Say, George, have you told my staff about all this?' 'Hell no,' Kenney replied. 'Don't tell them just yet,' MacArthur added. 'I don't want them scared to death.'[23] After further work on Marilinan and the connecting road, work on Tsili Tsili began on 20 June.

Meanwhile General Whitehead had told General Herring, 'you give us some troops to guard strips at Tsili Tsili and Bena Bena and we'll knock the Jap airforce out of the sky'.[24] Following General Blamey's approval on 8 June, Herring also agreed and Lieutenant Colonel Robert Marston's 57/60th Battalion was given the task of guarding the airbase development, coming under the direct command of New Guinea Force as the main component of Tsili Tsili Force.[25] Also attached were detachments of service corps personnel, engineers, signallers and field ambulance personnel. A platoon from the Papuan Infantry Battalion under Lieutenant Doug Stuart would provide a forward reconnaissance capability.

On 16 June Lieutenant Les Talbot's 17 Platoon was the first unit from Marston's battalion to arrive. Talbot's account of the landing gave a good indication of the rough nature of the Marilinan airfield. 'We were warned to hang on, and did and landed in what looked like an overgrown wheat field, with a cut grass cricket pitch about 500 yards long . . . The pilots were anxious to get back before the mountains clouded in again, and we helped as we could. They finally charged full pelt at the end of the short strip, just cleared the trees, and swung left back to Moresby, leaving a haze of clipped leaves and twigs from the tops of the taller trees.'[26] By mid-August Tsili Tsili Force had been built up to two infantry companies plus the mortar and machine-gun platoons. The entire battalion was not assembled at Tsili Tsili until mid-September.[27]

Major General Stan Savige, the Australian 3rd Division commander, had wanted Marston's battalion in the front line near Salamaua rather than at Tsili Tsili. 'Their alleged use to protect the Americans in building the airstrip in the valley was ludicrous,' he later wrote, and criticised General Herring for supplying the Americans with more than a company for the task.[28] Herring saw the bigger picture and knew the strategic importance of Tsili Tsili for the air war and told Savige on 25 June, 'I decided to put the whole Bn there because the threat to this valley may come down the Ramu and it makes your flank there secure against anything that may come down that way.'[29] The continuing spectre of another secret track, as used by the Japanese during the attack on Wau, clearly preyed on Herring's mind.

•

Lieutenant Colonel Harry Woodbury's US 871st Airborne Engineers Battalion, the first complete unit of its type to leave the continental United States, had arrived in New Guinea on 5 June 1943. Woodbury, a 27-year-old civil engineer, was 'the heart and soul of the Airborne Engineers' who had helped design the unit's equipment, each piece of which could fit into a C-47 transport or a glider and was limited in weight to about 2000 kilograms. Woodbury's battalion consisted of 29 officers and 501 enlisted men and on 10 July the first company was flown into Marilinan in 30 C-47s. The entire unit was not in place until 5 August.[30] The first thing the 871st engineers did was

The secret airbase

to mow a fake airstrip out of the nearby kunai grass to fool any Japanese aerial reconnaissance.[31]

Kenney gave Woodbury a month to build the airbase at Tsili Tsili so Woodbury worked his men day and night, making use of as much native labour as he could get. Kenney wanted space for a fighter group to be based at Tsili Tsili plus parking space for a medium-bomber group of strafers. Rather than build revetments from scratch it was proposed to 'scoop hard stands out of the side of hills' to save time. Storage space for 5000 drums of gasoline and 1000 tonnes of bombs was also required. Using light-gauge disposable fuel drums, the C-47s could carry fifteen drums per load and were already bringing them in.[32]

With fighter escort time over Marilinan limited to one hour, it was imperative to turn around as many transports as possible in that time. The key would be the loading and unloading procedures. Air Freight Forwarding Units were set up for the task and they used an old C-47 wreck at Port Moresby to train on. Prior to the training it would take about 40 minutes to load or unload a jeep from the transport, but after developing new procedures the men could do it in two and a half minutes. Using such techniques, some 30 to 35 transports could be unloaded each hour at Marilinan.[33] General Herring's staff complained about the amount of air transport allocated to Tsili Tsili in comparison to that provided to support Savige's 3rd Division in front of Salamaua. 'The Yanks are flying in hundreds of transports to Tsili Tsili and only five to 3 Div,' Savige told Herring. 'For goodness' sake what do you expect,' Herring countered. 'You ought to know better. It is all part of the big plan.'[34]

Vast quantities of equipment were flown to Tsili Tsili, not to mention fresh eggs and milk that came up from Townsville via

Port Moresby on most days. This was despite a parlous ration state among the Australians. 'The Americans', according to Colonel Marston, 'were too busy flying in cinema outfits, refrigerators and padded stainless steel furniture to concern themselves with even Australian rations for Australian troops.' The Americans also had a liberal supply of machine guns. Aside from the authorised eight .50 calibre guns, they had flown in another twenty twin .50 calibre mounts and twenty water-cooled .30 calibre guns. Marston coordinated their use with a fire plan to prevent 'a proper hellzapoppin'. This came at a time when intelligence warnings had been issued that a Japanese paratroop landing was possible.[35] If the Japanese were to launch a ground or air attack on Tsili Tsili they would certainly get a hot reception.

The engineers of the 871st spent 24 hours a day building the new airbase, 'working at night under a Hollywood arc light set up'.[36] A rough dirt runway was quickly completed so that any stray or crippled aircraft could make emergency landings. As Bud Seale observed, 'We got P-40s, B-25s and P-39s that had been hit or had fuel problems and the air corps mechanics would fix them up so that they could get back to their home base.'[37] With a need for vehicles larger than jeeps, two and half ton trucks were cut in half and flown into Marilinan in separate aircraft before being bolted and welded back together. 'It worked like a charm,' Kenney wrote.[38]

A detachment of Australian engineers from the 2/8th Field Company had been sent in to help grade the first airstrip. Sapper Vern Tuskin said 'we just cut a strip big enough for the Dougs to come in'. The initial task was to cut the kunai, but it had to be done correctly as 'the dirt underneath was that soft and . . . it was better to try and leave the roots in to hold the dirt together . . .

The secret airbase

Of course, when the Yanks come in they had these little miniature dozers things . . . if they'd seen a hump they'd just take that off but they went down to dirt level and of course theirs was too soft, so they bought these big steel strips in, they interlinked with one another.' This was Marston matting, interlocking perforated steel strips vital to prevent aircraft wheels, particularly those of fighters, from ploughing into the soft ground or mud. As Tuskin observed, 'When they landed you'd hear them clanker, clanker, clanker. Sounded like a train going past.' Tuskin noted that 'in about four weeks they put up five strips.'[39] By the start of September the 871st had constructed three dry-weather runways, about 150 hard standings (reinforced parking areas) and 19 revetments (for protection from bomb blast).[40]

On 14 August two squadrons of P-39 Airacobras from Lieutenant Colonel Malcolm Moore's 35th Fighter Group flew into Tsili Tsili. They were just in time as Japanese aircraft had finally spotted the airfield during a reconnaissance flight on 11 August.[41] The Japanese intelligence report noted that 'An airfield is being constructed at a point several kilometres north-east of Marilinan. There is a considerable number of men, and they appear to be gradually increasing in number, their plan being to attack the Nadzab and Chivasing areas.'[42] By the clever use of camouflage and careful timing of flights, the existence of the airfield at Tsili Tsili had been kept hidden from the enemy for around two months. As Peter Ryan observed, 'a major operational base had sprung from the earth just at the back door of Lae, the enemy's main stronghold'.[43]

Sergeant Major Akira Bomura was a wireless operator and machine-gunner in one of the Kawasaki Ki-48 Lily bombers of 3rd Hiko Chutai (Air Squadron) based at Wewak airfield. The 3rd was one of three chutais that made up Lieutenant Colonel

Akimitsu Oda's 208th Hiko Sentai (Air Group) which had flown from Truk to Rabaul on 9 May 1943 and then on to Wewak on 11 May. At full strength Oda's sentai had 45 Lily bombers but, due to a severe pilot shortage, no more than nine of the fifteen aircraft in each chutai were operational at any one time. Another Lily sentai, the 45th, was based at Boram airfield. The Lily only carried an 800-kilogram bomb load, had poor manoeuvrability, a slow rate of climb and was very vulnerable to enemy gunfire. Unsurprisingly, it was disliked by the Japanese airmen who nicknamed it the *Satsujinki*, the suicide plane.[44]

On the morning of 15 August seven Lily bombers from the 3rd Hiko Chutai led by Lieutenant Hidemitsu Imai left Wewak at 0600 and were joined over Madang by 36 escorting Oscar fighters.[45] The force targeted Fuaba airfield, the Japanese name for Tsili Tsili, each bomber only carrying six 50-kilogram bombs due to the distance involved, a three hour and twenty minute flight from Wewak. On arrival over Tsili Tsili at about 1000, the bombers were attacked by an estimated 30 US fighters and Bomura's Lily was shot down. Three of the four aircrew were killed in the crash but somehow Bomura survived. 'When I regained consciousness,' he wrote, 'my plane was burning and I was thrown to the ground.' Severely burned and unable to walk, Bomura rested the next day before deciding he must try to get to Lae. Three days after the crash he tried to walk out but was blocked at a river junction, still only about 200 metres from the airfield. He was captured on the following day, 20 August. Akira Bomura would prove to be one of the most valuable Japanese prisoners captured in New Guinea. He was extensively interrogated and the diary he carried gave a rare insight into Japanese air operations in New Guinea.[46]

The secret airbase

Despite the loss of their bombers, the Japanese Oscar fighters shot down two C-47s from the 21st Troop Carrier Squadron and forced the remainder back to Port Moresby, making their getaway by some skilful flying at treetop level. Ernie Ford's C-47 was carrying fresh vegetables to Tsili Tsili when an enemy fighter jumped his flight from above and behind. 'On the first pass he shot down both of my trailing wingmen,' Ford wrote. Despite also coming under attack, Ford, one of the most experienced transport pilots in New Guinea, was able to avoid the same fate by throttling back to almost stall speed as an enemy fighter closed in. 'As the fighter overshot and passed overhead, the "Meatball" of the Rising Sun insignia never was so big or so close,' Ford wrote. He also had to dodge a head-on pass by another Oscar before the escorting Airacobras came to his aid.[47]

'The Japanese fighters—Oscars—bounced our guys and bore down on our transports,' one of the escorting Airacobra pilots wrote, 'So there was a big soiree up there in the wild hills.'[48] The 26 Airacobras and three Lightnings soon engaged the attention of the Japanese fighters and, when the fight was over, four of the Airacobras had been lost, although three of the four pilots survived. All seven Lily bombers had been shot down along with three of the Oscars.[49] One of the Australian infantrymen, Max Hillberg, watched the fighting from below: '13 Japs down in 30 seconds,' he wrote.[50]

Damage on the ground had been slight although the 871st chaplain, Captain Keith Munro, was killed and three Australian infantrymen were wounded when one of the shot-down Japanese bombers crashed next to a church parade. One of the wounded men, Corporal Ray Taylor, later died. Colonel Marston's batman, Private William 'Herb' Doney, was one of the wounded, in shock with his right temple cut open. The American doctor, Captain Joseph Strauss, gave Doney a dose of plasma but expected him to die. However, a few hours later Doney was still alive. 'If a man wants to live that much,' Strauss thought, 'the least we can do is to try'. Operating on a raised stretcher with light bulbs hung from the trees overhead, Strauss went to work cleaning out the shrapnel and dirt from the wound, cutting and tying off blood vessels before packing the wound with sulfa and sealing it. Three of Strauss's men stayed with Doney all night, holding him when he got restless, before he was sent back to hospital in Port Moresby.[51]

The Japanese made another air raid on the following day, but Thunderbolt and Lightning fighters knocked down about fifteen of the strafing fighters. Thereafter, the Japanese aircraft kept away and it became evident that the Japanese air commanders at Wewak had decided to conserve their strength. That strength was about to be severely depleted by a devastating blow against the Wewak airfields.

•

The 6th Air Division of the Japanese Army had moved its headquarters from Rabaul to Wewak on 9 July 1943. The air division comprised five fighter and three bomber squadrons (sentais), 324 aircraft in all. The 7th Air Division, comprising three bomber squadrons and a fighter squadron, had also deployed to New Guinea in July and had a further 156 aircraft based at But airfield. Between them, these two air divisions had flown 1308 sorties in July 1943, 494 as convoy escort, 84 as intercepts and 190 as ground support.[52] However, up until a resupply convoy arrived

The secret airbase

in early August there were serious supply difficulties at Wewak. Aviation fuel was in short supply with fighter aircraft given preference while food rations were cut in half, even for the aircrew.[53]

General Kenney knew that the two Japanese air divisions had arrived and, with his reconnaissance aircraft now able to refuel at Tsili Tsili, he could keep a close eye on them.[54] The Japanese did not believe that the Allied medium bombers had the range to reach Wewak while the long-range heavy bombers presented less of a threat, particularly when out of range of escorting fighters. Two factors would change that situation. One was the construction of the Tsili Tsili airbase, which enabled escorting fighters to refuel and thus have the range to get to Wewak, and the second related to modifications made to the Mitchell medium bombers to increase their range and effectiveness.

When they had first arrived in Australia the Mitchells were equipped with a lower turret but, because the planes did most of their work in New Guinea at low altitude, this turret was removed and replaced with forward-firing guns in the nose. General Kenney's air depot at Townsville worked around the clock making this modification to 172 Mitchells during the period from July to September 1943.[55] Removing the turret also allowed an additional square-shaped 11,500-litre metal fuel tank to be installed, suspended by hooks from a bomb shackle and held in place by guide rails. Fabricated in Australia, these fuel tanks provided an extra two hours' flying time, enough to increase the range of the Mitchells to Wewak. However, these tanks were very vulnerable to catching fire in combat or on crash landing so would need to be used up during the first two hours of the flight. 'The auxiliary tank would be the first to empty,' John Henebry noted, 'and once empty, discarded.'[56]

Kenney's bombers would also enter the Wewak air campaign with a new weapon against enemy aircraft on the ground. The first parachute-retarded fragmentation bombs or parafrags had been developed from standard 10-kilogram fragmentation bombs which were carried in a honeycomb rack in the bomb bay. A small parachute slowed and straightened the bomb, allowing the bomber to get out of the blast range before they exploded. On Kenney's instigation, a new vertically suspended parafrag had been developed in the USA and would be used in the coming air offensive. Work was also proceeding on developing daisy-cutter bombs, which involved wrapping bombs with wire or strapping iron rods onto them to produce a ground-level fragmentation effect when used with a ground-proximity fuse.[57]

Kenney's bombers stayed away from the Wewak area until Tsili Tsili had been sufficiently developed and stocked with fuel to provide a base for escort fighters and an emergency landing field for the medium bombers. It was also hoped that time would encourage the Japanese to build up a juicy target at Wewak. By 13 August aerial photographs showed that this was certainly the case, with eight medium bombers, 31 light bombers and 69 fighters identified at Wewak and Boram, plus 34 medium bombers, 34 light bombers and 23 fighters at Dagua and But.[58]

General Kenney now had at his disposal two heavy bomber groups (the 43rd and 90th) with 64 bombers and two medium groups (the 3rd and 38th) with 58 modified Mitchells available to strike Wewak. The plan was for eight squadrons of heavy bombers to open the assault with night attacks on the four Wewak airfields followed by five squadrons of Mitchell strafers at minimum altitude to bomb and strafe every plane still on the ground. Fighter planes, which could refuel at Tsili Tsili, would escort the Mitchells.[59]

The secret airbase

Before midnight on 16 August, twelve B-17 Flying Fortress bombers and 38 Liberators took off in good weather from Port Moresby and all but two reached Wewak. For three hours from shortly after midnight the heavy bombers dropped their deadly loads on the four Wewak airfields. Three bombers did not return.[60] The next day, 17 August, two squadrons of Mitchell bombers from the 38th Bomber Group left Port Moresby for the 800-kilometre flight to Wewak. However, only three of these 26 aircraft, all from the 405th Bomb Squadron, reached their target of Dagua airfield, west of Wewak. None of them reached But airfield. Most of the Mitchells had great difficulty in jettisoning the new auxiliary fuel tanks and had to abort the mission. The three Mitchells that did reach Dagua strafed the airfield at low level, with their combined 24 machine guns firing at once. 'To my mind's eye, thousands of lightning bolts were pouring forth from my plane in a steady stream of reddish-white color,' Lieutenant Garrett Middlebrook wrote. 'The entire area erupted in dust, fires and explosions . . . I caught a glimpse of a fuel truck racing toward the jungle with its refuelling hoses dragging along behind.'[61] The three Mitchells fired over 5000 machine-gun rounds and scattered 105 ten-kilogram parafrags across the airfield, destroying or damaging at least seventeen aircraft on the ground. One of fifteen Oscar fighters sent up to intercept them was also shot down.[62]

Although based at Dobodura, the 3rd Bomb Group Mitchells flew out of Port Moresby to avoid the enemy airfields at Salamaua, Lae and Madang on the route to Wewak. Despite having eight Mitchells turn back, Colonel Donald Hall, the 3rd Group commander, led 29 Mitchell strafers across Wewak and Boram airfields, catching the newly arrived Japanese aircraft lined up on each side of the runways. The Mitchells also dropped 786 ten-kilogram parafrag bombs over the runways. The 3rd Bomb Group attack claimed some 60 aircraft destroyed or damaged at Wewak and Boram.[63]

According to 18th Army headquarters the Japanese 4th Air Army lost 60 to 70 planes on the ground during the 17 August attacks, leaving only 40 operational aircraft. A convoy due to arrive at Wewak on 25 August was postponed for two weeks due to the loss of air cover.[64] With the opportunity to refuel at Tsili Tsili, 99 fighters took part in these raids as escorts and 85 of those reached the target. Although there were no interceptions, it was an unprecedented level of fighter support for the 5th Air Force in New Guinea.[65]

Kenney's airmen were back over Wewak on the following day, 18 August, but poor weather meant that only half the 49 heavy bombers reached the target, and their bombing was inaccurate. Although most of the 62 Mitchells reached the target this time, the Japanese were waiting for them with heavy anti-aircraft fire and fighter cover. A flight led by Major Ralph Cheli, the commander of the 405th Bomb Squadron, was jumped by about a dozen Oscar fighters and Cheli's plane was badly hit, the right engine and wing catching fire. Despite that, Cheli led his flight across Dagua airfield before crashing into the ocean. Captured and sent to Rabaul, Cheli was later executed by the Japanese. For his brave action that day, Cheli was awarded his country's highest honour, the Medal of Honor. The escorting Lightning fighters, which had refuelled at Tsili Tsili, shot down fifteen Japanese fighters, for the loss of two.[66] One of the Australians at Tsili Tsili observed, 'fighters galore refuelling'.[67]

The offensive continued through to the end of August. Liberators carried out 102 additional sorties, and the Mitchells continued

The secret airbase

to attack land targets in the Wewak area. Other heavy strikes were carried out against important supply centres at Hansa Bay and Alexishafen. By neutralising Japanese air strength at Wewak, General Kenney's airmen had opened the way for the assault on Lae. His bombers and fighters had done their job over Wewak; next it would be the turn of his transport aircraft over Lae.

•

On 28 July Kenney had written to the head of the USAAF, General Henry 'Hap' Arnold, protesting at the low level of troop carrier crew replacements for the 5th Air Force. The level had been set at 7.5 per cent per month as against a 15 per cent figure for bomber and fighter units whereas Kenney wanted 25 per cent. 'The figures show that between weather and Nips a man lives longer in a P-39 than he does in a C-47 flying the troop carrier supply runs in New Guinea,' Kenney wrote. Despite the shortage of crews, Kenney was getting more transport aircraft with four new troop carrier squadrons reaching Port Moresby in the first week of July and two more soon thereafter. By September another troop carrier group had arrived giving the 54th Troop Carrier Wing a total of fourteen troop carrier squadrons. This force would provide the wherewithal to carry out an airborne operation at Nadzab and support the offensive to capture Lae.[68]

In the last week of August the C-47s made over 700 landings at Tsili Tsili.[69] Sergeant Alan Gray flew into Tsili Tsili on 29 August as part of the ground support crew for a flight of Wirraways from RAAF No. 4 Squadron. The flight of C-47s he was in had escorting fighters flying at three levels above and more fighters below. The transports crossed the main range at 3000 metres and after reaching the Watut River valley 'formed into line astern, made a wide circle and approached over the Watut'.[70]

What was later referred to as the secret airbase of Tsili Tsili had enabled the USAAF to largely eliminate the air threat at Wewak, which could have derailed the Lae operation. Now the secret airbase would provide a major staging post for that operation.

Chapter 6

MACARTHUR'S NAVY

Grand Allied strategy would shape General MacArthur's plans for operations against Lae. From 14 to 24 January 1943 the Casablanca conference in North Africa put in place the Allied priorities for the war. A decision was made at the conference not to go ahead with the cross-channel invasion of France in 1943 but instead to invade Sicily and then the Italian mainland. This would have a positive impact on the availability of landing craft for the Pacific in 1943.

What happened in New Guinea then depended upon what the US Joint Chiefs of Staff decided were the priorities for the South and South West Pacific theatres, the latter under General MacArthur's command. On 28 March 1943 a series of directives was issued known as the Cartwheel plan. Cartwheel had three stages, with stage one calling for the occupation and establishment of airfields on Kiriwina and Woodlark Island. The stage two objectives were to seize the Lae–Salamaua–Finschhafen–Madang area and occupy and establish airfields on Western New Britain. Stage three involved the seizure of the Solomon Islands including the southern end of Bougainville and the establishment of airfields there. This third stage would come under Admiral William 'Bull' Halsey's South Pacific Area of command, though General MacArthur would be responsible for ensuring proper coordination with his own forces.[1] General George Kenney, who was in Washington for the meeting, wrote 'Looks like it will be late summer before we can figure on take out of Lae.'[2] Late summer in the United States was six months away.

For MacArthur, the key to the Cartwheel plan was the occupation of areas capable of development into forward airbases and the subsequent capture of established enemy airfields.[3] Planning took place at advanced land headquarters in Brisbane under the direction of Deputy Chief of the General Staff, Major General Frank Berryman, assisted by Deputy Adjutant and Quartermaster General, Major General John Chapman. Other details were worked out at New Guinea Force headquarters in Port Moresby, firstly under Lieutenant General Iven Mackay and then from 23 May under Lieutenant General Edmund Herring. At this stage the operation to capture Lae, Salamaua, Finschhafen and Madang was given the code name Operation Postern.[4] General Berryman would be the key man in the extensive planning process that lay ahead. Berryman's biographer later characterised him as 'the architect of victory'. His planning and personal skills, particularly his relationships with the key American commanders, would prove critical in the months ahead.[5]

The original target date for Operation Postern was 1 August 1943 and would be in two stages: an amphibious landing on the coast near Lae and an air–ground operation against Nadzab airfield, 30 kilometres west of Lae. For the amphibious operation an Australian division would move to Milne Bay and then move in three brigade groups from north of Buna to land near Lae utilising small landing craft. On 21 May General Blamey met with MacArthur and it was decided that, for the amphibious phase, sufficient landing craft had to be available to carry a division of up to 10,000 men.[6]

•

It is doubtful that any army general other than MacArthur could have convinced the powers that be that he should have his own navy in the face of fierce opposition from the US Navy. The rationale for it was certainly there, paid for in blood by both American and Australian infantrymen fighting to reduce the stubbornly defended Papuan beachheads without the benefit of amphibious support. That experience convinced MacArthur that if the war continued in that vein then it was going to be a long and costly one and his troops would struggle to move beyond New Guinea, let alone reach the Philippines, to where he was determined to return.

Vice-Admiral Arthur Carpender was the commander of naval forces in the South West Pacific Area. In January 1943 he had a handful of cruisers and destroyers under his command, including Australian ships, but he was loath to deploy them among the treacherous shoals along the poorly charted Papuan coastline. They were mainly being used in Australian waters to protect convoys. However, the Royal Australian Navy (RAN) had taken a lead role in facilitating naval operations along the New Guinea coast. Three RAN survey ships had marked out a channel through the shoals around the eastern end of the New Guinea mainland and three Australian corvettes had used this route to bring the Australian 18th Brigade from Milne Bay to Oro Bay in December 1942. By late August 1943 the RAN had charted the New Guinea coast as far as Morobe and this would prove crucial for any naval operations against Lae.

The US Navy's Admiral Chester Nimitz was in command of the Central Pacific Area and the vast majority of naval assets in the Pacific were assigned to him. Nimitz's naval forces had given great support to the South West Pacific and South Pacific areas in 1942 when they were the critical areas of operations, but by 1943 Nimitz's eyes were on the Central Pacific, the most direct route to Japan. In the opinion of the US naval commander, Fleet Admiral Ernest King, that was where any naval resources available in the Pacific theatre should be sent.

Rear Admiral Daniel Barbey had been involved with trialling a new concept in the US Navy: seagoing landing craft. His understanding of their capabilities made him an ideal appointment to MacArthur's command. When Barbey had left for his new assignment, King had told him, 'You have the enviable opportunity to take into combat the ships you helped create.'[7] MacArthur's Assistant Chief of Staff, Brigadier General Stephen Chamberlin, briefed Barbey on how the US Navy must take a leading role in the Cartwheel plan, telling him that 'The general expects you and your amphibious force to do just that.' It was a difficult position for Barbey who, having met with Nimitz in Hawaii on the way to Australia, knew full well that the US Navy's focus was on the Central Pacific.[8]

On 10 January 1943, when Barbey reported to General MacArthur in Brisbane, 'MacArthur's navy' was born.

Starting from scratch, it was a difficult birth for Barbey's 7th Amphibious Force but by the end of the war MacArthur's navy had carried out over 25 separate amphibious operations from New Guinea to the Philippines. MacArthur's emphasis was on recapturing the Philippines, a task that would require an ocean-going amphibious capability. 'Your job is to develop an amphibious force that can carry my troops in those campaigns,' MacArthur told him.[9] As one of the few naval officers familiar with amphibious warfare, Barbey was the right choice for the job but the key factor was MacArthur's willingness to let Barbey get on with his task and not interfere in the details of his work. MacArthur's strength was finding the right people for a job and delegating the necessary authority for them to do it.

At the start of the Pacific War the US Navy had no dedicated amphibious capability. Even in Europe, amphibious warfare had hardly developed since the use of rowing boats at Gallipoli in the First World War. It was not until the fall of France in mid-1940 that serious moves were made to improve that capability in Britain and, with the start of the Pacific War, the need for an amphibious capability became vital to the Allied cause. However, such a capability was useless unless it could be effectively employed for operations, and Barbey's immediate focus was to develop a blue-water (oceangoing) amphibious doctrine suitable for proposed moves along the New Guinea coast to Lae and beyond.

The US Marine Corps had developed a doctrine based on using large troop transports to carry smaller amphibious craft, the same technique used by the Japanese. The advantage of this approach was that it could be rapidly implemented using converted passenger ships to carry the troops. Smaller ship-to-shore craft could be loaded aboard and then lowered by davits (cranes) for the troops to embark via scramble nets. The craft adopted for use in these operations was the Higgins Boat, developed in New Orleans from a pre-war design by the brilliant Andrew Higgins. Two types of Higgins Boats were produced, both with a hinged bow. The 11-metre-long landing craft, vehicle personnel (LCVP) could carry 36 troops while the 15-metre landing craft, mechanised (LCM), could carry either one tank or 60 troops. General Dwight D. Eisenhower later said Higgins was 'the man who won the war for us'.[10]

In concert with a British delegation, larger oceangoing landing craft capable of carrying and landing tanks, vehicles and supplies directly onto beaches were developed for European operations. The British proposed building a landing ship, tank (LST), landing craft, tank (LCT), landing craft, infantry (LCI) and landing ship, dock (LSD). Initially rejected due to the competing demand for naval and merchant ships from the major shipyards, the program was given the go-ahead following the outbreak of war in the Pacific. With the major American shipyards busy, the work went to smaller yards, and new ship-building facilities were constructed on inland waterways. The LSTs and LCIs for MacArthur's navy had to be sailed from the United States to Australia by their crews and, given their flat hulls, they were not the most comfortable of vessels for such a journey. An LST could carry 500 tonnes (either as eighteen tanks, 27 heavy vehicles or equivalent stores) plus 160 troops. For operations such as at Lae, where very few vehicles would be landed, an LST could carry 400 men. The smaller LCI could carry 120 tonnes, usually in the form of about 180 troops and their equipment.

Landing craft could be adapted to requirements. Due to 'the most crying need', Barbey had LST 464 converted to a 78-bed hospital ship at the shipyards in Sydney and nine months later notice came through from the US Navy denying his request to do so. One LCT was converted into a much-needed water barge and Barbey also made good use of small wooden-hulled luggers, coastal transport vessels known as APcs or the more familiar 'apple carts'. These served many purposes including tenders and flagships for LCT flotillas and one ended up as a floating post office.[11]

Auxiliary personnel destroyers (APDs) were First World War–era destroyers converted to carry troops. Equipped with four LCVPs, they could carry a company of troops and had been used in operations in the Aleutian Islands earlier in the war. The LCVPs could be offloaded and recovered using davits and the troops would embark and disembark between the destroyer and the LCVP via scramble nets. Barbey had four APDs allocated to his command: *Brooks*, *Gilmer*, *Sands* and *Humphreys*.

Given the ships available and the limitations imposed by the lack of naval power, particularly aircraft carrier cover, Barbey's doctrine for amphibious landings specified that the landing should be made at dawn, about two hours before high tide, and that all vessels should be gone within about four hours. The landing beaches also had to be carefully selected to be free of natural and man-made obstacles including significant numbers of enemy defenders. The approach to the beach should be at a time when there was no moonlight or otherwise under the protection of overcast weather.[12]

•

The US Army Engineer Corps operated its own amphibious force, the Engineer Amphibian Command. This had been set up in early 1942 when a means to cross the English Channel and make a contested landing on French shores had been recognised. The US Army amphibian force was confined to coastal operations within a 100-kilometre range of a land base.

Six US Engineer Special Brigades would be formed during the war, three of which would be assigned to the European theatre and three to the South West Pacific Area. The first brigade assigned to MacArthur was the Second Engineer Special Brigade (2nd ESB), which had been activated on 20 June 1942 and consisted of three regiments: the 532nd, the 542nd and the 592nd Engineer Boat and Shore Regiment (EBSR), plus the 562nd Engineer Boat Maintenance Battalion, a company of which was attached to each regiment during operations. Medical, signals, ordnance and quartermaster services were also incorporated into the brigade. Each regiment consisted of one boat and one shore battalion and was responsible for the operation and maintenance of the landing craft and for the loading and unloading of personnel and supplies. Colonel William Heavey took command of the 400 officers and 7000 men of the 2nd ESB in August 1942. On 24 January 1943 the personnel from the first regiment of Heavey's brigade, the 532nd, left San Francisco for Australia and the rest of the brigade soon followed. The 532nd landed at Townsville and then moved to its base 25 kilometres north of Cairns while the other two regiments were based on the coast north of Rockhampton.[13]

The main landing craft used by the ESB was the LCVP, one of the Higgins Boats. Colonel Arthur Trudeau, chief of staff of the Engineer Amphibian Command, knew the brigade's landing craft would take months to ship out to Australia, so organised to prefabricate the LCVPs and LCTs in sections that were easier to ship. The sections would then be assembled in Australia.[14] A boat assembly unit, the 411th Engineer Base Shop Battalion, arrived in Cairns in December 1942 and the first reassembled LCVP was launched in April 1943. Three assembly lines were built and, within a short time, seven boats a day were being launched.[15]

On 28 May a provisional battalion of the 532nd Regiment moved to Milne Bay and then to Oro Bay on 13 June. Five days later the unit suffered its first casualties of the war during a Japanese bombing raid on the port. The battalion then moved up the coast to Morobe where, on 25 June, Barbey's 7th Amphibious Force had taken over command of the 2nd ESB for the upcoming operations. This unified the amphibious command, though Heavey's brigade came under Lieutenant General Walter Krueger's US Sixth Army for administration purposes.[16]

The final point of departure for an amphibious operation against Lae, at that stage limited to the 2nd ESB's smaller amphibious craft, needed to be within 100 kilometres of the landing beach. The base at Morobe was too far away so an intermediate staging point south of Salamaua needed to be secured.[17] The first major operation for the 2nd ESB thus eventuated on the night of 30 June when units of the 162nd Infantry Regiment were landed at Nassau Bay, 30 kilometres south of Salamaua. Although the troops got ashore, the operation was a disaster for the landing craft with all but one of the 24 LCVPs being lost in the wild surf. Onshore, an Australian scout observed that 'those 12-foot breakers . . . hurtled the big square-snouted barges into the beach like so many match boxes, sideways and backwards and almost upside down'.[18] It was this operation that convinced General MacArthur that he would need to use the larger and longer ranged LCIs and LSTs for the Lae operation.

Nonetheless, the smaller landing craft would still be a vital component of the landing plan and beyond. So for the Lae operation about 65 LCVPs and LCTs from the 532nd EBSR were placed under Barbey's command for the landing, after which the unit would come under Australian control until the operation was complete. In early August part of the 532nd moved to Milne Bay to carry out further training with Australian 9th Division troops while the remainder concentrated at Morobe in time for the assault on Lae.[19] Meanwhile the rest of the 2nd ESB was also on the move.

In mid-July General Chamberlin said that the 2nd ESB was 'not worth a god damn at Cairns, but can be used in New Guinea'. Chamberlin added that, 'The whole thing is simple. Is brigade needed in Australia? No. Why not get it over to New Guinea. We cannot get ships unloaded there . . . I am going to order it forward now less training elements.'[20] However, only two of the three 2nd ESB regiments could be moved to New Guinea due to shipping constraints.[21]

When it had been initially proposed that the Lae amphibious operation only use the 2nd ESB, the requirement was for 420 LCVPs and 54 LCMs including a 50 per cent reserve. However, only 280 LCVPs and 30 LCMs would have been available, significantly short of the requirement and further reinforcing the need for the larger oceangoing landing craft to be used in the Lae landing.[22] On 25 May Chamberlin sent a memo to the Chief of Staff requesting that twelve LCIs, twelve LCTs and four LSTs should be made available by 1 September. They would allow the landing of 7000 to 10,000 troops east of Lae in successive movements. 'The Australians have requested them,' Chamberlin noted. 'It appears extremely risky to believe that the Engineer Brigade can accomplish the mission assigned without assistance. It is unanimously believed that substantial elements of the Amphibious Force must be employed.'[23] To enable the heavier landing craft to be assembled and the troops trained to operate from them, D-Day for Lae would have to be delayed by one month.

•

Rear Admiral Barbey left Brisbane for New Guinea in late June 1943. His first challenge was to organise Operation Chronicle, the unopposed landings on Woodlark and Kiriwina Islands, which commenced on 30 June 1943. Barbey was able to borrow four APDs and six LSTs from Admiral Halsey's Third Fleet for the operation to add to his own nine LSTs, eighteen LCIs and eighteen LCTs. Ten destroyers, eight submarine chasers and four minesweepers escorted the landing craft.[24] The convoy for Woodlark left from Milne Bay while the convoy for Kiriwina went directly from Townsville. Although both Woodlark and Kiriwina were unoccupied by the Japanese, they were surrounded by coral reefs through which entrances had to be blown for the landing craft. At Woodlark Island, Commander Richard Scruggs, who had carried out the initial reconnaissance, piloted each of the first six LSTs through the coral reefs and onto the landing beach. At Kiriwina no ships larger than LCIs were used due to the difficult reefs.[25] Because the landings were unopposed, shore parties of 200 men equipped with tools and beach matting had been put ashore a week before the landing. At Woodlark six beaching points, three beach exits plus dispersal areas and connecting roadways were constructed, enabling vehicles to readily move off the landing craft and the beach during the landing.

This enabled the first LST echelons to carry supplies and equipment in vehicles which could rapidly unload, an advantage that would not be available to the Lae planners.[26] Operation Chronicle benefited greatly from Admiral Halsey's landings at Rendova and New Georgia in the Solomon Islands, which attracted heavy Japanese air and naval attention.

Deception would also play a part in Operation Postern. On 11 May General Blamey's director of military intelligence, Brigadier John Rogers, proposed a plan to convince the Japanese that an operation from Darwin was being planned. Rogers suggested that Blamey visit the Darwin area along with an increase in troop and air movement. A landing craft would be sent there and other dummy landing craft and aircraft would be constructed.[27] On 30 May Rogers' Darwin plan came unstuck due to a lack of shipping activity and because some politicians were giving publicity to the boredom of the troops based there. The deception was also considered unconvincing due to heavy shipping at Port Moresby and Milne Bay. However, it was still proposed that increasing wireless traffic to India, moving troops around at Darwin and getting high-ranking officers to visit the town would help. However, this was still not considered convincing and on 16 June the Darwin deception plan was dropped.[28]

Although no specific deception plan was agreed upon, a very effective deception had been underway for many months. The Allied attack on Salamaua had drawn most of the Japanese combat troops from Lae. Ignoring the threats from air and sea, General Nakano saw Salamaua as the defensive shield for Lae and believed that as long as it was held then Lae was safe. General Blamey had identified this as a major flaw in the enemy strategy and had ordered that Salamaua not be captured at this stage.

Blamey stuck to the Salamaua feint strategy despite considerable pressure from General Kenney to capture the town for a forward airbase. General Berryman noted in his diary on 23 July that 'Original plan to be followed and NOT capture SAL but to continue present scale of ops there.'[29] Only days before the start of the Lae operation, Kenney was 'Arguing with Blamey about taking Salamaua and giving me a fighter field there . . . Blamey only wants to bleed Nips out of Lae to Salamaua.'[30]

•

The initial Postern plan had called for General Vasey's 7th Division to make the amphibious landing and some training had been undertaken by the division in Melbourne with the US marines. By early 1943 there were two main amphibious training centres in Australia, at Port Stephens near Newcastle and at Toorbul Point, on Moreton Bay near Brisbane. Intensive training of 7th Division troops began at Port Stephens before another training centre was established at Trinity Beach near Cairns to train for Operation Postern. However, due to the problem of malaria recurrence among previously exposed 7th Division troops in the tropical climate of Cairns, it was considered that the division could not be used 'without endangering the civilian population'.[31] Major General George Wootten's 9th Division, not yet exposed to New Guinea conditions and free from malaria, took over the amphibious role.

Under the command of Major General Leslie Morshead, the 9th Division had achieved great fame during the North Africa campaign fighting the German Afrika Korps. At Tobruk the division had made up a large part of the defenders and, by the time it was relieved, the 9th had held off the Axis troops for nine months. After a period in Syria, Morshead's division had moved to El Alamein where it had played a key role in the victory, though at great cost, with some 5800 casualties between July and November 1942.[32]

In March 1943 Morshead had been promoted to corps commander and Wootten, who had commanded the 7th Division's 18th Brigade with distinction at Milne Bay, Buna and Sanananda, took over. On its return to Australia the division had gone to the Atherton Tablelands inland from Cairns alongside 6th and 7th Division units already experienced in jungle fighting during the Papuan campaigns. Experienced training teams were allocated to each of the three 9th Division brigades for training and 9th Division officers were temporarily attached to 6th and 7th Division units to learn about jungle fighting.[33]

Brigadier David Whitehead observed that the 6th Division troops were experienced in 'high mountainous jungle country with narrow ridges' while the 7th Division trainers passed on their experience fighting through the swampy Papuan coastal plains. However, Whitehead found it more beneficial for his brigade 'to develop its own theories from first principles'. One of Whitehead's former battalion commanders, Brigadier Heathcote Hammer, who had been promoted to a brigade command in New Guinea, suggested training in higher country with steeper hills.[34] 'We train in jungle, wade mountain rivers, and at night debate where we'll go next,' Captain Ken Esau from the 2/3rd Pioneer Battalion, wrote.[35]

Starting at the end of June each brigade group went to Cairns for two weeks of amphibious training with the LCVPs of the 2nd ESB.[36] 'Crawling down scramble-nets draped over the side of destroyers into the LCVPs tossing back and forth,' Harry

Wells wrote, the men 'resembled prawns being shaken from a net.'[37] The men also carried out the same exercise by night using landing lights and torches. 'Wicked nights of rolling and pitching in rough seas,' Ken Esau wrote of this experience.[38]

The loads of stores, ammunition, jeeps and guns had to be weighed and then correctly placed in the landing craft. 'It was like some geometrical problem, and we realised that faulty organisation would ruin everything,' Corporal Patrick Bourke wrote. The greatest concern was what would lie ahead once the ramps dropped on the enemy shore. 'We feared the worst,' he observed.[39]

Initial plans were for Oro Bay to be used as the staging base for the Lae landing; however, it could only handle 60,000 tonnes a month and most of that was needed to supply the Dobodura airfields. Milne Bay was the nearest port that could handle the estimated requirement for August of 135,000 to 140,000 tonnes.[40] The 9th Division would therefore be shipped directly from Australia to Milne Bay and began the move north from Cairns on 26 July. The men of the 2/13th Battalion embarked on the 4600-tonne Dutch transport *Maatsuyker*. 'It was almost daylight as we staggered up the gangplank,' Patrick Bourke wrote, 'and were guided into hot, stuffy, over-crowded holds, overflowing with that nauseating odour that only those who have travelled on troopships know.'[41] The 9th Division, now under command of General Herring's I Corps, had completed the move to New Guinea by 12 August.

The day of the 9th Division amphibious landing would be designated D-Day and the start of the 7th Division operation against Nadzab would be Z-Day. For planning purposes D-Day was tentatively scheduled for 1 September with Z-Day on the following day. All over-water operations for Postern would come under Rear Admiral Barbey's command and the landing would be made entirely by his 7th Amphibious Force.[42] The smaller landing craft would only be used to land the EBSR shore battalion and for resupply along the coast. Buna would need to be developed as a staging port and a wharf was under construction and scheduled to be available by mid-July with an estimated capacity of 500 tonnes per day. However, loaded Liberty ships with their eight-metre draft couldn't get closer than 900 metres to the Buna shore so 25 DUKWs (amphibious wheeled vehicles) were allocated to help with unloading. Referring to the difficulties involved in unloading the Liberty ships with landing craft, it was said, 'If you don't use Libertys it is just like dumping a bucket out with a teaspoon.' With enemy submarine activity considered low, two ships were allocated to supply Buna, one Liberty ship from Sydney and a vessel of half that capacity from Brisbane.[43] With Buna as a staging port it would allow the loaded troops to disembark for a much-needed break on the journey between Milne Bay and Lae.

•

It was not until 27 July, following the completion of their work with Operation Chronicle, that Rear Admiral Barbey's amphibious force-planning staff became available to General Wootten at Milne Bay. As it was not possible to get a firm allocation of landing craft until a fortnight before the operation, the schedules for the allocation of troops and stores had to be continually changed.[44] After Wootten said he was happy with seven days of supplies, it was agreed that 7000 personnel and 2590 tonnes of stores would be landed on D-Day with another 2400 men and

1010 tonnes of stores to be landed on the following day, D+1. On D+2 another 3600 men would be taken from Buna to Lae.[45] Wootten wanted two hours of moonlight for the landing plus three brigade groups landed while Barbey wanted no moonlight and did not have the capacity to move and supply three brigades. On 25 July Barbey said he would be ready to go by 27 August and Wootten, despite his reserve brigade not yet fully trained on the large landing craft, said he would also be prepared.[46]

The 2nd ESB would provide amphibian scouts to go in on the first wave to establish red and yellow markers on both Red and Yellow beaches and to make a beach reconnaissance. Major Howard Lea, the Brigade Operations Officer, arranged the scout detail which he ultimately led during the landing.[47] The staff to organise beach operations came from Wootten's division and, although none of his officers had any training in this sort of work, the amenities officer, education officer and legal officer among others were all drafted in to do the job. Unfortunately no US Navy liaison officer was allocated to the division ashore during the operation and this would lead to frustrations and delays when landing craft needed to be diverted to beaches closer to the front line.[48]

From 20 to 22 August a full-scale landing rehearsal was carried out at beaches on the south coast of Normanby Island.[49] The construction of beach exits and dispersal roadways inland showed that the surfacing of tracks with steel mesh was too slow to allow the vehicles to clear the beach so it was decided that more stores would be loaded as bulk cargo and more labour provided to clear the landing craft.[50] On 29 August the 2/13th Battalion was taken up to Normanby Island on APDs where the men disembarked from the LCVPs up to their necks in the water. The difference between training conditions in Australia and New Guinea was stark: 'the country fringing the beach was the worst we had been in,' Patrick Bourke observed. 'Almost impenetrable jungle grew in waist deep swamps, crisscrossed by much deeper creeks.'[51]

•

A beach east of Lae out of range of the Japanese gun batteries needed to be selected by General Wootten's planning team for the Lae landing.[52] At least one Japanese 150 mm gun, which had a range of 20 kilometres, had been identified in Lae so the landing beaches needed to be beyond that range. The beach gradient also needed to be greater than 1 in 25 for LST operations and preferably on the steeper side to ensure that there was enough water under the stern when the landing craft were beached to make retraction easier.[53] Low-altitude photos were taken of possible beaches in late July to identify any underwater obstacles, beach defences and access to suitable beach exits.[54]

The beaches at Bulu Plantation and Singaua Plantation were considered the most suitable for the landing. Lieutenant Alastair Stewart, the 51-year-old former manager of Singaua Plantation, was able to provide a map and information on the area around the beaches. No enemy defence positions were evident east of the Busu River and the greatest hindrance to the advance would be the five rivers and numerous smaller streams between the landing beaches and Lae. All except the daunting Busu River were considered fordable if not in flood. The normal Busu crossing was at the river mouth and here the water depth was still one metre but any flooding from heavy rain would double this depth, making the Busu 'impassable for loaded men'. With maximum monthly rainfall expected in August and September (the average for September was 520 mm but had been up to 840 mm), it was obvious that the Busu River would be the problem.[55]

Two beaches were chosen for the landings. Red Beach was 22 kilometres to the east of Lae and was 720 metres long, stretching east from the mouth of the Buso River. Yellow Beach was 5 kilometres further east of Red Beach and was 540 metres long. It would protect the eastern flank of the main beachhead. The Bulu River and the adjacent Bulu coconut plantation separated the two landing beaches, which were approximately 20 metres deep and consisted of firm black sand with swamps behind.[56]

During initial planning, the time of landing (H-Hour) was scheduled to be between 0300 and 0400 in line with Wootten's request for two hours of moonlight before dawn.[57] Allowing nine to ten hours for unloading, the LSTs would then retract at 1300. However, once the landing date was postponed to 4 September, when there would be no morning moon, H-Hour could not be scheduled until after sunrise to allow time for the navy to identify the correct beach on a coast covered by low-lying swampy jungle devoid of prominent landmarks. This delayed the landing until 0630, 18 minutes after sunrise, resulting in the loss of about three hours' unloading time. This loss was compounded by a decision to retract the LSTs by 1100 as continuous air cover could not be guaranteed beyond that time. Unloading time was therefore reduced to four and a half hours. As it was thought that the troops would take one and a half hours to disembark, this would leave only three hours for unloading stores.[58]

•

Rear Admiral Barbey would use all the shipping he had for Operation Postern. For the landing he had four APDs, eighteen LCIs with two in reserve, sixteen LCTs with two in reserve and twelve LSTs with another in reserve.[59] The LCIs had proven to be the best troop transports during the Woodlark landings, with a carrying capacity of at least 150 men. However, they needed careful handling as the design of their propellers meant that any damage to them required docking back at Townsville for repair. The twelve LSTs had been used in Chronicle and all needed two weeks overhaul after being 'worked to death banging themselves out on the coral'.[60] For the Lae landing the LCTs would need to be better balanced than during the Chronicle landings where the bulk stores were loaded aft. Due to the bulk weight, particularly ammunition boxes, the craft had become unbalanced and in one case this resulted in the engine flooding via the submerged exhaust pipes.[61] Each LST was loaded with 84 tonnes of bulk freight, the amount that could be unloaded in two and a half hours. Bulk loaded 3-ton trucks and unit vehicles, 35 vehicles in all, took up the rest of the space aboard the LST tank deck. The 24 Bofors guns of the 2/4th Light Anti Aircraft Regiment were loaded onto the top deck and deployed for use against air attack while in transit. Each LST also carried 400 men.[62]

Morobe would be used as the operational base for the 532nd EBSR. However, the Japanese air threat was significant and on 3 September nine Rabaul-based Betty bombers, escorted by 27 fighters, carried out a high-altitude bomb raid, though without causing significant damage.[63] Brigadier General Heavey and his staff were in Morobe at the time having lunch when a red alert was sounded, but when the all-clear signal was given within ten minutes the alert was dismissed. When the sound of approaching aircraft was heard soon thereafter it was assumed the planes were friendly. 'Suddenly the harbor was filled with the sound of exploding bombs and it was realized belatedly that the planes were Japanese.' The bombs missed their mark, but with so many landing craft in the harbour the concern was 'What do the Japs know?'[64] That night PT boats from Morobe moved out on a sweep across the Huon Gulf to ensure that there were no enemy naval vessels lying in wait for the invasion convoy.[65]

With reports of enemy troops and supplies being moved down the coast from Finschhafen by night, Vice-Admiral Carpender ordered Captain Jesse Carter to make a sweep of the Huon Gulf by night and bombard Finschhafen. 'It will be worthwhile to prove the Navy is willing to pitch in, even if we get nothing but coconuts,' one of Carpender's staff noted. On 22 August four destroyers left Milne Bay and headed for the Huon Gulf, the furthest that Allied naval vessels larger than PT boats had ventured along the New Guinea coast since the start of the war. Early the next morning they opened fire on Finschhafen, firing 540 rounds of 5-inch shells within ten minutes before returning to Milne Bay. It was the first naval bombardment of Japanese forces in New Guinea.[66]

•

Two battalions from 20th Brigade were to land on Red Beach, the 2/15th Battalion on the right or eastern flank and the 2/17th Battalion on the left closest to Lae. A third battalion, the 2/13th, would land on Yellow Beach. The 2/23rd Battalion plus a company of engineers, a field ambulance, a troop of artillery and a light anti-aircraft section would also be attached to

20th Brigade for the landing phase. The 26th Brigade would follow-up the initial landings and move through the beachhead. With concern over Japanese naval action against the beachheads at night, as had happened at Guadalcanal and Milne Bay, the defence of Red Beach would be coordinated by the 2/2nd Machine Gun Battalion.[67]

Loading of stores, equipment and vehicles at Milne Bay was completed by 1 September. Patrick Bourke reflected the opinion of many of the 9th Division men waiting to board, who 'were anxious to prove that we would perform as well against jungle and Jap as we had against desert and German'.[68]

Chapter 7

AIRBORNE INFANTRY

The second phase of Operation Postern involved the capture of Nadzab airfield, 30 kilometres inland from Lae. The original plan called for troops from the Australian 7th Division to be taken by ship north-west along the coast from Port Moresby to the mouth of the Lakekamu River before transferring to smaller vessels for the journey up the river to Bulldog. From there the troops would move by vehicles along the proposed Bulldog Road to Wau and thence via existing and new roads down the Bulolo Valley to the Markham River. The final move across the Markham River to Nadzab would then require either amphibian vehicles or transport aircraft.

This plan was fraught with many difficulties and uncertainties. The obvious concern was that the challenging overland route from Bulldog to the Markham River would not be completed in time. Once completed, the Bulldog Road had to be able to supply a jungle division of 12,000 men with 250 tonnes of supplies per day across some of the most difficult country in New Guinea. For that to even happen it would also be necessary to provide suitable water transport from the south coast up the Lakekamu River to the start of the road at Bulldog, some 60 kilometres as the crow flies but over twice that distance as the river flows. Due to these concerns, it was sensibly decided that transport aircraft would be made available to take the 7th Division directly from Port Moresby into the overgrown pre-war landing ground at Nadzab.[1] The Nadzab operation was initially scheduled to precede the amphibious operation and would involve a parachute drop by an American parachute battalion to seize the airfield for the Australian 25th Brigade to be flown into.[2]

Despite accepting that air transport was required, General Blamey still had concerns as to whether the troops at Nadzab could be adequately supplied once they had landed. When he met with General MacArthur on 21 May it was agreed that the Bulldog Road would still need to be through to Wau before any operation against Nadzab commenced.[3] On 14 July Brigadier General Chamberlin sent a memo to General Herring stating the obvious: 'Present progress reports would indicate that this operation would have to be considerably delayed beyond the date in prospect.'[4] The next day General Blamey 'pointed out that lack of shipping from Port Moresby to the Lakekamu was a serious bottleneck'. It was now estimated that the overland route through to the Markham River would not be open until December 1943 and it would then require a full field-engineering company working for twelve weeks to build a bridge across the Markham River once Nadzab was secure.[5]

Airborne infantry

At a conference on 15 July Major General Berryman observed that 'Our American friends were very pessimistic about our Bulldog–Wau project.' Berryman bet General Kenney a bottle of whisky that a jeep would go over the route by 1 August but he would lose that bet: the first jeep convoy did not traverse the road until 23 August.[6] The Americans were right: 'this damn Wau-Bulldog road', as General Kenney called it, was a white elephant.[7] It would be air transport that would sustain the Markham and Ramu Valley campaigns and it was always going to be. However, it would take considerable resources to supply the 7th Division by air. To supply two infantry brigades and one parachute battalion, 770 planeloads would be required plus 290 extra planeloads to build up a seven-day reserve. Following that, 42 planeloads would be needed for the daily maintenance of the force.[8]

•

On 11 June General Berryman noted that 'Air superiority is the basis of future operations.' He stressed the need for forward fighter airfields at Bena Bena or Marilinan and that Nadzab should be captured as soon as air cover was available.[9] This would not be until mid-August when the new airbase at Tsili Tsili was complete. For operations against Lae it was considered that one fighter group at Tsili Tsili was equivalent to eight fighter groups operating from Port Moresby or Dobodura. By mid-August 120 transport aircraft would also be available and General Kenney planned to have 72 of those aircraft in use daily. However, Kenney also stressed the need to improve the port facilities at Oro Bay or he would have to continue to bring petrol and oil into Dobodura by air, thus tying up much of his air transport capacity. Air supply to the Australians at Wau and the drop zones behind the Salamaua front would also be cut back.[10]

General Kenney had a lot to do with driving Operation Postern forward and he found a willing ally in General Herring, the New Guinea Force commander, who was responsible for the planning and coordination of the land forces involved. After a meeting with Herring on 20 June Kenney wrote, 'The GHQ gang all think it would be September or October before we can start an amphibious expedition and Christmas before we capture Lae. At this rate we will all die of old age before the war's over.' He added that Herring 'realises that saving time also saves lives by ending the war that much quicker . . . Blamey is the stumbling block.'[11]

Kenney's air arm had a number of important roles in Operation Postern. His transport aircraft would need to form and maintain an air bridge from Port Moresby to Nadzab, while his bombers would carry out an intense preliminary bombardment of Lae and Salamaua and then closely support the ground operations. His fighters would escort both transports and bombers, provide a shield over the naval and ground operations and maintain an air blockade to prevent Japanese reinforcements and supplies reaching the operational area.[12]

As far back as May, General Chamberlin realised that how quickly Lae could be captured depended on how quickly control of the air over the Huon Gulf could be gained.[13] As Kiriwina airbase was not yet ready, convoy air cover was to be provided by the 8th Fighter Group flying from Goodenough Island. In addition, a P-38 Lightning fighter group would be ready at Dobodura by 15 August plus another two squadrons at Tsili Tsili. The final air plan, decided just before D-Day, had 32 fighters tasked for convoy air cover with other squadrons on ground alert.[14] A separate flight of reconnaissance aircraft from RAAF No. 4 Squadron, based at Tsili Tsili, would be allocated to each Australian division from D-Day with a squadron liaison officer based at each divisional headquarters.[15]

•

The Nadzab operation was originally conceived to prevent overland reinforcement of Lae and to assist the 9th Division operation to capture the town.[16] On 16 July a plan was submitted to send an infantry brigade across the Markham River in boats to support a parachute battalion that would be dropped to secure Nadzab. The logic of a plan to move a brigade across the Markham was queried as it meant first flying the brigade into Wau and Bulolo so the brigade may as well fly all the way to Nadzab once the paratroops had secured the site. This would also mean that the brigade would not be spotted by the Japanese gathering south of the Markham, a situation that could compromise the entire Nadzab plan.[17]

By 28 July the plan was still for one parachute battalion to drop at Nadzab followed by one infantry brigade brought into the airfield from Port Moresby. Following this, a second brigade was to advance to Nadzab from the Bulolo Valley.[18] Concerned that a single parachute battalion may prove insufficient to protect and clear the airfield, Major General George Vasey, the 7th Division commander, requested that the full regiment be deployed. 'He kept pressing me to get the US Paratroop Regiment and wasn't happy till he had the whole of it,' Herring later wrote. In the end Herring stressed that it was 'most vital' that the full regiment be used.[19] General Whitehead, who would have to provide the extra transport aircraft, added his weight, telling Kenney that 'The first time that we use parachute troops we must succeed. It would be better to drop the whole regiment and not need them than to drop one squad too few.'[20] General MacArthur agreed and the orders directing the full regiment to deploy to New Guinea went out on 8 August.

General Vasey arrived at Port Moresby with his advanced headquarters on 25 July and set up close to that of 5th USAAF so that he could work with General Whitehead on planning the Nadzab phase of Operation Postern. According to Lieutenant Colonel Bill Robertson, the cooperation between 7th Division and 5th USAAF was 'splendid and consistent'. Herring's attitude of 'bending over backwards' to cooperate with the Americans paid great dividends. General Kenney certainly had a great regard for Herring and this not only helped Herring gain access to the vital US air resources, it also gained access to MacArthur's ear via Kenney, a trusted confidant. Although Vasey wanted to use all three brigades of his division in the operation, he was told by Berryman that only two could be supported. Both Vasey and Robertson had been on Crete when a German airborne operation had led to the fall of the island so they understood the effect the air landing would have on the Japanese. As Robertson later wrote, 'The lessons of Crete were not entirely lost to us.'[21]

On 26 July Vasey attended a conference with General Blamey and was given the outline of the operation. Planning then continued until the final operational orders were issued on 27 August. General Berryman directed that the main role of the 7th Division was to prevent the enemy overland reinforcement of Lae while seizing Nadzab and helping the 9th Division capture Lae.[22] The commander of the 21st Brigade, Brigadier Ivan Dougherty, had no idea of the Lae plan until he arrived in New Guinea on 31 July 1943 and from then on it was a close-kept secret within the brigade.[23]

•

The planning for the capture of Nadzab began with the collection of all available intelligence and topographical information including terrain studies, aerial photos and interviews with those men who knew the area from before the war. Intelligence on the Nadzab area was quite sketchy so ANGAU patrols were sent in utilising native personnel. A map room containing all maps, aerial photos and a 2.5 by 3.5 metre topographical model was established and 700 copies of each area map were distributed. Photomaps (aerial photographs with annotated locations) proved particularly useful and each paratrooper was provided with one of the Nadzab area. Meteorological data was also analysed to determine the placement of a smokescreen to cover the air drop.[24]

Reconnaissance of the land and Watut River routes from Tsili Tsili to Nadzab as well as the Markham River crossing points were made. General Vasey and other key commanders also made a flight over the area of operations and, after two weeks of discussion, an outline plan was agreed between Vasey and General Whitehead, who was responsible for the air operation.[25] Much of the detailed planning was carried out between Lieutenant Colonel Bill Robertson and Colonel David Hutchinson, who was the 5th USAAF assistant chief of staff. The men became firm friends and this ensured the planning went smoothly. Together they flew over Nadzab in a Flying Fortress, a flight that attracted no ground fire, confirming that the area seemed deserted.[26]

A divisional order of landing was drawn up with each plane only carrying the personnel and stores from a single unit. With Port Moresby, Dobodura and Tsili Tsili all to be used as transport bases, the flight numbers were prefixed with M, D or T respectively. The first brigade to be flown in, Brigadier Ken Eather's 25th Brigade, was landed in tactical order, with the infantry and engineer units landed in two parts. The first was that part required for immediate effective action, the second part comprising the administration personnel and heavy stores not immediately required.[27] To differentiate from the amphibious operation, the first day of the Nadzab operation would be called Z-Day while H-Hour would indicate the time of the paratrooper landing.

•

Colonel Ken Kinsler's 503rd Parachute Infantry Regiment had arrived in Australia on 2 December 1942 and was based at Gordonvale in northern Queensland. From April to July 1943 training was intensive. At this stage only seven officers knew of the Nadzab operation, but once it was given the go-ahead all supply shortages were made good. Under the cover of preparing for an exercise with the 32nd Division, all troops practised extensively with their principal weapon and made themselves familiar with the other unit weapons.[28] In late July MacArthur ordered Kinsler and his planning officers to proceed to Port Moresby to work with New Guinea Force on the Nadzab plan.[29]

On 18 August Lieutenant Colonel George Jones' 2/503rd Battalion moved by truck to Cairns and then by air to Port Moresby, the move taking two days. On the night of 19 August the other two battalions boarded the *Duntroon* at Cairns and by

Members of C Platoon, 2/5th Independent Company, on the flight across the Owen Stanley Range from Port Moresby on 23 May 1942. (AWM 099998)

Heath's Plantation, ten kilometres north-west of Lae. At the time of the commando raid on 30 June 1942 most of the indicated defence positions had not yet been constructed. G indicates the Japanese field artillery position west of the house that was there at the time of the raid. K indicates the location where Major Kneen was killed during the attack. (MacArthur Memorial Library and Archives)

Tsili Tsili airfield. The airfield, secretly built out of the New Guinea wilderness, was crucial to the success of Operation Postern. (US National Archives)

Lae airfield under USAAF bombing attack. Off the end of the airfield lies the wreck of the Japanese converted minelayer *Tenyo Maru*, run aground after being damaged by US Navy carrier aircraft on 10 March 1942. (US National Archives)

Australian infantry disembarking from LSTs at Lae. (US Navy photo 054642, US National Archives)

Three US Navy seamen aboard LST 471 struggle to bring their crippled vessel alongside LST 458 using a makeshift rudder. (US Navy photo 54359, US National Archives)

Troops and supplies coming ashore at Red Beach. (Department of Information, Australia)

The paratroops drop behind a protective smoke screen at Nadzab, 5 September 1943. (US National Archives)

Pioneers from the 2/2nd Pioneer Battalion crossing the Markham River on a pontoon bridge built by the 2/6th Field Company engineers on 5 September 1943. (Photo by Private Edward A. Smalie, US Signal Corps, US National Archives)

An Australian pioneer shakes hands with an American paratrooper at Nadzab airstrip. (Photo by Private Edward A. Smalie, US Signal Corps, US National Archives)

Three US paratroopers pass by an Australian-manned jeep as the first transports land on a very dusty Nadzab airstrip. In the background, one of the airfield engineers' bulldozers is still at work. (US National Archives)

One of the trucks carrying 2/33rd Battalion troops impacted by the crash of the Liberator at Jackson's Strip on the morning of 7 September 1943. This was the second truck in line. (AWM 057404)

Aerial view of the Markham Valley road into Lae. The markings for Jenyn's and Jensen's need to be transposed. This road was the 7th Division's axis of advance between the Atzera Range and the Markham River. The 9th Division landings took place on the coast near Singaua. (MacArthur Memorial Library and Archives)

Aerial view of the mouth of the Busu River looking inland towards the Saruwaged Range. (US National Archives)

The Kunda bridge across the Busu River after being rebuilt. (Photo by Don Bain)

Australian infantry entering Lae on 18 September 1943. (US Navy photo 54230, US National Archives)

23 August the entire regiment was in camp at Port Moresby. Once there, the troops acclimatised and undertook extensive speed-marches with full equipment in preparation for the operation.[30]

The parachute maintenance platoon was flown over to Port Moresby with the 2/503rd to prepare storage facilities for the parachutes which were due to arrive on 23 August. These facilities were very makeshift, with log floors being built inside standard canvas squad tents. All parachutes and supply containers had to be inspected and, once issued, teams of riggers had to fit and adjust the parachutes for each paratrooper.[31]

On 31 August Colonel Kinsler, his three battalion commanders plus the operations, supply and communications officers flew over the drop zone in a Flying Fortress at very low altitude. This reconnaissance later proved invaluable. Meteorological reports were obtained to determine prevailing wind conditions in the jump areas, vital information to ensure a safe and accurate drop. These conditions were peculiar; up until about an hour before midday the prevailing winds blew down the valley and then switched direction up the valley.[32]

The 54th Troop Carrier Wing would carry the troops for the Nadzab operation. Prior to creation of the wing, the 21st and 22nd Transport Squadrons had been renamed Troop Carrier Squadrons and, together with the newer 6th and 33rd Squadrons, were allocated to the 374th Troop Carrier Group. It was from this group that the 54th Troop Carrier Wing was formed on 13 May 1943 under the command of Colonel Paul Prentiss.

Working with the 54th Troop Carrier Wing, the officers of the 503rd Regiment decided to use a drop formation of six planes, echeloned to the right rear with a 30-second gap between each formation. Each of the three battalions had a separate drop zone and the transports would fly in three separate columns. On each of the three days leading up to the drop, rehearsals were carried out and the bombers and fighters that were to provide air support joined in to ensure correct timing.[33]

The selected parachute drop zones had to be 900 metres long and 450 metres wide and clear of tree growth. These zones also needed to be out of range of enemy small-arms fire or screened from it, hence the decision to lay smoke. The drop zones also had to allow for the proper approach and manoeuvre of troop carrier aircraft and had to be reasonably close to the desired location for the later operation, the capture and defence of Nadzab airstrip. An alternative landing ground, preferably for the entire regiment, was also needed to allow for any last-minute changes in enemy dispositions.[34]

•

On 3 September, two days before Z-Day, the final plan was issued. The objective of the operation was to capture the Nadzab area and commence the preparation of the airfield site. A roadblock on the road leading to Lae also had to be established. Major John Britten's 1/503rd Battalion (less one rifle platoon) would jump on Field A with the task of securing the Nadzab airfield site, establishing a perimeter and immediately commencing work on the airfield. One platoon would jump on Field D to cover the assembly of the battalion.[35] A patrol from Britten's battalion was to effect liaison with the Australian 2/2nd Pioneer Battalion, which would cross the Markham River, and guide them to Nadzab airstrip. The pioneers would come under command of the 503rd and one of Britten's companies was to protect the native workers

Airborne infantry

attached to the pioneers. A runway would be cleared to a length of 740 metres with the airstrip and a glider landing area marked with ground panels. By 1720 the parachute battalion would occupy a perimeter defence of the airfield and twelve groups of paratroopers, each of one NCO and ten men, were to unload the first twelve planes to land.[36] An Australian officer accompanied by a native patrol was to cross the Markham River the night before Z-Day and mark the main landing ground at Nadzab with an L if there were no Japanese in the area.[37]

Lieutenant Colonel George Jones' 2/503rd Battalion would also jump on Field A with the task of capturing the Gabsonkek area and prevent any enemy moves from the north and northwest. Lieutenant Colonel John Tolson's 3/503rd Battalion would jump on Field C and capture Gabmatzung and prevent any enemy moves from the east.[38] A deception element was included in the operation with 22 dummy paratroopers and 22 dummy aerial-supply loads to be dropped in the forests south of Yalu at H+6 minutes, using the first 22 planes dropping the 3/503rd.[39] The dummy runs were to be made at a height of 300 metres to ensure enemy troops at Heath's Plantation observed the drop, after which Heath's would be strafed and bombed. It was hoped that the dummy drop would confuse the Japanese and delay any movement of troops towards Nadzab.[40]

•

One interesting detail of the plan was that an Australian gun detachment from the 54th Battery of the 2/4th Field Regiment would jump with the Americans to provide artillery support. When volunteers were first called for, the unit stepped forward almost to a man and a detachment of four officers and 30 men under Lieutenant Johnnie Pearson was chosen.[41] Norm Anderson enjoyed his three weeks training with the Americans, particularly given that they were flying in frozen beef from Townsville to Port Moresby for their men. 'With the Yanks you got prime beef for tea every night,' he said.[42]

The detachment was equipped with two of the recently developed light 25-pounder guns. The guns had been developed from a normal 25-pounder by shortening the barrel, cradle and recoil system, discarding the shield and modifying the carriage. The light guns were reduced in weight from 1630 to 1300 kilograms but this came with some major compromises. Although the light guns used the standard 25-pounder shells, the range was reduced from 12,250 to 9330 metres with a major reduction in accuracy. 'Each time it was fired, the gun leapt into the air and tried to stand on its tail; it came down again way off line,' one gunner recalled. Bernard Lord agreed. 'Every time you fired it,' he said, 'you had to send the gun crew out into the kunai to get it back!' Due to the shorter muzzle, 'the charge was still firing after the shell left the muzzle' and, without the shield, the gun blast was horrendous for the gunners who suffered severe ear damage and shell shock.[43]

The 7th Division had drawn eight of these new guns on arrival at Port Moresby but all had defects. Just five days before the jump an inspection revealed that 'they cannot be fired in present condition'.[44] Ordnance engineers could only produce two workable models from the eight and these were the guns that would be dropped at Nadzab. The guns were rigged for dropping using the same procedure as for the American 75 mm pack howitzer, none of which were available for this operation. Each gun was broken down into thirteen parts, each of which was packed in a separate container for dropping. All thirteen parts were attached to each other with loose webbing to facilitate recovery.[45]

The men of Pearson's detachment had seven days of jump training in Port Moresby before a practice jump on 30 August. After a gun that was dropped in training sustained damage to the sight bracket and the wheels, the gun packing procedures were also modified. The detachment plus the two guns would be parachuted from four C-47 transports while two Flying Fortresses would drop the 192 high-explosive rounds of ammunition.[46] The detachment flew across to Dobodura on 2 September only to return to Port Moresby the following day, having gone to the wrong airfield. On 4 September the detachment flew to Tsili Tsili, where the men would spend the night before jumping one hour after the main jump on 5 September. First Lieutenant Robert Armstrong, who had been responsible for the parachute training of Pearson and his men, would jump with them.

•

The timing of the landing had to take into account General Vasey's desire to land as early as possible so as to have the maximum amount of daylight available for operations, particularly the preparation of the airfield. The main concern for the air force was the weather at the base airfields, over the Owen Stanley Range and at Nadzab. A decision was made that the drop would not take place after 1100 and that it was up to the air force to choose a suitable time prior to that or postpone the drop.[47]

On Z-7 (seven days before the airborne operation), battalion commanders were briefed on the operation and began creating sand tables of the terrain. On Z-4 all company commanders were informed and on Z-1 their men were briefed, though not told the location. It was not until the troops entered the transport aircraft on Z-Day that they were given individual maps showing the area of operations.[48] On Z-2 all parachutes and aerial supply containers were issued and maintenance platoon personnel were sent to both airfields to make any necessary last-minute adjustments and to replace any parachutes if required. Some of the riggers would also take part in the parachute drop to recover the parachutes while the rest would repair and repack them once they had been returned. In the event, some parachutes would be lost due to a grass fire while most of the other chutes deteriorated due to exposure so all were only subsequently reused for aerial resupply drops.[49]

The paratroops would emplane in 82 C-47s from Jackson's and Ward's airfields at Port Moresby. At 1500 on Z-1, 82 trucks moved into the regimental area, each numbered to match one of the aircraft. As with the planes, the trucks were separated into three serials, each serial corresponding to one of the parachute battalions. At H-7 hours the first serial moved to the airfield followed at 30-minute intervals by the other two serials. Each truck moved to its corresponding plane and the troops embarked.[50] At H-3 hours the loaded planes took off and formed up and at H-2 hours the formations headed for the drop zone, soon joined by the bombers and fighters. In all there were 303 aircraft engaged in the operation.

Meanwhile, a two-day supply of ammunition and rations was flown to Tsili Tsili where three modified Flying Fortresses were made available to carry out any resupply drops. These aircraft had a platform built across one half of the bomb bay with the other half left open for dropping. An anchor line was set up between the bomb rack and the door of the radio compartment and the static line snap-fastener of the delivery parachute was attached to it. From the bombardier's compartment, the jump master would direct four men at the rear door and four in the bomb bay as to when to despatch the supply bundles. Other supplies could be stored in the main cabin and thrown out the rear door.[51]

Two of the modified Flying Fortresses flew into Tsili Tsili on Z-1 while the third plane would accompany the main force to drop heavier equipment for use at the roadblock on the Lae road. This load comprised land and anti-personnel mines, concertina wire, 60 mm and 81 mm mortars, machine-gun ammunition and extra hand grenades. The two Fortresses at Tsili Tsili took off and dropped their loads as soon as ground communications were established. Their loads were mainly shells for the two Australian 25-pounder guns and the mortars but included medical gear. At the end of Z plus 1 these bombers returned to normal service, while most of the supplies at Tsili Tsili were not required and were also later returned to Port Moresby.[52]

On 7 August General Blamey had asked MacArthur's headquarters if gliders were available for the Nadzab operation.[53] The gliders were included in the plan because it was considered important to fly in engineering equipment for the airfield's construction and guns to supply artillery support as soon as possible. The plan called for three to ten gliders to land with equipment on or adjacent to the Nadzab airstrip. They would be based at Dobodura and scheduled to land anytime after H+1 hour. Of the 14 glider loads that were allocated, the first nine carried three tractors, three mowers, two jeeps, a mechanised rake and a 2-pounder anti-tank gun. All equipment was to be landed with petrol and oil while the gun would be landed with its ammunition. The total weight for each glider was 1350 kilograms although the glider with the anti-tank gun weighed 1550 kilograms.[54] Although the nine gliders were loaded, they were never flown to Nadzab as the progress of the Australian pioneer battalion and engineers was so good.[55] There was also a concern over the provision of effective fighter cover for the lumbering gliders.[56]

•

As with the 9th Division amphibious training program, the 7th Division had to train with the transport that would carry its troops into battle, in this case C-47 aircraft. Emplaning needed to be as fast as possible and, with the air force only allowing 15 minutes for unloading, it had to be well rehearsed. Considerable practice using two unserviceable fuselages was required to achieve both emplaning and unloading efficiency that adhered to strict air force procedures.[57] As Sergeant James Milbourne later wrote, his 2/14th Battalion improvised: 'The Bn was being turned into airborne infantry and we practised at moving on and off aircraft drawn on the ground.'[58] Five operational C-47s were later made available by General Whitehead for further training.

The key considerations for aircraft loading were the total load and its distribution. The load limit for each C-47 was 2300 kilograms and the centre of gravity had to be between 6 and 6.7 metres from the nose of the plane. Any excess stores were loaded first and positioned well forward in the fuselage, over the wing. This was followed by the men, a normal load being sixteen men with each considered to weigh 115 kilograms fully equipped. Special ramps were developed for loading and unloading heavy equipment such as jeeps and artillery pieces, with the men responsible for such equipment comprehensively trained. To simplify the loading process, each plane was allocated a 3-ton truck which brought the men from their camps to the airfield. A separate detachment was formed to handle the unloading process at Nadzab, much in the nature of a beach master at an amphibious beachhead.[59]

The maintenance of 7th Division would commence on the second day of the operation and would have priority over other air movement. It would be based on a requirement of 11.5 kilograms per man per day and aircraft would be loaded with a balanced load of ammunition, food and other supplies. The amount of ammunition required would depend upon usage with any unallotted space used for 25-pounder ammunition. Petrol would be based on 38 litres per day per jeep plus oil and grease. It was planned to hold a seven-day reserve plus another seven days of hard rations once the move across to Nadzab was complete.[60]

Motor transport was an issue for both the 7th and 9th Division. Even though both had been designated as a jungle division with vehicle numbers at 25 per cent of normal, Operation Chronicle had shown that too much motor transport was being taken in early and that even the 25 per cent motor transport requirements for the Australian divisions could not be met.[61] For the 7th Division there was the added problem that most vehicles were unsuitable for air transport. Later in the campaign, three 3-ton trucks were cut up, sent over by air and reassembled, but for the initial landings only half-ton jeeps were able to be used. It was proposed that only 200 jeeps and 160 trailers be taken across to Nadzab by air. Native labour would do most of the carrying work, and the division was originally allocated 1000 native carriers, 800 of whom would come down the Watut Valley from Tsili Tsili and the other 200 down the Wampit Valley from Sunshine. As the campaign developed it was thought that more native labour could be recruited in the Markham Valley.[62]

There was a ground component to complement the initial parachute drop over Nadzab. The 2/2nd Pioneer Battalion, part of 7th Division, would trek in overland from Tsili Tsili before crossing the Markham River and helping prepare the airfield for use. Each man carried 35-kilogram loads and there were 700 native carriers to help carry the equipment needed to prepare the airfield. Sappers from the 2/6th Field Company would also be involved, bringing pontoon boats down the Watut River to help build a footbridge across the Markham River. Rubber boats would also be available to those troops using the Markham River crossing.[63]

•

On 11 August General Chamberlin told General Berryman that he thought that Operation Postern would be an easy operation with little opposition. 'They never seem to think there will be much when the AIF is concerned but when it is US then there are many,' Berryman observed.[64] On 19 August Berryman got to see the object of his planning during a trip to the Australian front line on the ridges above Salamaua. Over the shining blue waters of the Huon Gulf, Mount Lunamun was visible with Lae spread out below it.[65]

On 25 August General Herring took over command of I Australian Corps and moved his headquarters across to Dobodura. Herring had four divisions under his command: the 5th, 7th, 9th and 11th, plus 4th Brigade and Wampit Force. General Blamey took over temporary command of Herring's New Guinea Force in Port Moresby.[66] On 28 August General Vasey met Berryman and handed over the 7th Division operation plan. Berryman wrote, 'He was happy & optimistic but thought the reduction of Lae would take some time.'[67] Vasey knew how to play the game; optimistic generals tended to have short careers.

At MacArthur's headquarters, General Chamberlin was less than impressed with the final operational plans for the two Australian divisions. 'They appear to be completely independent,' he wrote on 28 August and considered the overall plan to be 'elementary and incomplete'. Chamberlin's main concern centred on a lack of planning beyond the assault echelons. This was in part corrected when the plan extended the operation west to the Leron River but no allowance was made for the clearance of the Huon Peninsula and the capture of Finschhafen. Chamberlin identified the key weakness in the Australian plan: there was 'no clear-cut plan of coordination' between the two divisions at corps level.[68]

General Herring had let both of his divisional commanders get on with the detailed planning, Vasey working closely with General Whitehead and Wootten with Rear Admiral Barbey. 'As far as I was concerned I just gave them my blessing and told them to go to it and get it all fixed,' he later wrote.[69] As would later become apparent, although the two plans were well put together, they were two separate plans and lacked the coordination that an abler corps commander should have provided.

The capture of Lae was only the start of operations to secure a major part of New Guinea. At this stage Rabaul was still MacArthur's objective and the current operations, beginning with the capture of Lae, were designed to secure the Huon Peninsula as far as Bogadjim using both a coastal and an inland advance.

Once Lae had fallen, the 7th Division was to advance along the Markham and Ramu valleys as far as Dumpu, thus providing General Kenney with airfield sites to both isolate the Huon Peninsula and to strike at Japanese supply convoys to Madang, Wewak and Hansa Bay. Simultaneously, the 9th Division was to undertake an amphibious operation against Finschhafen before exploiting along the coast to Sio and Saidor. MacArthur had also raised the possibility of capturing Cape Gloucester at the western end of New Britain once Finschhafen had been secured.[70]

With all the planning complete, the amphibious landing force left Milne Bay on the morning of 3 September, with D-Day to be the next day, 4 September. The Nadzab landing, Z-Day, was set for 5 September, the day after the amphibious landing.

Chapter 8

D-DAY DAWNS

'More than half a hundred craft of all descriptions moved on, relentlessly, majestically, in line of four abreast . . . What one of us will ever forget that sight,' Private John Holmes from the 2/13th Battalion wrote. Holmes had boarded the APD *Gilmer* at Milne Bay, climbing up a scramble net from an LCVP, helped by the strong arms of the American sailors. The empty LCVPs were then winched aboard. 'We trundled aboard somewhat in the fashion of overloaded donkeys,' Holmes wrote. Once aboard, the Australians then gave their rations to the American cooks, one of whom said, 'I wouldn't cook that stuff. We got grub that'll do you.' 'I still recall vividly the roast beef and tomato ketchup,' Holmes wrote. *Gilmer* left Milne Bay at 0700 on 3 September. 'Clapping on 22 of her 27 knots [41 km/h] the *Gilmer* steamed down the bay,' Holmes wrote.[1] Captain Ken Esau from the 2/3rd Pioneer Battalion had a more stifling experience aboard one of the landing craft: 'That night, cramped in the congested hull of the LCI, where miracles of compression provide a bunk for every man, but not enough room for a dog to bark or air to bark with, the fleet makes for its staging point at Buna. All night sweat rolls from you.'[2]

The men disembarked at Buna for a break and then re-embarked in the afternoon. It was only at this stage that they were told that they would be landing on the beaches east of Lae (see Map 9). Four APDs, *Gilmer*, *Humpreys*, *Brooks* and *Sands* carrying sixteen LCVP landing craft, made up the first echelon of the Lae landing. *Gilmer* and *Brooks* would land two 2/13th Battalion assault companies under Captain Paul Deschamps and Captain Edwin Handley at Yellow Beach. Two other assault companies, Captain Bill Angus's company from the 2/15th and Captain Philip Pike's company from the 2/17th Battalion, were aboard *Sands* and *Humpreys* destined for Red Beach.

The second echelon, ultimately comprising twenty LCIs in three sections, left Milne Bay first, at 1300 on 2 September, heading for Buna at 22 kilometres per hour, arriving there at 0800 on 3 September then departing for Lae at 2000 that night.[3] The second wave for Yellow Beach, carrying the other two 2/13th Battalion infantry companies, came from this echelon as did the second wave at Red Beach which comprised four infantry companies, two each from the 2/15th and 2/17th Battalions. The third wave at Red Beach, four LCIs carrying more 20th Brigade units including brigade headquarters, also came from this second echelon.[4]

The third echelon was made up of eighteen LCTs spread over three sections plus a section of ten LCMs and another of 40 LCVPs. This echelon, which carried a battalion from the 532nd EBSR and its equipment, left Morobe two hours after

D-Day dawns

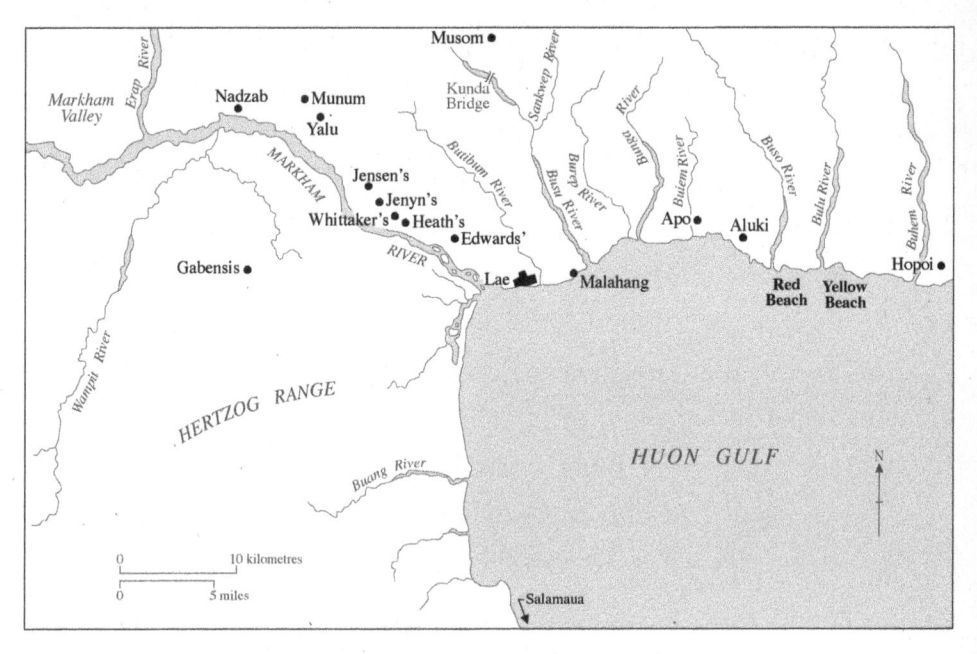

Map 9: Lae area of operations, September 1943

dark on 3 September. The ten LCMs and ten of the LCVPs were allocated to 9th Division for beach-to-beach ferrying. Echelons 4, 5 and 6 travelled from Milne Bay via Buna with a total of twelve LSTs and twelve LCTs. Fortunately, the sea conditions were favourable as the LCTs could only proceed at half speed in heavy seas. All six echelons would land on D-Day, 4 September. Another nine echelons were scheduled to land up until D-Day+13, that being 17 September.[5]

•

As the echelons of the invasion convoy assembled, the ABC journalist Peter Hemery watched. 'From every point of the compass ships were converging on us mirrored in the glassy waters,' he observed, 'a convoy of staggering size for these waters.'[6]

The waters remained smooth as the convoy crept along the coast past Salamaua and Lae in the dark of night. There were three separate routes to the landing beaches, all converging off the coast at the landing area. Only once the convoy was on the final leg to the landing beaches were most of the men told that Lae was to be the ultimate objective.[7]

There were a number of war correspondents accompanying the convoy. Bill Carty was one, working as a cameraman with the Australian Department of Information. Carty's first job in New Guinea had been at Buna where he had met General Wootten. Wootten had told him to 'go wherever you like, but keep your bloody head down'. Carty would follow the same approach at Lae despite being told to stay on the ship rather than land with the troops. 'I dismissed it as a ridiculous order,' he later wrote.[8]

The first landing craft would hit the beach at 0630 on 4 September, 18 minutes after sunrise. The landing force had wanted to go in at dawn, around 0515, but as the beach was backed by low-lying swampy jungle with no prominent features, 0630 was considered the earliest time that the beach could be identified with any certainty. At both Red and Yellow Beach there was a small coconut grove at the beach to aid identification and these clumps of coconut palms and a river bend were the main features used to identify the beaches. This job was given to the headquarters ship USS *Conyngham*. Identification took place at 0550, at which point the APDs lowered the landing craft carrying the first wave.[9]

•

On one of the two APDs off Yellow Beach, the 2/13th Battalion infantrymen waited to be called onto deck to board the landing craft. 'Faces looked strained in the dull blue light of the "black out" lamps,' Patrick Bourke wrote, 'and the occasional snatches of laughter that arose from several quietly conversing groups were just a few notes too high pitched.' The two APDs lowered four LCVPs each and then the men boarded. 'We climbed carefully down the swaying net ladders,' Bourke continued, 'carefully because the weight and awkwardness of our gear made us clumsy, where a false step would mean drowning or being crushed between the tossing barge and the mother ship.'[10] 'Away the landing force!' shouted the voice from the loudspeaker as the shore bombardment commenced.[11]

Five destroyers provided a preliminary bombardment for six minutes from H-11 (0619) by which time the first landing craft were 1100 metres from the beach.[12] 'Your ears soon hear the rolling thunder of a naval bombardment, a pleasing sound when it's yours,' Ken Esau wrote.[13] Peter Hemery watched as 'The slowly clearing darkness split with light as flame stabbed from the warship's guns.'[14] 'We could see a brilliant flash from their guns and the destroyers seemed to jump with the recoil,' Harry Wells observed.[15]

From his guard post at the anti-aircraft position overlooking Lae airfield, Kiichi Wada could hear the sound and see the flashes from the naval bombardment out in the Huon Gulf. 'Suddenly, there was a booming sound from the sea,' Wada wrote, 'and in a split second, I sighted red and yellow tracers come flying on a half moon ballistic arc.' 'Where would the huge fleet land?' he pondered. 'Aren't they, in fact, landing right here in Lae?' The Lae garrison had been given orders to fight to the death and Wada thought, 'If I must die, I will fight with courage and die like an imperial navy man without shame.'[16]

Aboard the eight landing craft heading for Yellow Beach were the two assault companies from Lieutenant Colonel George Colvin's 2/13th Battalion. 'What Japanese enemy lurks in that tall proud jungle?' John Holmes pondered. Holmes felt the relief, determination, fear, amazement and wonder 'at this strange mechanised mission intruding upon the beauty of the tropic dawn.' 'We squatted down, our heads beneath the gunwhale, gazing at the outline of our bayonets against the pale blue sky.' Some of the men then raised their heads and watched as the bombardment burst along the shoreline. Then 'the naval guns fell silent, the barges revved and shot for the shore'. At the same time, the machine gunners on the barges opened fire at the shoreline. The landing craft were unarmoured but fortunately there was no return fire from ashore. At 0633 the ramps dropped and the platoon commanders and Owen gunners scrambled for the jungle. Ten minutes later the first wave of the 2/13th had reached its objective.[17]

The second wave then approached the beach in the larger LCIs. 'Bayonets were fixed and actions cocked,' Patrick Bourke noted. The first LCI beached correctly but the second hit a reef 20 metres from shore and the men had to wade ashore in water up to their chests. The LCTs of the third wave came in an hour later and the first metal strips were laid out to ensure that the disembarking vehicles did not bog down in the heavy black sand. 'Men loaded with gear scurried back and forth across the beach, and there was a continuous babel of orders,' Bourke observed.[18] There was no enemy resistance at Yellow Beach after some 30 Japanese defenders abandoned their strongpoint, leaving behind weapons and equipment at the former Bulu Plantation manager's house. 'They had departed in some haste,' Bourke wrote, 'there

D-Day dawns

were signs that most of the garrison had been in bed when the assault began . . . there were gaping rents where shells and HMG [heavy machine-gun] bullets had torn through the walls.'[19]

By mid-afternoon the 2/13th had extended the Yellow Beach perimeter 3000 metres inland, 2000 metres east and the same distance west from the landing beach. 'The swamps had proved narrow, if nasty; the scrub had been neither as dense nor as tall as thought,' Bourke wrote. 'Two o'clock and all's well.'[20] 'As far as we're concerned everything went according to plan,' Les Clothier noted.[21] The Australians went looking for a fight, with two companies moving east along the track towards Hopoi mission station where opposition was expected.

The first wave for Red Beach was also carried in two APDs, each of which lowered four LCVPs holding one of the assault companies. From the 'Tojo' observation post in the Buang Ranges south of the Markham River, Captain Vic Tuckerman watched the 'landing craft spread out in fan like formation'.[22] As the landing craft approached the beaches, Harry Wells watched as 'their machine guns chattered away spraying the beachhead with a continuous stream of tracer bullets'.[23] The gunfire was only going one way and both companies had landed unopposed by 0615.

The three battalions of Brigadier Victor Windeyer's 20th Brigade plus the attached 2/23rd Battalion, which was to act as brigade reserve, also landed without opposition. 'As each wave discharged its load and drew offshore to reassemble, another wave grounded in the shallows,' Peter Hemery observed.[24] General Wootten had specified that the brigade commander had to be ashore early and Windeyer landed 15 minutes after the first wave. 'I always felt out of touch, impotent and useless until I was ashore,' Windeyer noted. 'Once ashore I hoped I could be useful.'[25] Although the landing had been unopposed on the ground, danger lurked above.

•

On the day before the landing, 21 Allied bombers had struck Lae airfield but, despite the damage, six Oscar fighters and three Sonia reconnaissance aircraft had managed to land there late in the afternoon, probably intending to carry out further reconnaissance of the concentration of landing craft at Morobe the next day. The three Sonias were from the 83rd Independent Air Chutai which had been based at Wewak and Madang since April 1943. The unit's Sonia aircraft, often mistaken for Val dive bombers due to their fixed undercarriage, had been involved in operations around Salamaua and at Nassau Bay from May to July 1943. By the end of July only five of the Sonias were still operable.[26]

On 2 August 1943 one of the remaining Sonias had been involved in a mission to bring the 18th Army commander, Lieutenant General Hatazo Adachi, from Alexishafen to Lae, escorted by nine Oscar fighters. However, the ten aircraft ran into an American air raid over Lae and became engaged with Lightning fighters. While the Oscars took on the Lightnings the solitary Sonia dropped down low and headed for Tuluvu on the western tip of New Britain, landing safely with Adachi. At 18th Army headquarters back in Wewak, Lieutenant General Kane Yoshihara and the other staff officers 'passed an anxious night, but fortunately next morning . . . there was a report that he had made a forced landing, so we were greatly relieved'. Adachi flew on to Salamaua on 3 August before he was returned to Madang in the trusty Sonia three days later.[27]

D-Day dawns

Now on the morning of 4 September, 'like a peal of thunder in a clear sky', word had come through that an amphibious landing had taken place east of Lae and the three Sonias and six escorting Oscars were hurriedly readied for action and took to the air at around 0700.[28] Kiichi Wada watched as the planes flew past his anti-aircraft position east of the airfield. 'Hei, the Rising Sun, our planes!' he wrote.[29] Only minutes after taking off, the aircraft were over Red Beach flying east along the coast into the rising sun. At 0704, half an hour after the initial landing, the aircraft came in low over Red Beach and, before any Allied fighters could intervene, the six Oscars strafed the landing craft followed by the three Sonias on a bombing run (see Map 10).[30] 'Suddenly the dull roar of barge engines was drowned by the staccato crack of ack ack,' Peter Hemery observed, 'as warships opened up on eight enemy bombers which had slid over mountain tops in background to bomb and strafe the tight formation of barges.'[31] 'Japanese bombers screamed down', Harry Wells wrote, 'Like large silver birds they sped onward dropping their eggs of death.'[32]

Troops from the 2/23rd Battalion, who were on seven LCIs about 30 metres apart approaching the beach, spotted the six low-flying Oscar fighters heading straight for them, the puffs of

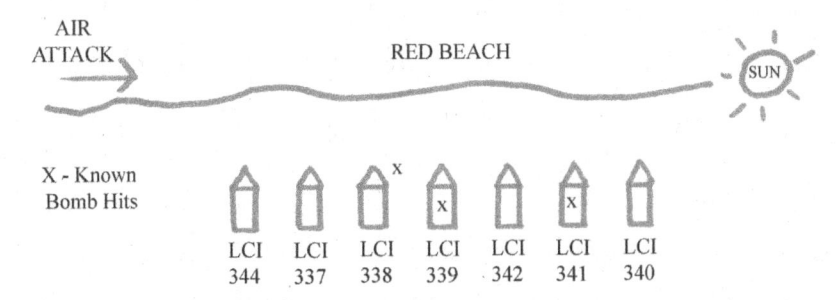

Map 10: Japanese air attack at Red Beach on 4 September 1943 as witnessed by the commander of LCI 338 (drawn from original, in US National Archives)

smoke along the wings signifying their intent. 'Cannon shells are hitting the bridge,' Ken Esau wrote, 'but the strafing is just too high to hit the packed mass of men on the deck.' The fighters made one pass but behind them were the three bomb-loaded Sonias. One bomb crashed through the main deck of Ensign James Tidball's LCI 339 forward of the pilot house and the ship caught fire, listed to port and quickly began to take on water. Ken Esau watched from LCI 338, worried that it was 'sinking, out of control, and may ram you as she yaws wildly'. The stricken landing craft was run ashore and abandoned by the crew, ten of whom had been wounded. Lieutenant Fay Begor later died.[33] 'There were 3 bombers with the Zeros & it was them that done the bombing,' Les Clothier noted.[34]

Another bomb narrowly missed LCI 341, exploding near the bottom of the ship and blowing a large hole amidships on the port side, flooding two compartments. A list to port was corrected and the LCI was run ashore where it was salvaged a month later. The commander, Lieutenant Robert Rolf, remained with the ship and was killed during another air attack two days later.[35] Nine men from the 2/23rd Battalion were killed including the commander, Lieutenant-Colonel Reg Wall, while 45 more were wounded.[36] The LCIs had restricted exits from troop holds and this contributed to the heavy casualties. Upon landing, Major Eric McRae took over command of the battalion. Bill Carty watched the air attack from LCI 340, the LCI at the eastern end of the line and next to LCI 341. 'Out of nowhere, a Japanese plane headed directly towards the beach,' he wrote, 'the plane dropped its bomb just before it skimmed over the top of my ship.'[37] 'The force of the bombs of our friendly planes astounded me,' Kiichi Wada wrote. 'I saw with my own eyes the immense power of the black gunpowder . . . Unlike the enemy bombs, it sounded harder and the blast more powerful . . . The smoke was black.'[38]

Allan Dawes was another war correspondent at the landing and was on one of the bombed LCIs: 'I saw in the haze of the dawn the flash of the warships' guns as salvo rolled on salvo and a bombardment of upwards of a thousand rounds softened whatever resistance might be offering; saw the first waves of light landing craft go into the coconut grove which was the agreed pointer to the landing beach; saw Japanese aircraft flash down, bomb, strafe, and kill.' Dawes was lucky to survive. 'Swinging by a stanchion, burning hot, over the huddled body of an Australian soldier whose clenched hand still held the Bren [light machine gun] he was taking ashore when he was struck down by the same blast which skittled a case of mortar bombs, I plunged into the hold of a still-smoking landing craft to retreat hastily before the stench of smoke and high explosive,' he wrote.[39]

Harold Guard, an American war correspondent, was aboard LST 458 heading for Red Beach. During the trip to Lae the steering gear had broken down and Guard, who had once served on a submarine with the same steering mechanism, was able to help get it fixed. 'Good Lord!' the engineering officer exclaimed, 'a bloody correspondent has put the steering gear right!' As the LST approached the shore, Guard could 'see the wire meshed landing strips that had been laid down' to help any vehicles to get off the beach. He could also see the beached LCI 339 was still on fire and LST 458 beached alongside it to help douse it with fire hoses.[40] Petty Officer Fay Fielder was a crewman on LST 458. 'When we got there one was already hit, they strafed it or something and it was burning so our forward damage control guys went over there and they put out the fire,' he recalled.

'They secured the engine and they said the ship was abandoned. There was no one on her. So they just left it there beached.'[41]

Three weeks after this attack, the 83rd Independent Air Chutai was awarded a citation by General Adachi. In that citation the attack by the Sonias at Hopoi (Red Beach) was highlighted alongside the earlier operations around Salamaua and Nassau Bay. 'It is a deep regret that the majority of their personnel were either killed or wounded during all these operations,' Adachi added.[42]

•

Two flights from RAAF No. 4 Squadron with eight Boomerangs and two Wirraways based at Tsili Tsili were supporting the Lae operation. Though obsolete as fighters, both aircraft types were well suited to reconnaissance and observation in support of ground troops. Flying Officer Ron Dickson watched the landing from his Boomerang, circling over the beachhead protecting the small aircraft that were directing the naval gunfire. 'It was a fantastic sight, seeing this huge fleet of vessels disembarking the troops, supplies and equipment onto the beaches,' he later wrote.[43]

Following the landings, the engineers at Red and Yellow Beach quickly got to work clearing the beachhead and constructing roads. By nightfall all objectives had been achieved. The 2/17th Battalion had crossed the Buso River and by 0730 the following morning the 2/7th Field Company had built a single-girder bridge across it. To protect the beachheads from further air attack, a battery from the 2/4th Light Anti-Aircraft Regiment had landed two detachments at Red Beach and another at Yellow Beach.

The three assault waves had landed 3780 troops while the follow-up echelons brought in another 2400 plus anti-aircraft

D-Day dawns

batteries, vehicles, ammunition and stores. The 1050 men making up the shore battalion of the 532nd EBSR also landed at this time, having moved up the coast from Morobe on their own LCVPs and LCMs plus some navy LCTs. A total of 7800 personnel and 3300 tonnes of equipment and supplies had been landed on D-Day.[44] The Japanese command estimated that 15,000 men, almost twice the actual number, had landed. Given the same naval resources, the Japanese probably would have landed that many.[45]

Unloading of the landing craft required air cover and this could not be guaranteed after 1100, giving only a four and a half hour window for unloading. The unloading parties had all LSTs cleared within 2 hours and 15 minutes and by 1050 all but one of the LSTs from Echelon Four had retracted from Red Beach. LST 452 was hard aground but was finally pulled off an hour later by the tug *Sonoma* while three destroyers made waves across the beach to help jolt it free.[46] Clearing the stores from the beach was the greater challenge and, after the next echelon of LSTs bringing in the 24th Brigade arrived, uncleared stores were still on the beach at daylight. Fortunately the enemy aircraft that came over did not attempt to bomb or strafe the stores or the men and vehicles trying to move them to cover.[47]

The LCTs, each carrying 120 tonnes of bulk stores, took much longer to unload. Despite a 2 hour and 30-minute limit, and much to the exasperation of the craft commanders, those LCTs that landed at 0800 were not all cleared until 1430, over six hours later. Two LCT echelons had to withdraw with a large proportion of their load still aboard.[48]

The original plan was for loaded vehicles to drive off the landing craft ramps and then unload at dump areas before re-embarking on the next incoming echelon. However, this was not possible due to the number of other vehicles that were using the exit routes, resulting in congestion and confusion. This led to later echelons arriving bulk loaded rather than on vehicles and unloading took much longer.[49] Lieutenant Colonel Bertram Searl, the 9th Division quartermaster, was responsible for beach organisation, assisted by the beach master, Second Lieutenant Bruce Campbell from the 532nd EBSR who had set up a loudspeaker system to help keep the beach under control. Lieutenant Colonel Edwin Brockett, the commander of the 532nd, coordinated his shore group and some of the Australians to clear the stores as promptly as possible.[50]

Allan Dawes watched the build up. 'The beach . . . was throbbing with business, like a market place. Bulldozers, caterpillar tractors, and trucks rolled out of the great holds of a long line of ships straight into the work of making roads, laying steel-mesh strips over soft earth, and transporting supplies. Dumps of crates, cases, boxes, drums, and cans mounted,' he observed.[51] The operation was 'mainly in the hands of the engineers and quartermasters who have been grappling with appalling difficulties and beating them,' Merv Weston wrote. 'Routes had been slashed into the jungle with machetes,' he added, 'steel netting had been laid along the sandy beach to carry heavy transports, guns had disappeared inland, and huge bulldozers were already pushing earth to and fro by the ton.'[52]

As was the case during the rehearsal landings, vehicles backed up on Red Beach because there was only the one track leading inland through the swampy ground behind the beach. This was somewhat alleviated by sending all vehicles and artillery except jeeps down the beach and up the bed of the Buso River in order to clear the beach. This was helped by the firmness of the beach, which could be traversed without wire mesh being laid down. Any wire mesh that had been put in place proved a hindrance as the ends of each sheet could not be anchored and tended to turn up. It was also useless on the swampy ground behind the beach and was therefore discarded in favour of using logs to form corduroy roads.[53]

The routes from the beach to the supply dumps were the first to be corduroyed. From Apo fishing village onward the beach narrowed, though it could take jeeps despite the numerous streams. The Burep River had a firm base and, with a limited catchment area, did not rise appreciably when it rained so was not a major barrier to supply. The gravelly bed of the river was therefore used as a supply route for vehicles while LCVPs were used to bring the supplies forward from Red Beach to the west bank of the Burep.[54]

Having spent the day carrying equipment and supplies from the beach to dumps inland, it was soon obvious that too much equipment had been brought in and this would hinder any rapid advance. As Brigadier Windeyer later noted, 'methods and technique for loading and unloading landing craft were not fully developed until later, when for Borneo a very high degree of efficiency was attained in this art throughout 9 Div, and MLOs [Military Landing Officers] became very skilled'.[55]

•

Air attacks against Japanese airbases had been arranged for the morning of D-Day. At 0745 thirteen RAAF bombers hit Gasmata, at 0900 24 Liberators bombed Lae and at 0930 nine Mitchells attacked Cape Gloucester. However, the main Japanese airbase at

Rabaul was not heavily attacked. At 1317 the US destroyer *Reid*, acting in an early warning role off Cape Cretin to the east of the landing force, picked up three clusters of enemy aircraft on its radar. They were 126 kilometres away approaching from Rabaul. Captain Ball, the fighter controller aboard *Reid*, knew that there was one US fighter squadron escorting landing craft back to Buna and another over the beachhead at Lae but did not know exactly where the American fighters were. Once a minute Ball sent out the grid reference of the incoming enemy aircraft across the airwaves, knowing that each pilot was on his frequency and had a grid map in his cockpit. Ball then watched his radar scope, knowing the aircraft would soon reach the isolated *Reid*. He then went out on the deck and counted around 60 Japanese aircraft pass by heading for Morobe. 'That was a nasty moment for us,' Ball noted.[56]

The attacking force of 81 aircraft from Rabaul was made up of twelve Betty bombers, eight Val carrier bombers and a mixed formation of 61 Zero fighters.[57] Captain Ball was able to guide 40 Lightnings and 20 Thunderbolts into the fray with contact made in the vicinity of *Reid*. Three Val dive bombers bombed *Reid* without success while the remaining enemy planes headed for Morobe.[58]

At 1420 that afternoon the six LSTs from the 6th Echelon with the Australian 2/4th Independent Company and 2/2nd Machine Gun Battalion aboard were about 33 kilometres east of Morobe and heading north towards Lae in two columns. Many of the commandos had served on Timor where they had fought with guile and success in a harsh and isolated environment. Cooped up in a landing craft they waited anxiously to reach the landing beaches east of Lae. Their anxiety proved well founded as the Japanese aircraft from Rabaul came into sight.[59]

D-Day dawns

At 1355 observers aboard LST 473 sighted eighteen enemy aircraft, a mix of bombers with escorting fighters. Two minutes later the landing craft was attacked by at least four Val dive bombers from the south-east. Men from the 2nd Machine Gun Battalion watching from the nearby LST 471 spotted four Vals 'very high and right in the sun' dive down on LST 473 'with a shrill whine'. The Vals flattened out at about 100 metres above the water and released their deadly load. 'The bombs are falling,' the men observed, 'little black ones from each ship as it flattens out.' They saw four bombs strike LST 473 which was astern of LST 471. 'Poor blighters,' the watchers thought, 'wonder what their casualties are?'[60]

LST 473 sustained two direct hits and two near-misses. The first bomb destroyed the starboard side Oerlikon anti-aircraft gun and four ammunition lockers as well as the pilot house and with it the control of the vessel. Keith Hanisch had been watching four men playing cards on the deck as the stern was lifted out of the water. 'I can still see the four blokes, cards, money and blanket floating in mid air,' he later said.[61] The second bomb penetrated three decks and destroyed both drive shafts. Fortunately, as Bob Phillips observed, the bomb did not explode. Fire broke out but was soon brought under control by the well-drilled crew. Meanwhile, with power to the ammunition hoists knocked out, the commandos were helping to pass shells up to the anti-aircraft guns. One of the commandos, Brian Jaggar, had even taken the place of a wounded American gunner and was helping to fight off the attacking aircraft.[62]

During this first attack, the LST 473 helmsman, Seaman Frederick Erickson, was blown clear and Seaman Johnnie Hutchins, though also badly wounded in the blast, took over the helm. Then, as the dive bombers left, at least six torpedo bombers attacked from the west about 25 metres above the waves. After the torpedo wakes were sighted Hutchins turned the ship sharply to starboard but it turned very slowly due to the bomb damage. One torpedo passed under the LST and one passed astern. When other shipmates reached the pilot house they found Hutchins dead at the wheel and had to prise it loose from his fingers.[63] Hutchins was awarded his country's highest honour, the Medal of Honor.

Meanwhile LST 471 had been hit in the stern by one of the torpedos that had missed LST 473. 'A torpedo passed in front of our bridge and went slap bang into the stern of the next LST,' Bob Phillips observed.[64] The LST had been targeted by two torpedo planes at mast height, both of whom were shot down but not before they had released their torpedoes about 1000 metres out. 'A torpedo seems to float down to the water and hits with a splash,' an observer noted. The first torpedo passed the bow but the second struck the stern of the LST and, for those aboard, 'the LST lurched violently, throwing everyone off their feet'. 'Wounded are now staggering up from the after hatchways, covered in blood,' one of the men observed. When rescuers reached the stern, they found 'a mass of twisted, jagged steel plates, strewn around with most shockingly mutilated bodies and human remains'.[65]

Jim Rae was one of the commandos on board, locked into a compartment down below behind watertight doors and bulkheads. 'We were being tossed about like rubber balls. Then it was still,' he later said. 'All I could see was water down below and sky up above—nothing in between . . . The back part of the ship was gone.' Rae was one of only five commandos on the ship still physically able to carry on.[66] Ralph Coyne was another one of the survivors. 'Rising to my feet, I was confronted by horror,' he wrote. 'Tiers of bunks collapsed on one another. All men on their bunks were dead.' Once he made his way up to the deck, Coyne saw how 'The stern of the vessel where we were quartered was turned up like a scorpion's tail, the stern gun pointing up into the sky.'[67] One officer and six men from the landing craft crew were killed but the greater loss was among the 2/4th Independent Company commandos, 34 being killed and seven wounded, 'a calamitous loss for a small unit'.[68]

At the time of the attack, six LSTs from the 4th Echelon escorted by four destroyers were also east of Morobe but heading south after the landing.[69] Two of these LSTs, LST 454 and LST 458, were ordered to divert from their course to assist the two LSTs damaged by the air attack. Petty Officer Fay Fielder was aboard LST 458 when it reached the damaged LSTs. 'They were both helpless in the water,' he said. At 2000, some six hours after the attack, LST 458 came alongside LST 471 and using hawsers they 'reeled it in and tied it up with cables' using buckler guards to keep the two vessels from clashing. 'It would crush them but it kept them enough apart,' Fielder recalled. Fifteen minutes later LST 458 and LST 471 were secured, and using the engines of LST 458 the two vessels were safely beached at Morobe five hours later. The cables were then cut and the LST 458 retracted to continue its journey south.[70]

Before LST 458 left Morobe the medical corpsman, accompanied by Fay Fielder, was sent to see if there were any survivors down below the decks of LST 471. Descending a stairway to the tank deck by flashlight, the two men moved through the crew quarters in about half a metre of water. 'He's shining the light there and these guys sitting at the table, they must have been eating, all Australians,' Fielder said. 'From what I could see some of those guys didn't have a mark on them. I mean no cuts, no bleeding, they were dead. Concussion killed them I guess . . . We realised then that the war was going on.'[71]

Conyngham accompanied the damaged LSTs to Morobe and assisted with medical treatment, later taking on board 40 wounded who were taken to Buna. The four APDs were ordered back to Morobe from Buna and, once they arrived, another 40 wounded men were put aboard *Humphreys* which returned to Buna. *Gilmer* acted as an anti-submarine screen at the Morobe harbour entrance while *Brooks* and *Sands* were sent to reinforce the escort for Echelon 6, which had continued on to Lae. Meanwhile the cargo on the two damaged LSTs was offloaded onto LST 454 and LST 458 and they returned to Lae with the five LSTs of Echelon 8 the following day.[72] During the air attack the Japanese had lost four Zeros and three Bettys with another three Zeros, seven Bettys and five Vals damaged.[73]

Meanwhile back at Red Beach more enemy aircraft had appeared at 1700, setting fire to an ammunition dump and killing two US shore engineers and wounding twelve. The two stranded LCIs that had been hit in the morning attack also received further damage. Low-level bombing and strafing attacks were stymied by the anti-aircraft guns but high-level bombing took a toll. There were nine air attacks on Red Beach during the first two days of the landing.

At Yellow Beach the Australian infantry appreciated the air cover. 'All day squadron after squadron of fighters had circled above us,' one observed, 'and squadron relieved squadron according to such an accurate timetable that there was scarcely a minute that we were without air cover.' However, just as the last sixteen

D-Day dawns

Lightning fighters left the area at 1630, four Lily bombers, escorted by Zeros, bombed and strafed the beaches.[74]

With US air units responsible for attacking the Japanese airfields at Wewak, Lae and at Tuluvu on Cape Gloucester, the RAAF got the job at Gasmata. At 0730 on the morning of 4 September, ten Beaufort bombers from RAAF No. 100 Squadron, backed up by three A-20 Bostons (the Australian name for the A-20 Havoc) from RAAF No. 22 Squadron, bombed the airfield despite heavy anti-aircraft fire. One of the Beauforts, piloted by Flying Officer Tom Allanson, was shot down and the four-man crew were lost. Another Beaufort pilot, Flying Officer John Baker, later wrote, 'I dodged and weaved all I knew. It was the most thrilling experience of my life.' Three Bostons returned to Gasmata later in the afternoon and bombed and strafed the airstrip. 'Strip considered unserviceable,' the 22 Squadron War Diary noted.[75]

On the following morning of 5 September the three Bostons returned to Gasmata, knowing how important it was to put the airfield out of action following the previous day's Japanese air attacks. When the attack went in at around 0600, it was clear some repair work had been carried out but this time the Bostons left the airfield 'definitely unserviceable'. Nonetheless, just after 0700 ten Beauforts followed up with another attack but they faced unexpectedly heavy Japanese anti-aircraft fire and, as the Beauforts made their bomb run in a shallow dive, five of the aircraft were hit. Flight Lieutenant Roy Woollacott's aircraft, which led the flight, was one of them, but with his Beaufort in flames he continued the bomb run and dropped his four bombs on the runway. He and his four crewmen were killed as were the crew from two other Beauforts, one of which crashed into the sea and the other into the hills to the north-east.

The other two damaged Beauforts made it back to Goodenough Island where one was destroyed on landing, though the crew survived.[76]

•

Although a direct attack on Lae had been expected by the Japanese at some stage, as Kane Yoshihara noted, 'for the front line units it was like a peal of thunder in a clear sky'.[77] The initial Japanese response was as expected. At 1700 on 4 September orders were issued that 'The division must defend Lae and Salamaua to the death.'[78] Kamesaku Iwata, a naval medic with the 82nd Naval Garrison, wrote that he 'strangely felt calm thinking that finally I can die for my country'. Iwata had come to Lae in the wake of the loss of the Bismarck Sea convoy where his vessel had been sunk and the survivors left to drift at the mercy of the strafing Allied aircraft. 'It will be different this time,' he wrote. 'Being killed while killing the enemy is my long cherished ambition.'[79]

It was specified that 'Commanders in the Lae area will combine and lead army and navy units, and must defend Lae with all their strength.' That night further orders came from 18th Army headquarters specifying that the 51st Division must concentrate its forces at Lae and take over command of the naval forces for the defence of Lae. Based on these orders General Nakano decided that Salamaua would not be defended to the death and the units there would begin the withdrawal to Lae on the following day, 5 September. Engineering and anti-aircraft units would be the first to move.[80]

Chapter 9

'THE WOLF AT THE BACK GATE'

The first plane over Nadzab early on 5 September was able to report that the weather conditions were suitable for the second phase of Operation Postern to proceed (see Map 11).[1] Once given the green light for Z-Day, the three battalions of the 503rd Parachute Regiment embarked on the 82 C-47 transports from the 54th Troop Carrier Wing and headed across the Owen Stanley Range to Nadzab. Over Marilinan the aircraft manoeuvred into their six-plane groupings for the parachute drop.

At one minute before H-Hour three squadrons of Mitchells bombed and strafed the wooded areas adjacent to the drop zones. The Mitchells were followed by three flights of Havocs which laid down a smokescreen in front of those wooded areas. Other air support came 30 minutes after the H-Hour drop when

D-DAY NEW GUINEA

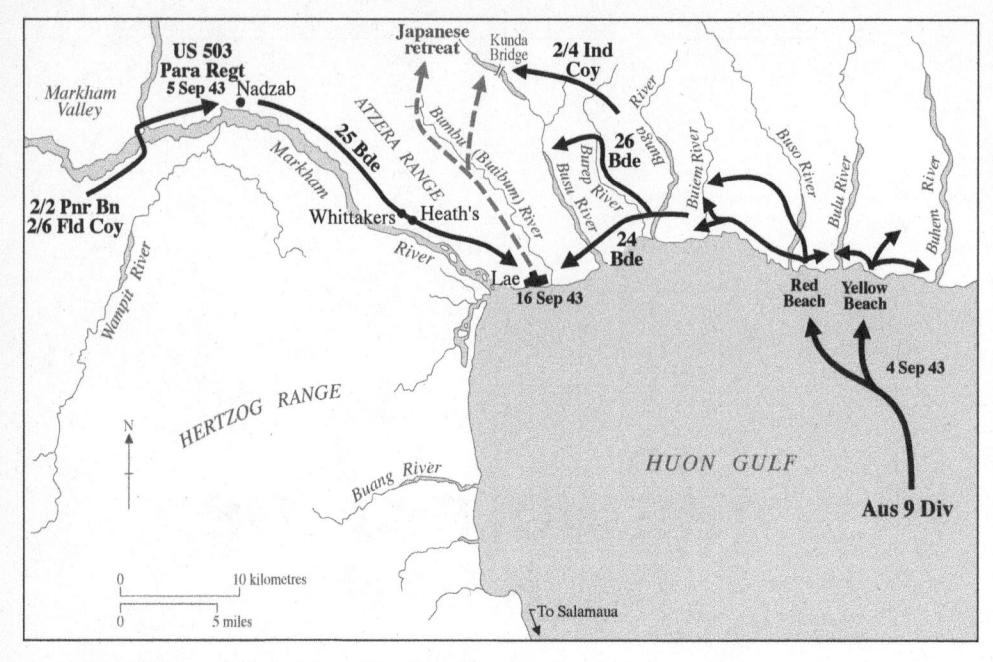

Map 11: Lae operations, September 1943

Liberators and Flying Fortresses dropped bombs on Gabmatzung, Gabsonkek and the Markham Valley road to Lae. Another squadron of Mitchells provided direct support to the paratroopers on the ground, with one-third of the squadron on call for 90 minutes at a time. There was also a squadron of Airacobra fighters on call from Tsili Tsili and they carried out armed reconnaissance flights over the Lae road looking for any Japanese troops moving towards Nadzab.

•

On the ground, a company from the Papuan Infantry Battalion (PIB) patrolled the south side of the Markham River upstream from the Watut River junction to prevent any crossings by local natives

'The wolf at the back gate'

until the operation was well underway. Once the paratroops had dropped, the PIB company would cross the Markham and patrol the north bank from the Erap River junction to Chivasing and into the Markham Valley, looking out for any Japanese movement west of Nadzab. Another PIB patrol at the former Diddy camp would detect any enemy moves from the north. Further downstream the infantrymen of the 24th Battalion kept a close eye on the Japanese troops holding Markham Point.[2]

Both General MacArthur and Kenney watched the landing from Flying Fortresses circling above Nadzab. Kenney had told MacArthur he wanted to be there because 'they were my kids'. 'You're right, George,' MacArthur replied, 'we'll both go. They're my kids, too.'[3] General George Vasey, who had seen German paratroops in action over Crete in 1941, also watched the drop from above. 'I wanted to see [paratroops] land from the top rather than the bottom as in Crete,' he wrote to his wife.[4]

Lieutenant Colonel John 'Smiling Jack' Tolson, the commander of the US 3/503rd Battalion, would make the first combat jump in the Pacific. He could see the airfield below but, as he looked up for the green light to jump, it didn't flash on; the excited pilot and navigator had failed to press the button. 'So I hesitated for a few moments,' Tolson later recalled, 'then saw we were over the middle of the field, and I jumped.' The delay meant that quite a number of Tolson's men ended up in the trees at the end of the drop zone.[5] Three columns of C-47s with escorting fighters above and on either side deposited their troops over the three landing grounds in four and half minutes. Three men were killed in the jump, two of whom were 'streamers' whose chutes failed to open, plus one man who got hung up in a tree before falling about 20 metres to his death.[6] One of the

82 transports did not drop any men after the door blew out as it was being removed, leaving it hanging from the side of the plane, thus endangering the life of any jumper.[7]

There were seven war correspondents aboard the troop carriers that morning and Merv Weston was one of them. 'It was all over so quickly,' he wrote, 'that all one was left with was of a vision of parachutes billowing briefly, and then a big concentration on the ground that looked like so many sheep.'[8] RAAF Boomerang pilot Alex Miller-Randle watched the drop from well above: 'I saw below me dozens of DC3s [C-47s] and the parachutists tumbling from open doors and floating down like little mushrooms.'[9] Although all drops were successful, the two to three metre high kunai grass hampered the assembly of the battalions. Nonetheless, two hours after the jump all units were in position and work on clearing the airfield had commenced. General Kenney was suitably impressed by the near faultless parachute drop. In a letter to his superior, General Henry 'Hap' Arnold, Kenney wrote that 'the operation really was a magnificent spectacle. I truly don't believe that another air force in the world could have put this over as perfectly as the 5th Air Force did.'[10]

An hour after the initial 503rd jump, Lieutenant Johnnie Pearson's gun detachment successfully jumped with the two light 25-pounder guns.[11] Lieutenant Alan Clayton took part even though he had not made a training jump, having replaced another officer who had broken his ankle in training. David Wilson had also fractured his ankle during training but kept quiet about it and made the jump.[12] Norm Anderson remembered how the men were shouting out to each other as they descended, joking about the experience until the final 6 metres or so when the ground 'came rushing up at you'. Like most of the gunners, Anderson 'landed pretty hard', but all of them got down safely though a crosswind scattered them along the kunai-covered Nadzab airstrip. They had all jumped on the first pass across the strip and the equipment came down on the second and third passes. The gun crews managed to get the first gun into action soon afterwards although its support was not immediately required. However, the parachute load containing the buffer and recuperator for the second gun was not found in the head-high kunai grass until three days later. 'It wasn't fun trying to find the parts,' Norm Anderson recalled.[13] There was no Japanese resistance to the landing and Pearson's gunners didn't get to fire a shot in anger on this occasion.

Lieutenant General Kane Yoshihara, the Chief of Staff of the Japanese 18th Army, later wrote, 'While the Lae units were keeping at bay the tiger at the front gate, the wolf had appeared at the back gate.'[14] What the Japanese didn't know, but soon came to realise, was that General MacArthur had ordered that the paratroopers were not to be employed on infantry tasks and would therefore not be advancing into Lae.

•

After flying into Tsili Tsili on 1 September, the 2/2nd Pioneer Battalion and 2/6th Field Company, plus medical and signals detachments, trekked to the south bank of the Markham River on foot. Using concealed routes east of the Watut River, the men took two days to reach Kirkland's camp about 10 kilometres from Nadzab. The pioneers made the strenuous journey helped by 700 native carriers and with 35-kilogram loads on their own backs. 'A lengthy column of troops and carriers toting stores,' one of them noted. A separate engineer party in twenty folding boats with outboard motors moved down the Watut and Markham rivers to Kirkland's with instructions not to reach the Watut–Markham junction before 1800 on Z-1. The boats, each of which could carry eight men, were then brought down the Markham by night to cross the river once the parachute drop began at H-Hour. Two boats were lost and one sapper drowned during this difficult move which was made using oars rather than the unreliable motors. The boats were to carry the 2/2nd Pioneers and later the native carriers across the Markham to Nadzab.[15]

The sapper who had drowned after his boat got snagged in the Markham and capsized was Lance Corporal Harry Fagan. Fagan was a shearer from Coonamble in western New South Wales who had enlisted with his twin brother Maurie early in the war. One of his mates in the 2/6th Field Company was Bert Beros, who had penned the iconic 'Fuzzy Wuzzy Angels' poem during the Kokoda campaign. Beros also penned a poem in memory of his mate. 'We left you sleeping, Harry, where the Markham waters flow,' wrote Beros, 'A sapper cobber whom we'd known so long.'[16]

The 2/6th Field Company arrived at Kirkland's on the night of 4–5 September and, once the men saw the parachutes fill the skies the next morning, the sappers began crossing the Markham. The river was divided into four streams, the first three of which were fordable but the fourth, the main river channel, requiring an improvised footbridge. The sappers used eight of the motorised folding boats, anchoring seven of them across the river, joined by timber cut from saplings along the river bank. The eighth boat was used to ferry troops across the gap to the bridge until more boats arrived to complete the bridge. Two upstream anchors were used on each boat with a breast line connected to the middle boats from each bank. By 1230 the pioneers were crossing the 64-metre-wide fast running river. To get the carriers across, a chain of rubber boats was suspended from a 64-millimetre steel cable that had been strung across the river. The system, which required an anchored A-frame and considerable cable and rope management, was installed within 30 minutes. Each rubber boat carried two or three men plus stores across the river.[17]

As soon as they saw the paratroops drop, the 2/2nd Pioneers moved off in extended order over the sandbanks to the main channel of the Markham. The pioneers were all across the Markham by 1400 and then made their way to Nadzab to help clear the airstrip. Rather than wait for mowers to be flown in, the pioneers burned the grass off the airstrip and cleared away any rubbish. The burning did not go well as considerable stores and equipment also went up in smoke. More seriously, with no layer of grass to bind the soil once the aircraft began landing, the baked unbound surface subsequently broke up, and within a week the landing ground had to be closed for repair.[18]

The minimum dimensions for the transport airstrip at Nadzab were 840 metres long and 27 metres wide with a 62-metre-wide cleared area overall. The airstrip would later need to be expanded to the more desirable 1200 metre length and 45 metre width with a 110-metre-wide cleared area. Although a gradient of two degrees across the runway would normally suffice, in tropical conditions it needed to be three degrees to disperse any rainfall. A drainage system to cope with the water from the airstrip also needed to be constructed, in this case using ditches running either side of the strip. Two landing strips were to be constructed as soon as possible, with unloading facilities for 24 aircraft.[19]

The first aircraft to land at Nadzab was a Piper Cub at 0940 on 6 September with Lieutenant Colonel Woodbury on board ready to get his airborne engineers to work. At 1050 the first of 32 C-47 transport aircraft landed, all of them coming from Tsili Tsili. The first two C-47s brought in the engineering headquarters for 7th Division along with loading ramps. The next seven planes carried equipment from Woodbury's 871st Airborne Engineer Battalion including a D4 bulldozer which had been dismantled and spread over three planeloads. The tenth plane brought in US airfield control personnel and the next 17 aircraft brought in the US 707th Airborne Machine Gun battery for airfield defence.[20]

Other aircraft acted a ferry service for 7th Division troops from Port Moresby to Tsili Tsili and then onwards to Nadzab on the following day, 7 September, when 66 planeloads would land at Nadzab. General Vasey's 7th Division headquarters and signallers landed first, followed by the first infantry from the 2/25th Battalion and the 2/4th Field Ambulance. Next to land was the 54th Battery of the 2/4th Field Regiment with four standard 25-pounder field guns. The 7th Division troops carried their own ammunition plus three days of hard rations and two days emergency dehydrated rations. One field ration per man was also carried on the plane plus two extra bandoliers of small-arms ammunition which were to be dropped off after disembarking.[21]

•

Captain Reg Seddon had one of the toughest jobs in Port Moresby, arranging a marshalling area within range of all 7th Division units but with sufficient space to disperse 100 trucks. It also had to be in reasonable proximity to the three major Port Moresby airfields

'The wolf at the back gate'

and have good two-way all-weather road access. Seddon began looking for a suitable site on 30 August and, with vacant space at a premium, he took one and a half days to find one. He chose the area at the southern end of Jackson's airfield, believing the site 'was the only one that was eminently suitable'. It was 800 metres from the end of the runway and about 7.5 metres lower.[22]

On 5 September Seddon organised eleven planeloads for embarkation, all of which flew to Tsili Tsili. On the following day he arranged another 68 planeloads, also to Tsili Tsili. Well before dawn on the morning of 7 September, Seddon had eighteen trucks carrying much of Lieutenant Colonel Tom Cotton's 2/33rd Battalion ready and waiting at the new dispersal area, scheduled to head to Durand airfield to embark for the trip north across the Owen Stanley Range.[23] Jackson's airfield was also a key base for the USAAF heavy bombing units and the long-range bombers were busy ensuring that the major Japanese base at Rabaul was kept under surveillance and control. At the same time as the Australian troops were gathering for their flights, the USAAF ground crews were preparing heavy bombers for their own flights north.

The morning was cold and Doug Marshall had jumped aboard a truck next to his big mate Ivan 'Slim' Whittle, the son of one of Australia's most highly decorated soldiers of the First World War. 'Come up here and I'll keep you warm,' Whittle had told him. At 0420 Marshall heard the roar of the first of the Liberator bombers taking off, only clearing the trucks by about 30 metres. Sergeant Bill Crooks heard 'a deep throated blast and roar of aircraft engines'. 'Christ! He was close,' one of the other men quipped, 'I hope we don't stay here too long.'[24]

Five minutes later another Liberator, *Pride of the Cornhuskers* from the US 403rd Bomb Squadron, loaded with four 500-pound bombs and 10,500 litres of fuel, took off. Piloted by Second Lieutenant Howard Wood, the fully laden bomber struggled to gain lift. 'This plane was much louder,' Doug Marshall noted.[25] The men in the trucks looked anxiously towards the end of the airstrip off to the right where the plane 'seemed to hang just above the ground'. Then it 'came crashing through the trees, its engines roaring' and after the left wing sheared off, the Liberator 'smashed down like an arrow into the trucks'.[26] 'Everything went white. The sky went white with flame,' Doug Marshall recalled. Ivan Whittle was killed but 'as he got hit he just pushed me clear, over the side of the truck'.[27]

The point of impact was 640 metres from the end of runway with the aircraft wreckage zone scattered forward another 120 metres over a 70-metre width.[28] Five trucks had been hit and four of them were on fire. The other, the second truck in line, was blown over onto its side. Private Fred Ellis was in the last of the five trucks hit and saw the Liberator come over a rise. 'Gee it's low,' he said, just before it struck a tree, lost the left wing and crashed into the hillside nearby. The blast from two explosions blew Ellis out of his truck. Firefighting was ineffective and the vehicles could not be approached due to exploding ammunition and had to be allowed to burn themselves out.[29]

Reg Seddon, who was in the control tent, heard the normal sound of the first aircraft taking off from Jackson's but soon after heard a tremendous crash and the sound of exploding bombs accompanied by a great ball of fire rising above the marshalling area. He immediately phoned through to request the dispatch of all available ambulances, medical officers and firefighting units to the crash site. He also ordered all trucks still in the Durand dispersal area to move to the nearby Jackson's dispersal area and used the loudspeaker to call for all able men to help with the injured. Private Harry Davies, Reg Seddon's batman, was walking from the cookhouse to Seddon's tent when he heard the crash and explosions. His immediate thought was that it was an air raid and he went to ground. Then he saw the flames and heard the screams.[30]

Captain Eric Marshall was second-in-command of A Company. The company was in trucks moving slowly in the dark along the top of a rise at the end of Jackson's Strip. 'The whole scene was vividly lit by an intense light, a wave of heat hit the top of the ridge, plane wreckage was hurtled up over our vehicles and everyone rushed for the leeward side of the ridge,' he later wrote. What seemed to be only minutes later the men jumped back on the trucks and drove on, 'past what appeared to be a nightmare scene', Marshall wrote. 'The fire was still burning fiercely, small-arms rounds were exploding, incendiary bombs were alight.'[31]

Ray Fewings put his hand up to protect his face. 'It burned down the side of my face,' he said. 'Some were completely alight, desperate, running around and yelling "put me out".'[32] Fred Caldwell saw how, 'Flaming high-octane fuel sprayed the vehicles, men became blazing torches.' Ammunition exploded, killing some who tried to rescue others. 'We did our pitiful best . . . horribly burnt men pleaded to be shot,' he recalled.[33]

Bill Crooks sat on the tailgate of the end truck involved in the accident. A two-year veteran of the war at the age of 17, he was one of the most experienced soldiers in D Company, although still one of the youngest. Crooks was chatting with Frank Smith and Billy Musgrave as the Liberator took off, exhaust sparks and flames obvious as the plane clawed for height off the runway. 'Christ, it's going to hit us!' somebody screamed, 'Look out!

Look out!'[34] 'The trucks were wood lined and open,' Crooks related, and the men on the right-hand side copped the worst of the blast. The men were all carrying cloth bandoliers of .303 cartridges and a box of grenades was shared between two men. Each also had two mortar bombs, all to be dropped off on landing at Nadzab. 'The rear bomb fuses stuck out of the men's pockets,' Bill Crooks remembered, 'the men were loaded up with so much ammo.' The blast flung Crooks out the back of the truck into a tree where he hung by his belt from a branch. He wondered where the heat was coming from and soon realised his bed roll was on fire so used his knife to cut himself free and then joined up with Jimmy Laing. They could smell fumes from the petrol that had soaked into the gravel track and gathered in the culverts like a fire grate. The two men watched the rivulets of flaming petrol running down the hill 'giving off tremendous heat'.[35]

Three of the four 500-pound bombs carried by the Liberator had exploded in the crash. With his leg badly damaged, 'Big' Jim Condon lay next to the unexploded bomb for some time, unable to move. Bill Crooks, Jimmy Laing and Billy Musgrave found him, seemingly stuck to it. 'I'm bloody glad you found me,' he quietly told them, 'my eyes are sore staring at that great bomb and waiting for it to go off.' The impact of the crash had knocked the caps off the nose fuses of all four bombs, thus removing the safety blocks. However, the striker head on the fourth bomb had apparently not hit the ground and Captain Vince Berger, a USAAF ordnance officer, was able to remove the nose and tail fuses, thus disarming it.[36]

Captain John Balfour-Ogilvy watched men running in all directions to escape; some already burning. 'Some of our members who I personally assisted were blackened all over,' Balfour-Ogilvy wrote, 'clothes were on fire and their clothes had been completely burnt off and when I grabbed them, skin just came off wherever I handled them.' With such intense heat there was a limit to what could be done and even two American Air Force firefighters 'wearing asbestos suits and walking into the inferno' had to retreat. 'The heat was so intense very little could be done, and to those able to assist, we now saw friends being burnt alive.' Unable to help the living, Balfour-Ogilvy took on 'the grim self-appointed task of organising and laying out the bodies and bits and pieces of bodies that the firefighters brought out.'[37] A stunned Bill Crooks 'walked to the control tent to report to the adjutant that D Company was no more'.[38] Brigadier Ivan Dougherty arrived and asked Lieutenant Colonel Cotton if the emplaning should proceed after such a tragedy. Cotton asked his three remaining company commanders the same question. Captain Dave MacDougal replied, 'We go sir, we can't stop. Morale will drop like a lead balloon, sir.' The other officers agreed and the remainder of the battalion headed for Durand airfield.[39] There was a battle to be won at Lae.

Despite what they had just been through, Bill Crooks and Johnny Beck jumped aboard a C-47 transport for Lae. However, as it roared down the runway, the port engine caught fire and the engineer told everyone to 'lie down and hold on' as the pilot tried to stop the plane before takeoff. It finally slewed to a halt against the side of a revetment with a burst tyre, and Crooks and Beck, their nerves shot to pieces, were ordered to hospital and treated for shock.[40]

The bodies of fifteen Australians and the eleven American airmen were recovered from the crash site. John Balfour-Ogilvy could 'clearly recall 14 bodies, burnt beyond recognition, heads, legs and arms completely burnt off, leaving bodies only, like charred blocks of wood'.[41] It was only the beginning: another 47 would die from their burns and 89 more were injured, many of them horrifically maimed. Of the 62 Australian dead, 60 were from the 2/33rd Battalion and two were drivers from the 158th General Transport Company.[42] Dave MacDougal summed it all up: 'so many mates gone'.[43]

•

The work of the 871st Airborne Engineers at Nadzab continued full-time under lights, at times in torrential rain and always under threat from Japanese ground and air forces. The first transport aircraft landed on the new gravel strip at 0800 on 10 September, less than 48 hours after work had begun. Three days later a parallel gravel strip was in operation with a taxiway and eighteen hard stands also completed.[44]

On 8 September the 2/25th Battalion's pioneer platoon was flown in to help the engineers working on the airfield. Later that afternoon, C Company of the 2/33rd Battalion also arrived and by midday the next day the rest of the weakened battalion had flown across from Tsili Tsili. That night a heavy rain storm flooded Nadzab airstrip and, much to General Vasey's annoyance, this delayed the arrival of the 2/31st Battalion until 12 September. Over the six days from 6 to 11 September 420 planeloads had landed at Nadzab. Of these, 333 planeloads (79 per cent) flew in from Tsili Tsili and 87 directly from Port Moresby.[45] The secret airfield at Tsili Tsili had proved vital to the success of Operation Postern.

Sergeant John Rutherford was one of the men who flew to Nadzab from Port Moresby. 'We are to be airborne to Nadzab,' he wrote. 'We back our truck to the gaping doors, transfer our load into the bowels of the waiting monster, and take our seats.' For many of the men, powered flight was a new experience. 'The motors roar furiously, our monster vibrates alarmingly,' Rutherford wrote, 'then slowly, ever so slowly, we trundle forward, gradually picking up speed until, soon, we are literally hurtling along as though bent on destruction.' Crossing the Owen Stanley Range, the men watched 'Huge jagged peaks, seemingly within reach, thrust their sinister tops menacingly through the clouds.' Once over the range, Rutherford saw 'a rough-looking burnt clearing on which descending planes were playing a game of "follow my leader" as, in a whirlwind of black dust, they jolted down the short runway.' After disembarking, Rutherford observed 'Nadzab! A centre of confusing noise and bustling activity; of shouted orders and jabbering natives; a hell of dust and heat and roaring planes.'[46]

•

Major General Ryoichi Shoge, the commander of the 41st Division infantry group, was put in command of the defence of Lae. Lieutenant General Kane Yoshihara later praised Shoge's attitude of cool courage as the ideal for a commander. Yoshihara considered him the original taciturn samurai, who would go for a day or two without opening his mouth if there was no reason to do so. Yoshihara wrote that 'silence is superior to eloquence on the battlefield' and that Shoge 'was a fighting man who did not display signs of joy or sorrow, pleasure or pain'. Shoge held the 'enemy back to the east and west, even while they were within such close range, he was a model of coolness . . . the composure of the commander made the officers and men steady down'. Yoshihara also singled out an operations staff officer, Major Masatake Mukai, for note, writing how Mukai acted as platoon and company commander as he went to the most forward positions to direct the fighting.[47]

The lack of a mobile Japanese force that could respond to the Nadzab landings was a major flaw in the Japanese defence plan. A section of artillery within range of the airfield, directed from any number of excellent lookout positions in the hills above the airfield, would also have significantly delayed operations at Nadzab. On 5 September General Berryman wrote that 'enemy is weak and fully occupied at Lae by 9 Div. However if enemy had a strong mobile force our [position] could be serious if he attacked Nadzab in strength.'[48]

Prior to the Lae operation, Rear Admiral Kunizo Mori had been ordered to replace Rear Admiral Ruitaro Fujita as the commander of the 7th Base Force at Lae. This command covered most of the naval forces present at Lae. On 9 September, at the height of the battle for Lae, Mori arrived at Lae from Rabaul on the submarine *I-174*, and Fujita returned to Rabaul on the same vessel.[49] With most of the naval forces in Lae allocated to support tasks, it would be the Japanese army units from Salamaua that would bear the brunt of the front-line fighting in defence of Lae.

•

While Vasey's 7th and Wootten's 9th Division provided the main clout for Operation Postern, there was a third division involved, that being Major General Edward Milford's 5th Division, operating south of the Markham River and engaged in the battle at Salamaua. Milford's role in Postern was twofold. The first role was to maintain the pressure on Salamaua to hold the Japanese

'The wolf at the back gate'

troops there and prevent them from moving to Lae. The second role was to directly threaten Lae by pushing along the coast from Salamaua and by driving the Japanese from their major position on the south bank of the Markham River at Markham Point (see Map 12).

Lieutenant Colonel George Smith's 24th Battalion, which had operated in the vast area between Salamaua and the Markham River for three months, was given the task of attacking Markham Point. On 11 August Smith's battalion, less one company but with a PIB company attached, was designated Wampit Force and came under the direct command of New Guinea Force. Its initial role had been to prevent any Japanese incursion into the Wau and Bulolo area and to continue building a jeep track through to the Markham River.[50]

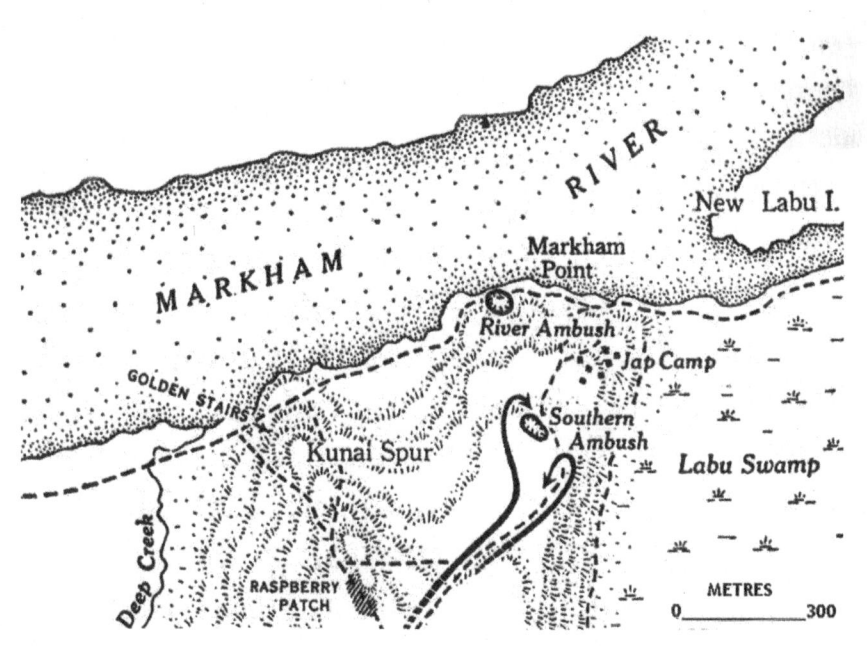

Map 12: Markham Point, 4 September 1943 (from Dexter, *The New Guinea Offensives*, p. 342, Copyright Australian War Memorial)

Smith's battalion was now ordered to make a company-sized attack on Markham Point, the dominating enemy position on the southern bank of the Markham River, which covered the best crossing point of the Markham where it split into two channels either side of Labu Island. The position was garrisoned by just over 100 soldiers from the 2nd Battalion of the 238th Regiment.[51] The attack was originally to take place on 5 September, but on 3 September Smith received orders to attack the next day, 4 September, the day of the amphibious landing. The attack would act as a diversion for both the amphibious and airborne phases of Operation Postern. As Captain Clyde Bunbury later wrote, the attack was 'a diversion from NADZAB . . . Hence there was NO intention or need to destroy the MARKHAM PT garrison'. However, Smith was hampered by a poor air-supply situation which had left essential supplies that had been dropped on 2 and 3 September scattered, and a chronic shortage of native carriers to bring those supplies forward. Smith had less than 90 carriers available to move some 2200 loads. Captain Ted Kennedy excelled by accompanying the carriers on four return trips from the supply base at Wampit to the front line in the time normally allocated for a single trip.[52]

Captain Arthur 'Reg' Duell, the C Company commander, would have four platoons available for the attack on Markham Point plus two Vickers machine guns and two 3-inch mortars in support, about 120 men in all. However, due to the need for security leading up to Operation Postern he had minimal time to study the Japanese defences and deploy his men. He was also hampered by having to wait for his battalion commander at Deep Creek, well back from the start line. Lieutenant Fred Childs' 14 Platoon would make the initial attack from the south-west

'The wolf at the back gate'

followed by Lieutenant Maurie Young's 13 Platoon, which would push down off the ridge to the river. The other two platoons would cover the company base area while the mortars would target the Japanese camp on request and the two Vickers guns would fire on Labu Island to hamper any Japanese reinforcement or retreat.[53]

The Japanese defenders had been dug in behind barbed wire for several months astride a razorback ridge abutting the fast-flowing Markham River to the north. It was a well laid out position with a small village of living quarters and training areas about 400 metres back from the front lines.[54] Having only reached the area on the afternoon of 3 September, Fred Childs had little time to plan an attack that would be based on next to no knowledge of the enemy strength and dispositions. Another problem was that Childs had only just taken over command of the platoon so he had not yet built up the rapport with his section commanders that was vital for controlling such an action.[55]

Childs' platoon moved up towards the start line late that afternoon accompanied by Young's platoon and the Vickers gun section. The men struggled with the Vickers guns on the steep slopes and dropped behind, further delaying the deployment. When dark came, the two platoons were unable to find the track which led to the start line so laid up for the night further back.[56] The lead elements would rely on surprise so there would be no preliminary mortar bombardment, but, without enough signal wire to connect a line to the forward units, there would be no mortar support on call either. 'It cannot be wondered that the troops were feeling that they too were expendable,' one of the mortar men observed.[57]

Before first light on 4 September Childs' platoon moved out. The men in the two lead sections formed an extended line below the ridge and advanced up to the enemy position. A one-metre-high barricade made of dead logs extended along the slope below the top of the ridge with five firing lanes cut into the grass facing north towards the river. The men of Corporal Harold Blundell's and Corporal Henry Gray's sections moved across the fire lanes and climbed over the chest-high barricade, fortunately into an unoccupied enemy position with empty weapon pits strung out along the ridge. However, the Japanese had laid a number of booby traps and, when one was set off, John Sullivan was killed and four other men wounded. One of the wounded, Private James Walker, pulled a shard of metal from his chest and continued. Blundell moved east down the trench and then along a track that continued up the spur. Here he encountered an unarmed Japanese soldier moving towards him along the track, probably to check what had set off the booby trap. Blundell fired three bursts from his Owen gun at four paces and then went back to find Childs. Blundell then shot another enemy soldier moving down the track before moving off the ridge. He was with three other men when heavier fire came their way, wounding Len Whitby in the leg as he crossed a barricade. Blundell then pulled his men back out of the fighting.[58]

Fred Childs had led one section past the first line of weapon pits and along the track towards the Japanese camp before heavy machine-gun fire forced the men to ground. Childs was wounded in both legs by a burst of fire and was left behind within 15 metres of the enemy lines. He could hear the Japanese defenders talking and moving about, firing regularly down the cut fire-lanes and throwing grenades. Just after dark, Childs decided to try to crawl out and after about 10 metres he met up with the four men from Gray's section. Afraid of the noise they would make in the dark, they all waited for the dawn when they were able to move back through a swampy area. However, the Japanese heard them and followed. Childs despatched one with his pistol but the other four men who were further away got involved in a fierce firefight with their pursuers. When Childs got to them only two were still alive: James Walker, who had been shot through the legs and had a broken arm, and Herbert Wilson, who was in a very bad way after enemy fire had broken his back.[59]

Childs, Walker and Wilson lay there all day and throughout the next night, with Wilson delirious, calling out for water. On the morning of 6 September, with no prospect of help, Childs and Walker began to crawl out, leaving the immobile Wilson, who asked Walker to arrange for his mother to be written to. Coming across an enemy position, Childs and Walker waited until the night to move past. It was now the night of 6–7 September and as the two men crawled through the Japanese camp they were grateful for the rain which provided much-needed water to allay their thirst. Next day they continued on past enemy weapon pits towards the Markham and on the afternoon of 8 September they met up with an Australian patrol along the bank of the Markham River. The rest of Gray's section never made it back. Henry Gray had been killed and Bill Hellens shot through the ankle. Allan Betson and Russell DeLacy helped carry Hellens out but the three men were never seen again.[60]

Captain Reg Duell then went forward with Maurie Young to see what was happening. The two officers moved up along the west side of the spur, entered the Japanese position unopposed and found two of Childs' men there. Leaving Young just outside the position to await his platoon, Duell returned to the start line and sent the rest of Young's men up; however, when the platoon arrived, Young could not be located. Although Duell said that 'his body was discovered later'—and despite that claim being repeated in the Australian Official History—Maurie Young's body was never recovered and remains missing to this day.[61]

The action had been a costly failure for the Australians, with twelve men killed or missing and another six wounded. Duell's new orders were just to contain the enemy position.[62] George Christensen, who was with the mortar section at Markham Point and later wrote the battalion history, called the operation 'The Balls Up'.[63] The fact that the remains of four Australian soldiers from this action remain missing to this day indicates that 'The Balls Up' didn't end there.[64]

Chapter 10

'A TERRIFYING BUT MAGNIFICENT SPECTACLE'

The decision to make the amphibious landing 22 kilometres east of Lae had its pros and cons. The key advantage was that it ensured the beachhead could be established out of range of enemy artillery fire but, with the advance now underway, the difficulties of the terrain had an immediate impact. The ground over which the troops had to advance was a coastal plain about 5 kilometres in depth covered by dense jungle inland with kunai patches and mangrove swamps closer to the coast. The major terrain problem came in the form of the six rivers and many minor creeks between Red Beach and Lae. All these watercourses were liable to flooding when rain fell on the adjacent Rawlinson Range, and that was pretty much every night.

Having established the two beachheads on D-Day with no significant resistance on the ground, the Australians began the advance on the following day, 5 September. After the 2/13th Battalion advanced east from Yellow Beach and reached the Buhem River, two companies crossed over and occupied the overgrown Hopoi airfield. This secured the eastern flank of the beachhead against any Japanese counterattack from Finschhafen.

After a strenuous day moving west towards Lae from Red Beach on 5 September, a patrol from the 2/23rd Battalion, now commanded by Major Eric McRae, reached the Buiem River without any enemy contact. At dusk Sergeant Don Lawrie was ordered to take out a patrol to establish a forward post at the mouth of the Bunga River, about 4 kilometres further west towards Lae. That night Corporal Alan Schram woke with a fright, a hand clamped across his mouth by one of the men from his section. The other hand was pointing to a line of enemy troops filing past almost within touching distance of the two Australians hidden in the shoreline scrub. The Japanese were moving along the beach from the direction of Lae. Schram started counting as a group of 40 men passed followed by another 87; 127 troops in all. Nearby, Don Lawrie had counted the same number, 'all big fellows, heavily armed with machine-guns and mortars'.[1]

The Japanese, a company of naval troops from the 82nd Naval Garrison, were heading east towards Singaua Plantation, cutting off Lawrie's route back to the battalion.[2] With the radio not working, some other means of alerting battalion headquarters of the enemy incursion had to be found. Stripped of arms and equipment, Dave Fairlie and Schram waded into the sea and then made their way back towards the 2/23rd lines, at times almost neck deep in the ocean. Once he thought he was past the Japanese positions, Schram moved inshore but, when a match flared at the edge of the scrub, he could make out an armed enemy soldier.

'A terrifying but magnificent spectacle'

Schram and Fairlie then slid back into deeper water but the noise alerted the Japanese sentry who moved to the shoreline and cocked his rifle. The men ducked underwater until out of breath, letting the current carry them further away from danger. Day was breaking when they finally emerged from the water at the mouth of a creek where men were washing. They had found their battalion lines but had only arrived with the warning fifteen minutes before the enemy patrol would have reached the perimeter. Schram told his company commander, Captain Joe Dudley, that the enemy company was only 200 metres away. 'Good, we'll bash em,' Dudley replied. Fairlie and Schram also met Major McRae, the new battalion commander, who went forward to where he could clearly see enemy troops digging in.[3]

At 0635 Dudley sent two platoons down the coastal track and within 100 metres they had clashed with the Japanese in dense jungle near a copra shed on Singaua Plantation. Bill Harrison was shot and killed by a waiting sniper before Lieutenant Jack Atkinson's platoon attacked. Atkinson's men were soon forced to ground while Lieutenant Stan Morey's platoon fared little better with three men including Morey wounded. Meanwhile, Captain Max Thirlwell's company had been sent through swamp and dense scrub to get in behind the Japanese position, followed by a second company tasked with hitting the Japanese flank. At 1030 Atkinson's platoon attacked again and forced the Japanese to pull back along the beach past Thirlwell's positions.[4] By early afternoon resistance was overcome with 30 enemy troops killed and the rest fleeing. The Australians had hit them before they had had time to dig in. Nonetheless the Japanese naval troops had fought hard and some committed suicide with their own grenades rather than surrender. All of the Japanese wore life vests so had apparently been landed by barge on the east side of the Busu River.[5]

Those Japanese troops that did withdraw came up against Sergeant Lawrie's platoon, still trapped further west. Lawrie's men held off six attacks between 1400 and dusk, each time warned by bugle calls and shouting. Lawrie noted that, 'the closer the attackers came in the faster they fell . . . after each futile attack the Japs walked back to their start line like bowlers in a cricket match'. Lawrie took care of at least ten enemy soldiers himself while directing the actions of his sections, at all times conscious of conserving ammunition.[6] By nightfall McRae's battalion had crossed the Bunga River having taken 30 casualties during the day's fighting.[7]

•

Following up the air attacks on D-Day, Japanese aircraft returned the next day with two attacks in the early afternoon, one on Red Beach and the other on the Aluki track, the route heading west from the beachheads to Lae. There were other air attacks on 6 September, the major one against Red Beach by seventeen bombers with a heavy fighter escort. However, only nine bombers managed to bomb the beachhead, the rest driven off with four of the escorting fighters also shot down. On the same day a Boomerang reconnaissance aircraft, flown by Flying Officer Tom Laidlaw, was shot down by a Zero east of Hopoi.[8] Laidlaw had been flying close to the ground directing artillery fire while another Boomerang, piloted by Flying Officer Syd Carter, provided top cover. Neither plane had any chance in a dogfight against so many Zeros but Carter managed to evade them by

'A terrifying but magnificent spectacle'

heading into the mountains to the north. After this incident the Boomerangs arranged to have American fighters patrolling as top cover during such missions.[9]

As always in New Guinea, the toughest fight was against the terrain. The construction of corduroy log roads through the swampy terrain from the beachhead to the front lines was slow and difficult. At times the use of a bulldozer exacerbated the problem as it would tear up the ground surface while clearing the jungle. An angled dozer was preferred as there was less backing up and slewing around, but in the end it was found to be more efficient to cut through the jungle by hand and then lay the corduroy track onto better ground. Steel mesh runner strips were then laid along the top of the corduroy road to prevent the trucks from ripping the road to pieces with their chained wheels.[10] Brigadier Victor Windeyer later said that he had 'never seen a more devoted effort than men building roads through hopeless swamps towards Lae'.[11] Merv Weston also knew how important the development of a suitable road was to the operation. 'Most of the work has been done by American and Australian engineers and by Australian pioneers who work in the fierce sun with a fury I have never seen equalled,' he wrote, 'stopping only to throw themselves into ditches or foxholes when the ack-ack [anti-aircraft fire] opens up at their elbows.'[12]

Greater problems started in the Apo–Singaua area where the jeep track was blocked by swampy ground west of Aluki village. Without firm ground, the corduroy road could not be laid so from there on it just became a foot track. However, due to the demand for men for unloading work at the beach, none were available to bring supplies up to the front line. Brigadier David Whitehead's 26th Brigade landed on 5 September and Whitehead soon realised that supply by landing craft was necessary. Later in the day he was told that landing craft would come into Apo fishing village that night if the beach was suitable. The boat engineers looked at the beach that night and, despite the offshore reefs, two LCMs arrived at dawn on 6 September.[13]

The further the Australians advanced towards Lae, the greater the need was for that amphibious supply. On the night of 6 September, another LCM was diverted to Apo and on to Singaua Plantation where it was guided ashore by 2/24th Battalion troops. The solitary Australian Army Service Corps corporal on the beach worked like a Trojan to break down the bulk loads for distribution to ensure the brigade could continue the advance on the next day. It was upon the broad shoulders of such men that this battle was to be won.[14] On the night of 5–6 September, Wootten's third brigade, Brigadier Bernard Evans' 24th, disembarked at Red Beach. The weather had been fine for the first three days of the operation but on the night of 6–7 September very heavy rain fell, turning all creeks into major obstacles and making the tracks near impassable. 'That night it rained as it has never rained before,' Harry Wells wrote.[15]

On 7 September Evans' 24th Brigade took over on the coast while Whitehead's 26th Brigade moved further inland up the Burep River. That night landing craft were requested to land at the mouth of the Burep where brigade headquarters had been established and supplies were subsequently landed on G Beach, west of the river mouth. Two jeeps and an amphibious DUKW were also landed but without a petrol reserve; by mid-morning the DUKW was idle and one of the jeeps had broken down. That day Whitehead's brigade reached the east bank of the Busu and the 2/48th Battalion, up until then used for labour at Apo, had rejoined the brigade.[16] G Beach became a key supply point, considerably shortening the supply line to the front; if a landing craft left Red Beach at 1730 then they could make three supply runs per night.[17] On the night of 8–9 September two 25-pounder guns were brought down to G Beach to provide artillery support.

The 2/48th commander, Lieutenant Colonel Robert Ainslie, noted the difficulties of moving through the jungle where it was impossible to determine the swampy ground from aerial photographs. It was only while cutting through the jungle that the swamps were discovered and the heavily laden troops then had to just plough on through—'an exhausting and slow process'.[18]

On 8 September the 26th Brigade moved across country from the Burep to the Busu River without any enemy contact. When Lieutenant Ed Shattock's platoon from the 2/24th Battalion reached the Busu, Shattock was told not to cross, although he thought he could do so. 'The Japs were not in position opposite me; we could have done it,' Shattock said. It then rained heavily during the night and the river rose.[19] Brigadier Whitehead also thought that there were no Japanese forces on the west bank of the Busu at this stage. However, the battalion had reached the Busu at its narrowest point where the locals had formerly constructed kunda-vine suspension footbridges. The river current was at its fastest at this point with the central river channel producing standing waves over a metre high, making crossing without a bridge nigh on impossible.[20]

Meanwhile the brigade was trying to build up a three-day ration reserve before crossing the Busu. Ammunition was less of an issue given the light fighting up to that time but there was a shortage of 3-inch mortar rounds and, until regular artillery support was available, this was a concern. On 8 September five landing craft brought in supplies plus four more jeeps and two 2.5 ton vehicles to G Beach. A bulldozer was also landed but it had given up the ghost a few hours later. The following day the entire brigade was used to carry supplies forward and to widen the track between the Burep and Busu into a jeep track.[21]

As the principal outlet for the tropical rains that fall across the mountain range to the north and then funnel down towards Lae, the Busu River always runs fast and strong. Swollen into a raging river by heavy rains and with enemy defenders behind it, it was the most daunting of obstacles. After seeing that the river was running at full spate at over 20 kilometres per hour, Whitehead informed General Wootten that bridging equipment would be required to get across. When Wootten replied that the movement of artillery had priority, Whitehead argued that artillery fire would be ineffective against the heavily wooded western bank and that his mortars could handle the suppression job. He urgently needed a box-girder bridge brought forward before enemy opposition built up and severely hampered any bridging work.[22]

•

On the coastal flank Brigadier Bernard Evans' 24th Brigade also reached the Busu River. Evans later wrote that 'The advance was gruelling . . . we had unloaded our own gear, pressed on with the march, overtaken the leading troops of the day before and continued the advance in contact with the enemy—cutting our way through mangroves.' He noted that 'The advance to the Busu was very fast but could have been faster with two LCVPs.'[23]

The West Australians of Lieutenant Colonel Colin Norman's 2/28th Battalion led the way along the coast. 'The worst factor

'A terrifying but magnificent spectacle'

was the stifling heat in the kunai patches plus boots full of water,' Allan Henderson said of the advance. 'It always rained at night and you virtually slept in water.'[24] When Norman asked Major Keith Mollard, who was second-in-command of the 2/32nd Battalion and who had spent two years in Lae before the war, 'Where do we cross the river?', Mollard told him that the natives always crossed at the mouth or else at the narrower point further inland. However, Mollard thought Norman 'wasn't in the race to cross higher up'.[25]

'We were told to push as fast as possible through fairly thick jungle and keeping in earshot of the ocean close on our left,' Allan Henderson noted of his company as the men approached the Busu. 'We proceeded cautiously towards that ominous roar.'[26] The 2/28th Battalion reached the east bank of the Busu River on the afternoon of 8 September and at dawn the next morning a patrol under Lieutenant Peter Rooke tried to get across 250 metres upstream of the mouth. However, they only made it across the minor channel to the island in the middle of the river. A few hours later a platoon tried the local route directly across the mouth to see if it would be suitable for getting the mortars and Vickers guns across. Captain Leo Lyon watched as the two leading scouts moved across the sandbar about 50 metres apart with their rifles at high port. The lead scout was about 80 metres from the far bank when the Japanese opened fire from near the mouth of the river on the west bank. Both men fell and were quickly washed out to sea but one was only wounded and 'fought his way back through the current to our side of the river'. The platoon withdrew under covering mortar fire. Lyon 'reported the incident to CO by phone who decided it was too dangerous to cross at the mouth'. Nonetheless, soon after midday Norman received orders to somehow cross the Busu and establish a bridgehead.[27]

Ed Benness led a patrol upstream to look for another way across. His men made a number of attempts but it was hopeless, so 'as a last resort I persuaded the signaller who had accompanied the patrol to allow his cable to be tied around my waist', Benness related. However, he soon lost his footing and was swept downstream before he was dragged back to shore by the cable. Norman now considered that the best place to cross was directly across from the island where there was a slight bend in the river with the current drifting towards the west bank.[28]

With the island and the raised opposite bank offering some cover, Norman decided to send the battalion across the main channel from the island in four lines just before dusk. It was anticipated that this time of day was Japanese 'rice time' and surprise was possible. The men would carry minimum equipment but maximum ammunition. Having waded across several narrow channels to the island during the afternoon, Lieutenant James 'Pat' Hannah's company was the first to step out into the raging torrent of the main channel, which was about 50 metres wide. Some men 'couldn't swim and must have had grave reservations as to their long term future,' Benness observed. It would be like going into battle without a weapon. Following 22 rounds of artillery fire on suspected Japanese positions at the river mouth, Hannah gave the order and the company entered the water in extended line led by Hannah, who was also the first to emerge onto the far bank. Many of the men lost their weapons as they were swept off their feet but most of the men were washed up on the far bank. The bank was over a metre high and provided shelter from enemy fire although most of that fire was being directed towards the river mouth. However, an enemy machine gun soon found its range. 'One of my men, a young lad and recent reinforcement raised his head above the kunai and was killed instantly,' Ed Benness noted. Corporal Neville May went forward alone and found the machine-gun position about 100 metres inland from the coast. Using grenades and his Owen gun he wiped out the post.[29]

Leo Lyon's company followed with similar results although helped ashore by human chains formed on the far bank by Hannah's men. The rest of the battalion followed, 'as though on parade until the current hit them'. The companies went across in line, the men not hesitating as they entered the swirling waters and were swept onto the far bank, generally still in formation. There was now intermittent enemy fire from the far bank and the Bren gunner next to Colonel Norman was hit and went under. He was one of 30 men that were swept away during the crossing. Of these, thirteen had drowned, the remainder able to scramble out at the bar about 50 metres out to sea beyond the river mouth where the water was only one metre deep.[30] As William Loh later wrote of the river crossing, 'It was a terrifying but magnificent spectacle.'[31]

Keith Mollard watched the men crossing. 'If it was included in a Hollywood film it would have been panned by the critics as a highly improbable possibility,' he later wrote, 'it looked for all the world as though a giant hand was snatching them across to the far bank . . . this was the most dramatic event I saw during the entire war'. Mollard and two other men were trying to get across at the river mouth, having waited until five minutes after Norman's men began their crossing. They figured that the Japanese defenders would have their attention diverted by the main crossing and that they wouldn't be seen in the low light at dusk. 'We couldn't have been more wrong,' Mollard later wrote. 'I am reasonably sure that not one shot was fired at the battalion and the three of us copped a veritable hail of lead . . . the three of us fell flat on our faces in one of the shallow water channels and paddled away from the shootin'.' Given his earlier advice to Norman to cross at the mouth, Mollard later reflected, 'I still go hot and cold when I think what would have happened if Colonel Norman had taken notice of me.'[32]

The Japanese noted how they had stopped the morning attempt to cross at the mouth and thought they had killed 20 to 30 men in doing so. They also thought that the attempt by 200 to 300 men later in the day had also been stymied despite there being 'insufficient men to protect the upper stream of the Busu River'.[33] As General Herring observed on 12 September, 'The Jap missed a great opportunity of cracking the 28 Bn when isolated across the river in a small perimeter.'[34]

Norman's men had lost about 25 per cent of their weapons during the crossing and the signals gear was not working. Despite slight wounds, John Crouchley swam back across the river that night to tell Brigadier Evans what had happened and supplies were organised despite the river continuing to rise. John Threnoworth and Bill Swift also swam back across with a signals line and communications was established later that night. Organising the defence of the newly won bridgehead was difficult, with companies mixed up in the five-metre-high kunai grass along the river bank, but fortunately there were a few sandy patches that were covered with low scrub instead of the kunai and they were slightly higher than the swamp. As Norman later wrote, 'we had a perimeter and were in a position to fight'. Despite the cold and rain, the men waited out the night. During that night Alec Wilson, who had been swept out

'A terrifying but magnificent spectacle'

to sea during the crossing, managed to get ashore behind enemy lines and reach the bridgehead.[35]

Around midday on the day after the crossing, the bridgehead came under attack from machine-gun and mortar fire. 'Right out of the blue hand grenades were exploding all amongst us immediately incurring casualties,' Allan Henderson recalled. The Japanese had obviously got up very close but could not be seen in the kunai grass. The platoon sergeant, Alex 'Sandy' MacGregor, slid over the bank and down onto the beach for a better view. He saw that about six enemy defenders were holed up in a drain-like depression in front of the Australian lines. It was probably where the nearby swamp drained out to the sea. Sandy was able to point out the enemy party to his platoon but because of his exposed position on the beach he was killed by machine-gun fire while directing the platoon's weapons.[36]

Lieutenant John Brooks was a quiet, unobtrusive man who had never so much as raised his voice to his men during training. He was considered the perfect gentleman. However, following the loss of the courageous MacGregor, Brooks was 'fighting mad'. 'Right chaps, fix bayonets, follow me,' he told his men as he led the way forward. The men crossed about 150 metres of open ground before enemy fire broke out from a large kunai patch immediately ahead. 'All hell broke loose,' was how Allan Henderson described it. 'John Brooks was everywhere, exhorting us to keep up the momentum, completely oblivious to personal danger.' The three platoons of C Company were involved in the attack, moving forward a section at a time searching out the Japanese positions on small sandy islands scattered about the waist deep swamp. As Allan Henderson struggled out of the swampy ground, 'suddenly my luck ran out,' he recalled.

An enemy rifleman hiding in thick kunai grass to his left waited until Henderson had passed by before shooting him, 'bringing to an untimely end my aspirations and my military career,' as Henderson saw it.³⁷ Nonetheless, the attack succeeded and 63 Japanese soldiers lay dead in its wake.

Further inland, B Company also moved forward through freshly prepared defensive positions that fortunately had been abandoned. The men then turned towards the coast, moving through two-metre-high kunai grass to the beach before turning west for Lae. Again, as Ed Benness observed, 'there was plenty of evidence of Japanese occupation with slit trenches, machine-gun posts and bush shelters but fortunately all were unoccupied'.³⁸

Meanwhile Brigadier Evans stripped his 2/43rd Battalion of weapons and ferried those weapons across to the 2/28th to replace the ones they had lost in the crossing. 'This battalion was spent after so much effort but I had to keep them going,' he later wrote of the 2/28th. Evans also tried to get one or two LCVPs allocated to help land supplies and troops on the west bank of the Busu mouth to support Norman. The request was refused, although one boat did turn up.³⁹ Lieutenant Henderson McPherson's boat crew had volunteered to ferry the remaining troops around the river mouth and for 48 hours their landing craft took fresh troops across the Busu and brought back the wounded under Japanese fire. The landing craft's rudder was shot away but the crew improvised another while McPherson sat exposed in the stern, steering the boat. The LCVP made 40 trips, taking some 1200 troops and considerable supplies across to the west bank of the Busu.⁴⁰

•

'A terrifying but magnificent spectacle'

Both the 24th and 26th Brigade had been ordered to cross the Busu and establish bridgeheads in depth with fighting patrols to gain and hold contact with the enemy. Whitehead's 26th Brigade had been held up at the Busu for 36 hours waiting for rubber boats and suitable rope to get the men across. An attempt to span the river with fallen trees failed when the river rose and all attempts with the rubber boats ended in them being swamped. 'Rubber assault useless,' the brigade report noted.[41] On the night of 9 September bridging supplies were landed at G Beach but the urgently needed material remained on the beach until it was discovered the next morning.[42]

The 2/24th Battalion worked with the engineers to get across the Busu at a place where the river separated into three channels of 20, 30 and 14 metres wide and ran at about 25 kilometres per hour with a depth over 2 metres. After the heavy rain of the previous night, it was apparent on the morning of 10 September that 'a crossing was impossible with the materials available'. Nonetheless, at midday Warrant Officer Bill McCallum and two engineers swam the river with signal wire and managed to then drag a rope across and secure it to the far bank. Despite enemy fire, boats were then hooked to the rope but they were soon swamped and this method had to be abandoned.[43]

On the next day, 11 September, the men began to build a bridge using felled logs supported on stone pylons to bridge the first 20-metre stream. That night the river again rose and the logs had little chance against the raging torrent. The 'current was so strong that logs, anchored at both ends by pylons of rocks, would break in the middle,' Lieutenant Colonel Andrew Gillespie later said. The next day, with the river dropping, the men again tried to bridge the river with logs. The first bridge was replaced but all attempts to get a log across the second stream failed and the attempt was once more abandoned.[44]

On the morning of 13 September a span of box-girder bridging arrived to bridge the 30-metre-wide second stream. Although the crossing point was still under enemy fire, the box-girder bridge was launched soon after midday, but, when almost across the gap, it overbalanced and was swept away downstream. Later that afternoon more box-girder sections arrived and another attempt was made. A 25-metre single box-girder bridge was assembled using three box and two hornbeam sections. A box section from an auxiliary loading ramp was then fastened to the near shore end of the bridge to provide an additional counterweight. One hundred men then picked up the bridge and carried it through water over a metre deep across the first 20-metre channel to a mid-river island from where it was launched across the main 30-metre channel. However, it did not reach the far bank and the launching nose provided the last six-metre length. It was a unique operation, launching the box-girder bridge with no bridgehead on the far bank with only a mortar barrage to keep the enemy at bay. Once the bridge was secured on the second island a third section was put in place early on 14 September. The first infantry company from the 2/24th Battalion crossed the Busu at 0630 that morning and headed north, mopping up one enemy strongpoint by 0830, leaving 30 defenders dead and capturing a 20 mm anti-aircraft gun.[45] 'Two platoons across before the Japs woke up,' Brigadier Whitehead later said.[46] By early next morning the rest of Whitehead's 26th Brigade had also crossed.

Closer to the coast, Brigadier Evans' 24th Brigade finally moved out of its bridgehead on 14 September and reached Malahang anchorage and airstrip. It was expected that the

'A terrifying but magnificent spectacle'

Malahang area would be strongly held, so the plan was to bypass the area and push on to the Butibum River to cut off any enemy defence positions. However, on reaching the outskirts of Lae, only Japanese stragglers were encountered and on the afternoon of 16 September a signal came through indicating that troops from 7th Division were already in Lae. 'Have occupied Lae prevent your troops engaging my troops,' the message read.[47]

•

While the infantry brigades advanced on Lae, a major part of General Wootten's plan to capture the town, the artillery component, was struggling to get forward. Wootten's experience at Buna as the commander of 18th Brigade had undoubtedly influenced his planning for the Lae operation. At Buna his men had paid a heavy price attacking strong interlocking defence positions with very limited artillery support. Here at Lae he had wanted to ensure that he had the artillery that he had so lacked at Buna.

Although General George Kenney considered that aircraft could do the job of the artillery in New Guinea, General Wootten knew that it was not that simple and that artillery had considerable advantages over air support. The aircraft were based at Port Moresby or Dobodura and there would be a significant delay in reaching the target and it would be difficult to cancel or adjust air strikes. Any friendly forces would have to retire a safe distance back from the bomb line beforehand. Artillery missions were easier to control with the forward observation officers in the front line. Wootten also stressed his experience with artillery at Milne Bay, Buna and Sanananda where what artillery he had had been very effective. Wootten had a lot more artillery available at Lae and, as he later noted, 'At this stage as far as was known the Japanese were defending Lae and intended to continue to defend it.'[48]

One battery from the 2/12th Field Regiment was landed in the first wave at Red Beach on 4 September with the remainder following in later waves. The regiment deployed sixteen standard and eight light 25-pounder guns. Subsequently a further twenty standard 25-pounder guns from the 14th Field Regiment plus another battery of eight light 25-pounder guns and a medium battery of two French 155 mm cannon from 2/6th Field Regiment were also landed. Twenty-four 40 mm Bofors guns from the 2/3rd and 2/4th Light Anti Aircraft Regiments provided anti-aircraft support. Because the light 25-pounder guns had a shorter range, they had to be moved more often, but this proved difficult. The wheels were smaller than on the normal gun and were too small for the rigours of jungle tracks and the guns had to be loaded onto the back of trucks or onto landing craft to relocate. The Bofors guns were even harder to shift.[49] By 11 September, fourteen 25-pounders, eight light and six standard, had been brought forward to provide close fire support and were in operation east of the Burep River. With Australian troops now across the Busu, the impact of these first artillery rounds was profound. Following this shelling, the Japanese command considered that 'Lae's doom was imminent.'[50]

The two First World War–era French 155 mm guns were the toughest to move. Wheel chains and considerable manhandling was required just to get the guns from Red Beach to positions about one and a half kilometres inland. On the night of 12–13 September the two guns were moved down to G Beach by LCT but unfortunately one of the LCTs returned to Buna without unloading its ammunition. The gun personnel had had limited

'A terrifying but magnificent spectacle'

training with these guns and did not get them into action until the afternoon of 14 September.[51]

For the final attack on Lae, General Wootten had 52 field guns and two medium guns available and each was allocated 1000 rounds. The 2/12th Field Regiment was firing from positions along the Burep River while the guns of the 14th Field Regiment only reached the Busu River late that afternoon. The convoy consisted of twenty tractors and guns, eight heavy trucks and half a dozen other vehicles which had to cover 25 kilometres of track including 4 kilometres of corduroy road. The 2/3rd Field Company sappers had worked tirelessly to get the road finished. On 16 September 22 guns were in range of Lae town and eighteen of these began firing, but were soon told to stop as they were firing on troops from the 7th Division.[52]

•

With the deployment of so much artillery alongside three infantry brigades and other support services, there was enormous pressure on the supply services and a major conflict between the US Navy and Australian Army requirements played itself out on the landing beaches. While General Wootten required the landing of a considerable supply reserve to guard against the supply line being broken, the US Navy considered the best way to guarantee the supply line and particularly the supply vessels was to limit the time the landing craft remained on the beach. The US Navy also wanted to gain the maximum cover of darkness while at sea moving to and from Lae. Once landed, the army had its own problems moving the supplies forward from the beaches as all carrying was being done by the troops.[53]

Every man had carried two operational and three emergency rations when they had landed. One of each type was dumped at the beachhead to create a reserve so each man initially had rations for three days.[54] However, after those three days most of the men ended up on short rations. On 11 September Captain John Davies, the Regimental Medical Officer from the 2/23rd Battalion, reported, 'Over the past five days quantity of rations has been quite inadequate, considering the strenuous physical exertion involved... men are constantly complaining of weakness and inability to stand up to the work. Unless the quantity of food is increased the men will not be able to carry on under the existing conditions.' On the next day Davies was killed when an enemy shell hit a nearby tree.[55]

Brigadier Whitehead had questioned the adequacy of the ration scale for his brigade during operational planning at Milne Bay and the other two brigades had raised similar objections. At that time Whitehead had been told that the reduced scale was to be used for the first seven days and normalised thereafter but this never happened and the troops were on low rations for 24 days.[56] The 2/23rd Battalion commander later noted that 'Physical conditions have been extremely hard, and were by no means improved by the shortage in quantity and lack of nutritive value of rations available during the campaign.'[57] One of the 9th Division signallers, Lieutenant Ken Lovell later drew a cartoon captioned 'Tokio radio reported—40,000 Australians are lost and starving near Lae. Lies—there were 30,000 and we were not lost.' Under another cartoon he captioned 'Never before have so many been fed by so little!'[58]

Without a balanced 'one man' or even section ration pack, the breaking down of bulk supplies into individual amounts also became a huge issue, delaying the time units could move off in the mornings. The front-line troops were also feeling the lack of tea, coffee and sugar, staple fare for hard working infantrymen. The rain and damp also affected clothing and such supplies as salt, Atebrin anti-malaria tablets and water sterilising tablets. As no replacements came up in resupply, these problems only got worse.[59]

Whitehead was later told that the ration scale was based on what the 7th Division had used during the earlier campaign in Papua. Vasey's division had actually increased the ration scale for Operation Postern despite the fact that the division would be supplied by air transport where weight was such a critical factor.[60] It was only when an American base moved into Lae that food could be bartered for. This was because the Light Aid Detachment from Whitehead's brigade managed to get three of the freezing chambers from the Burns Philp plant back into operation. This cold storage space was then offered to the Americans in exchange for an adequate supply of eggs and butter which could be issued to the Australian troops.[61]

Operations had also been hampered by communication difficulties with the radio link between General Wootten's headquarters onshore and the US Navy offshore inoperable. Any communication had to go via I Australian Corps headquarters at Dobodura and then via the command ship *Conyngham* if it was at Buna or else via naval command in Port Moresby. An army radio set on *Conyngham* would have been useful but its radio channels and coding facilities were already overloaded, as was its limited accommodation. The radio link between the 532nd EBSR shore battalion and its bases at Morobe and Oro Bay also didn't work.[62] Due to the tropical conditions there were difficulties with both the 108 radio sets and the walkie-talkies used by the army and the sets had to be systematically and continuously maintained to stay operable. Communications were also affected by the supply shortcomings. Of 50 kilometres of signal cable that was available to the 9th Division, only 26 kilometres was D3 type on drums suitable for infantry carriage, the rest being D8 cable on heavy wooden drums.[63]

Nonetheless, despite the difficulties of terrain, rainfall, supply shortages, communications failings and a fanatical enemy, General Wootten's 9th Division had managed to reach Lae within two weeks of the D-Day landing.

Chapter 11

'FIX BAYONETS'

The first units of Lieutenant Colonel Richard 'Drover' Marson's 2/25th Battalion left Jackson's Strip at 0900 on 6 September and flew into Tsili Tsili. The troops remained there throughout that day and most of the next before A Company was flown into Nadzab at 1700 on 7 September, with the balance of the battalion arriving the next morning.[1] The commander of 25th Brigade, Brigadier Ken Eather, also landed at Nadzab that afternoon with orders from General Vasey to advance on Lae as soon as possible. The 2/25th began the move down the road towards Lae that day and reached Yalu the next (see Map 13). Marson later noted how 60 to 70 per cent of the men in his infantry companies were reinforcements taking part in their first battle so the leadership of the experienced men was crucial. The first contact with an enemy patrol came on the afternoon of 10 September at Jensen's Plantation, about two-thirds of the way from Nadzab

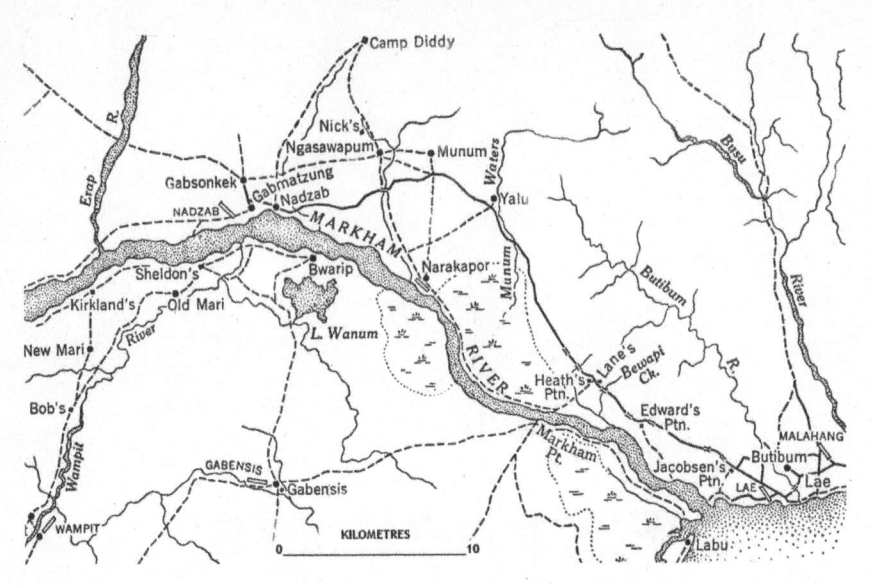

Map 13: The road to Lae, September 1943 (from McCarthy, *South-West Pacific Area—First Year*, p. 87, Copyright Australian War Memorial)

to Lae. Australian moves on either flank forced the Japanese patrol's withdrawal under cover of darkness.[2]

The Australians had taken five days following the capture of Nadzab to contact Japanese positions west of Lae and this delay staggered the Japanese commanders. 'The movement of the units which had dropped on Nadzab were very sluggish; if they had attacked with their vast strength, it would have been the hour of death of Lae in a matter of a few hours,' Lieutenant General Kane Yoshihara later wrote. Considering it 'a piece of good luck in the midst of misfortune', the Japanese command, although 'unable to understand the reason', was given time to bring troops across from Salamaua to defend the western approaches to Lae.[3] On 8 September, 200 men from the 15th Independent Engineer Regiment were sent to block the advance from Nadzab along a line from Markham Point to Yalu. The following day a

'Fix bayonets'

machine-gun company was sent to Munum and Ngasawapum to keep the route open to Boana.[4]

Meanwhile the two companies of Australian pioneers that had been working at Nadzab had been relieved and moved to Narakapor to patrol the tracks north of the Markham River. While the two light 25-pounder guns remained at Nadzab, further artillery support in the form of eight standard 25-pounder guns from the 2/4th Field Regiment had arrived at Nadzab by 11 September to support the advance on Lae. Four of these guns were brought down the road to a cleared point 3 kilometres west of Heath's Plantation. 'It was a heart-breaker of a trip trying to move the guns,' the unit history noted. Overnight rain on 9–10 September made the track very sticky, and, with numerous streams to cross, the engineers of the 2/5th Field Company were kept very busy opening up a route for the jeeps and guns. Two jeeps and considerable manhandling were needed to move each gun along the track as wooden culverts gave way and the corduroy log track was ploughed under by the weight of the guns. The two pioneer platoons from the 2/25th and 2/33rd Battalions were attached to the engineers to help in the work. When the guns finally arrived, the forward observation officer Lieutenant Bill Stokes quickly had them firing.[5]

Back at Nadzab the condition of the landing strip had deteriorated. The ground had begun to break up, particularly in the aircraft touchdown area, because the grass had been burned off rather than mowed in the rush to get the airfield operational. This also caused considerable wear on the transport aircraft and would no doubt lead to a major accident if nothing was done about it. Allied to the bad weather, the need to repair the landing strip meant that the number of flights into Nadzab on 10 and

11 September was halved, delaying the arrival of the 2/31st Battalion until 12 September.[6]

On 11 September the 2/25th Battalion, with artillery support from the 25-pounders back at Yalu, attacked an estimated 200 enemy troops at Jensen's, the Australians killing around 30 of them as they advanced through the plantation. Meanwhile the 2/33rd Battalion sent out three long-range patrols from Yalu into the Atzera Range to the north to ensure that there was no danger from that flank to the advance.[7] The next morning a company from the 2/25th Battalion made contact with Japanese forces at Jenyn's Plantation and cleared the position. Another company encountered heavy opposition including three enemy light machine guns further down the road at the bridge at Whittaker's Plantation (see Map 14). After Brigadier Eather ordered the 2/25th to continue to push forward, the two remaining companies were sent north in a wide flanking move to get in behind the enemy positions. Colonel Marson went in with them but the difficult terrain made any progress slow. A Japanese flank position was contacted in the afternoon; however, the two companies did not link up with the company at Whittaker's bridge and the Japanese still held the crossing at nightfall.[8]

•

Seeking to delay the Australian advance, Japanese defence positions were strung out back along the road behind Whittaker's bridge, with strong positions at Heath's, Edwards', Jacobsen's and a strongpoint north of Lae airfield.[9] On 13 September Lieutenant Colonel Ewan Murray Robson's newly arrived 2/31st Battalion took over from the American paratroopers at

'Fix bayonets'

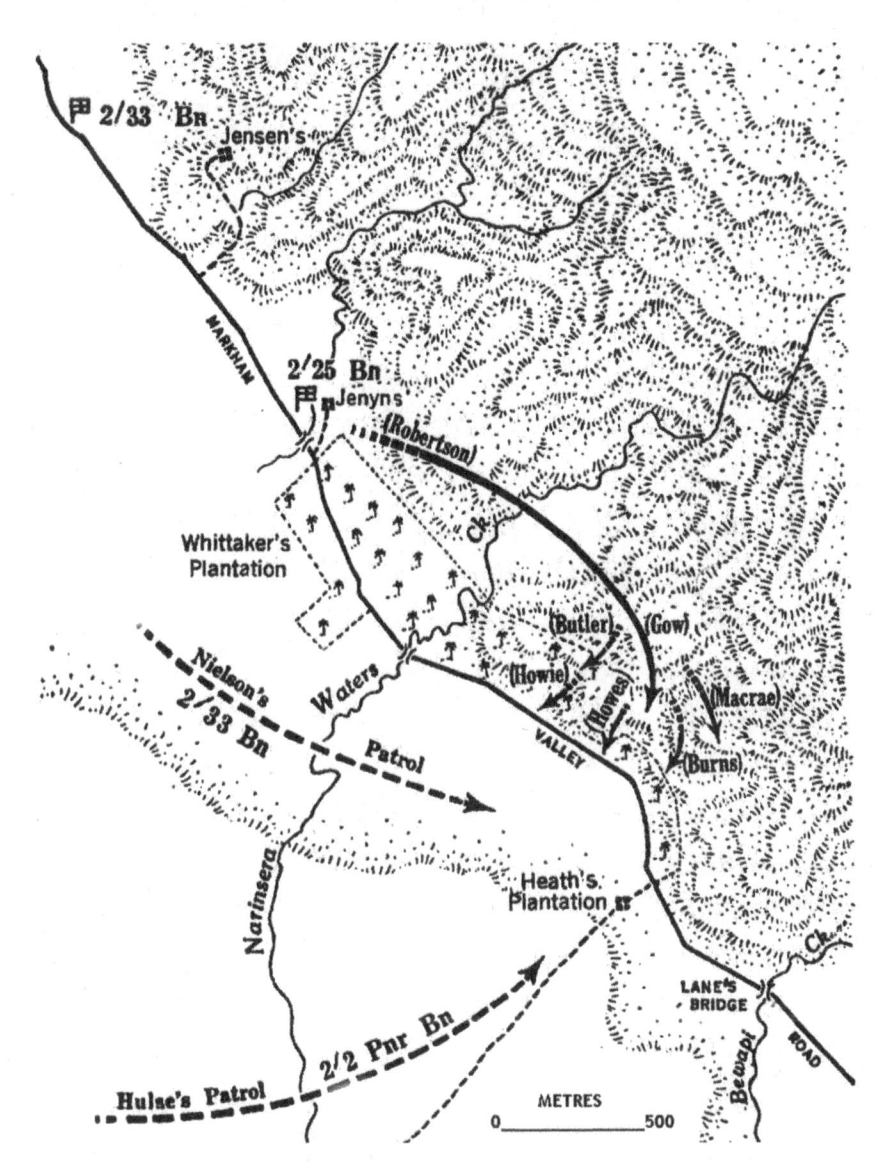

Map 14: Whittaker's Plantation, 13 September 1943 (from Dexter, *The New Guinea Offensives*, p. 375, Copyright Australian War Memorial)

Nadzab while Lieutenant Colonel Tom Cotton's 2/33rd Battalion moved up behind the 2/25th. The Japanese still held the bridge at Whittaker's but, after the Australians pulled back 50 metres, forward observers brought down artillery and 3-inch mortar fire onto the enemy positions. Two of the forward Australian troops were wounded by the close fire support but it had a greater effect on the enemy defenders and the bridge was captured.[10]

As part of the attack, the 2/25th also advanced around the left flank while the 2/33rd moved around the right side of the road with a patrol from the 2/2nd Pioneers moving up from the southwest. All three units would converge on Heath's Plantation, where the enemy was believed to be holding a strong blocking position. Marson told Captain Gilbert Gow to head towards Heath's on a compass bearing and engage any enemy defenders on the way. Using walkie-talkies to stay in touch in the close country, Gow's men moved forward through thick scrub across numerous boggy streams. Marson was anxious about his platoons losing contact so the advance was slow.[11]

Captain Jimmy Howes commanded 12 Platoon out on the left flank among the foothills of the Atzera Range where the going was at its toughest. Looking for easier ground, Howes directed his men down a gully into a cocoa plantation north of the Lae road. Expecting such a move, the Japanese opened fire along the cleared corridors between the cocoa trees and Howes' two forward sections were pinned down. With thorny acacia growth along the tree lines, the troops could not move out of the open corridors, which were about 4 metres wide. Howes sent his third section in but the men came under fire from another position, forcing them to ground. Meanwhile Lieutenant Geoff Burns moved his 11 Platoon in behind Howes and down the hills towards Howes' left flank.[12]

Corporal Stuart Sawers' section from Burns' platoon linked up with the left side of Howes' platoon with Corporal Billy Richards' section spread out in an extended line on their left. Corporal Jack

'Fix bayonets'

Duckham's section was even further out on Richards' left flank. The idea was to find just where the enemy right flank was north of the road but the Japanese were also well spread-out and all three 11 Platoon sections came under heavy fire. Captain Gow now sent in his last platoon, Lieutenant Don Macrae's 10 Platoon. Macrae's men moved up onto a ridge even further to the left of Burns' platoon, still trying to outflank the enemy positions. The 'experienced and fearless' platoon sergeant, Bernie Hill, cleared one of the light machine-gun posts along the ridge before finally getting around the flank into the Japanese rear, capturing a headquarters position. The men found a large wireless there and cut the phone lines to the forward defenders.[13]

Closer to the road, Burns' platoon continued to take heavy fire and Stuart Sawers was killed at the head of his section. The Australians were up against strongly entrenched positions held by Japanese marines along a ridge overlooking the Australian advance. The Australian section leaders were trained to lead from the front and, in doing so, Billy Richards was badly hit, shot through his shoulder, back and stomach. Despite that, he was still trying to direct his section's fire onto the enemy machine gun that had stitched him up but his position, lying wounded out on the forward slope of a rise in front of his men, made him extremely vulnerable.[14]

Two of Richards' men, Richard Kelliher and Johnson Bickle, had found some shelter in a small dip further back with a tree stump for cover. Both knew Richards was in an untenable position and it was Kelliher who decided to do something. 'I'd better go and bring him in,' he told Bickle. 'You'll get shot to pieces,' Bickle replied.[15] Nonetheless, the dour 38-year-old Irishman rose from behind the tree stump and rushed towards the enemy machine-gun post which was on a narrow spur. Four short hardwood logs protected the front of the post and it had a galvanised iron roof covered with earth, the material having been taken from buildings at nearby Whittaker's Plantation.[16] Kelliher flung two grenades into the position, killing some of the occupants but not all. He then dashed back to his section and grabbed a Bren gun from the wounded gunner, Tom Ramsden, before returning to the fray. Kelliher emptied one Bren magazine into the position then returned for another. This time he lay down and directed accurate fire onto the machine-gun post to finally silence it. Eight Japanese marines and their officer lay dead around the machine gun, half of them accounted for by the courageous Irishman. Kelliher now went out under covering fire and brought the wounded Richards back, despite coming under fire from another position. After bringing Richards in, Kelliher then helped recover two other men, both of whom had been wounded trying to get to Richards.[17]

Richard Kelliher was awarded the Victoria Cross, his country's highest military honour. 'I didn't think of doing it to get a medal,' he would later comment, 'my primary purpose was to bring my cobber Billy back, and that was the only way to do it.'[18] For Kelliher it was also a case of redemption as nine months earlier at Gona he had refused an order from his company commander to advance. To Kelliher, under heavy fire at the time and unable to see ahead through the thick kunai grass, 'It was madness to go forward.' For that decision at Gona he was court martialled but the finding was quashed three months later and he had returned to the battalion in time for the Lae campaign.[19] Three years after the Victoria Cross award was announced, the native Irishman was personally presented with his medal by King George VI, as

'Fix bayonets'

was his right. For his own staunch bravery, Billy Richards was awarded the Military Medal.

Captain William Butler's company was on the right flank of Gow's. Butler had been decorated for his leadership on the Kokoda Track and he had prepared his men well for fighting in such difficult terrain. Back in Port Moresby his men had trained with the grenade discharger cup, which was attached to the end of a rifle and fired grenades using a blank cartridge. A rough range-table was worked out for the 5-second and 7-second fused grenades to try to detonate the grenades some 2 to 5 metres above the ground and send deadly shards down onto sheltering defenders. Butler's two forward platoons were now also held up by the Japanese defences, forcing his men to take shelter in ditches at the cocoa plantation. Grenades were fired against the enemy defenders who were also sheltering in deep drains, and, when the position was later taken, one of the defenders was found with his head almost blown off by an explosion above ground. 'Maybe he was just unlucky,' Butler observed.[20]

By the end of the day the 2/25th Battalion was astride the road at Whittaker's bridge with two companies overlooking Heath's Plantation from the north. Lieutenant John Anderson took a party of men forward that night using lanterns to guide the way for the wounded men from the two forward companies to be evacuated, at times moving through Japanese controlled terrain. Great sacrifices were made to recover the wounded, with two stretcher bearers, James Riccalton and James Palmer, killed during the day's fighting.[21]

Despite heavy rain, there were two counterattacks on the 2/25th positions north of Heath's that night, but both were repulsed. Corporal Mokato Yamamura, who was wounded during the attack, was captured by the Australians the next morning. Yamamura served with the machine-gun company from the 2nd Battalion of the 66th Regiment and had only come across to Lae from Salamaua on the night of 11–12 September. His battalion, now down to only 130 men after four months of fierce fighting among the ridges around Salamaua, had been immediately ordered to break through the Australian lines west of Lae and advance towards Madang. Once the battalion reached Heath's, they were joined by 150 SNLP marines and a detachment of engineers. Although Yamamura said that his unit was left by the marines and engineers to take the brunt of the fighting, he also noted that casualties among both were heavy and included the 5th Sasebo SNLP commander, Commander Shizuka Takeuchi, who was killed in an air attack on 12 September. Yamamura, who had been serving with his regiment since August 1941, told his captors that he was 'tired of war'.[22]

On the next morning of 14 September, the two other 2/25th Battalion companies moved up and crossed Whittaker's bridge to attack Heath's Plantation. However, they found that the Japanese had gone, abandoning considerable ordnance including 20 mm anti-aircraft guns, 37 mm anti-tank guns, 85 mm mortars and Juki machine guns. 'There were piles of ammunition beside them, but they had not fired a shot against us,' Merv Weston wrote. A bombing raid on 5 September had demolished the plantation house. 'It was not directly hit, but it is flattened and its timber mangled to a fantastic degree. Three 1000 lb bombs—judging by the size of the craters—fell within 15 yards,' Weston noted.[23]

Lieutenant Henry Weitemeyer probed down the road towards Lae to see where the next enemy position was, following a scout towards Lane's bridge. As both men closed in on the bridge, the

'Fix bayonets'

scout dropped to one knee and indicated a group of Japanese ahead, apparently playing marbles on the bare earth of the road at the bridge crossing. The scout and Weitemeyer opened fire, inflicting casualties but attracting a response from Japanese positions in the jungle on the far side of the road clearing. Weitemeyer, the former drum major of the battalion pipe band, was killed. He was the second platoon commander from Major Campbell Robertson's company to die during the advance on Lae. Lieutenant John Shaw had been killed two days previously, though his body was never recovered and remains missing to this day.[24]

•

Brigadier Eather moved his headquarters up to Heath's to keep his brigade on the move to Lae and the 2/33rd Battalion was brought forward to attack Lane's bridge. As Dick Fletcher said, 'Now it was a race to see who could get in and take Lae first.'[25] Major Dave MacDougal's company attacked out of the tree line west of the bridge. Following the loss of so many front-line infantrymen during the plane crash at Jackson's airfield, many of the rear-area men in the 2/33rd had been transferred to the weakened front-line platoons. One of these men, normally a bandsman and now serving as a rifleman, lined up for the attack with the rest of the men, but unlike them he held what was an empty rifle reversed with the butt pointed forward. As the men from his company were about to break out of the timber, Dave MacDougal looked across to his right, saw the situation and sent the man to the rear where he was correctly re-assigned as a stretcher bearer, a task he performed admirably. 'He was a conscientious objector and was prepared to die for his conviction,' MacDougal later said.[26]

Captain Harry Cullen's company had the toughest job, with both the brigade and divisional commanders up at his forward headquarters telling him to get a move on. His battalion commander then sent him off to the higher ground on the left flank. 'Fix bayonets... let's all get at it,' Cullen ordered and, with some of his men firing from the hip, he led a charge at the enemy positions some 200 metres ahead. It was too much for the defenders. 'The Japanese, yelling and screaming, bolted', leaving twelve dead and considerable equipment behind.[27] The defenders pulled back to their next defensive position at Edwards' Plantation (see Map 15).

It was apparent that most of Eather's brigade would be needed to overcome the strong enemy positions around Edwards' as the defenders were being supported by Japanese artillery emplaced

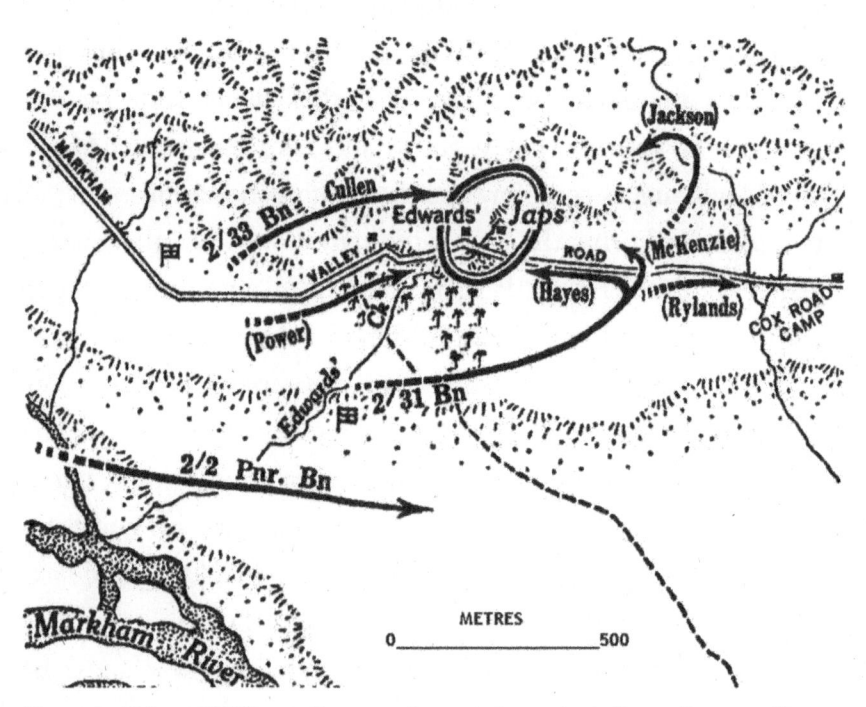

Map 15: Edwards' Plantation, 15 September 1943 (from Dexter, *The New Guinea Offensives*, p. 383, Copyright Australian War Memorial)

further back near Jacobsen's. Cullen's company advanced through the foothills along the north side of the road before coming under fire near Edwards'. The lead scout, Peter Kelly, was killed. Cullen then moved forward and tried to get a platoon up onto a ridge on the left flank, but the move was stymied by close-range Japanese fire. Pushing ahead, more men fell in bitter fighting. Hampered by the absence of his fourth company, all but lost in the air accident at Port Moresby, Colonel Cotton ordered Cullen to hold fast and wait for two wider flanking moves to get in behind the Japanese positions.[28]

As part of the attack on Edwards' Plantation, Dave MacDougal's company was sent further up the ridge to the left to outflank the enemy position to the north. Corporals Pat Maloney and Dave Green led the two forward sections from 10 Platoon into the attack. The ridge ran parallel to the road and the men followed it for some 500 metres until the forward scouts could see the Japanese defenders in trenches along a spur below them, holding firm against the attack along the road. Throwing grenades ahead, Maloney led an attack down onto the spur as other troops came in from the west, routing the defenders, eleven of whom were killed.[29]

On the right flank south of the road, two companies from Colonel Robson's newly arrived 2/31st Battalion were ordered to move around behind Edwards' Plantation and cut the road. Once the two companies reached the road, Captain Chris Rylands' company took up a defensive position around a bridge while Captain Horace Hayes' company advanced west back down the road towards Edwards' with Lieutenant Horace Hamilton's platoon south of the road and Lieutenant Sid Sawyer's to the north. Major Ken Hall noted that 'the undergrowth was so dense along the route that machetes were used almost continually . . . Often men were up to their waists in water and mud.' One of the tactics used in such close country was for the men to fire their Owen guns into the undergrowth ahead to speed up the attack. The road between the two platoons could not be used as it was 'under intense fire' and this also made it difficult for Hayes to maintain control over the two platoons. 'It was practically suicidal to attempt a crossing,' Hall later wrote. However, under attack from both sides, the Japanese defence at Edwards' was confused and crumbling. A Juki machine gun was still pointing down the road to the west when captured by Hayes' men coming from the east.[30]

Hamilton's platoon got hit pretty hard as the men crossed an open clearing. After Lisle Rowe was shot in the throat and arm, one of the stretcher bearers, Alfred Scott, went out for him under heavy fire. As Scott wrapped a dressing around Rowe's throat, Rowe was hit again, this time in the foot. Holding the dressing in place, Scott carried Rowe back to safety and then went out again to treat and bring in two more wounded men. Unfortunately Lisle Rowe would not survive his wounds.[31]

After the attack by Hayes' company had stalled, a number of men kept it going. One of those men was Corporal Jim Gordon, who had been awarded a Victoria Cross for his bravery during the campaign in Syria. 'Gordon, the VC, sized up the position in a flash,' Colonel Robson later told Merv Weston, 'he yelled "Come on men let's into them!" With that Gordon and Sergeant Norm Pepper led a wild charge . . . the rest joined in with them and it was all over in a few minutes.' Gordon was recommended for another decoration but told battalion headquarters that he wasn't interested.[32]

Harry Cullen's company from the 2/33rd now continued the advance. An enemy machine-gun position had to be knocked out first, so Cullen took over a Bren gun and, using the gunner's shoulder to support the gun, proceeded to fire three magazines into the enemy position. He took care of the machine gun, but in doing so Cullen took a bullet through his arm, into his shoulder and out his back, putting him out of action.[33]

Major James Jackson's company from the 2/31st was responsible for cutting off the enemy retreat. With daylight fading, Lieutenant Duncan Campbell took up a Bren gun and from his two-metre height was able to fire at the retreating Japanese as if using a rifle. With darkness fast approaching, Campbell's and Lieutenant Jack Scott's platoons then formed a circle in the jungle to wait out the night. Japanese artillery fired 46 shells at the Australian positions that night but all landed over 300 metres away and caused no casualties. In the middle of the night a Japanese group attacked the western side of the perimeter, trying to break through to Lae and, as Scott later wrote, 'From absolute silence the night erupted into mayhem.'[34]

Some of the Japanese got out to the south-east that night, but most fell to the Australian infantrymen. The Australians also had heavy casualties, with the 2/31st suffering 13 killed and 25 wounded during the fighting. Four stretcher bearers were killed bringing the wounded into the makeshift 2/31st aid post which itself came under fire. Padre John Robinson helped out by keeping a primus stove operating under a groundsheet while the rain tumbled down. He was in the process of rigging a stretcher using another groundsheet when the man helping him fell dead across the stretcher, shot through the chest.[35]

Further south, the 2/2nd Pioneer Battalion was positioned to prevent anyone from the Japanese garrison at Markham Point crossing the river and reinforcing Heath's. The pioneers were also in a good position to provide support fire onto Markham Point and thus aid any further attack by the 24th Battalion troops, still the main component of Wampit Force. Despite the 'balls up' on 4 September, General Herring was keen to get Wampit Force involved again but General Vasey thought it was best to just isolate Markham Point and thus prevent any of the garrison crossing the river and reinforcing Heath's. On 14 September a pioneer patrol moved uncontested along the north bank of the Markham River all the way to the river mouth to confirm that there was no further large-scale reinforcement of Lae by troops moving overland from Salamaua. By the time the Japanese garrison finally withdrew from Markham Point on the night of 16–17 September, Lae had already fallen.

•

With units from Brigadier Ivan Dougherty's 21st Brigade now arriving at Nadzab, the three battalions of the US 503rd Parachute Regiment were flown back to Port Moresby from 14 to 19 September. Before the paratroops flew out, American Lieutenant John Rucker, who had witnessed the Australians in action on the road to Lae, told the Australian war correspondent Bill Marien, 'When I saw these soldiers first I thought they were the worst disciplined, worst dressed rabble of men I had ever seen. I had to see them in action and preparing for action before I realized what a terrible asinine mistake I had made. Then I knew that they were the best disciplined, the best dressed and the greatest body of fighting men that anyone in the world could hope to have fighting for or with them.'[36]

The support of the engineers during the advance to Lae was also vital. They built 32 bridges and culverts and laid 360 metres of corduroy road. 'All finer points of bridge building were discarded and structures made sufficient to carry jeeps and guns,' the 25th Brigade report later noted. A lot of corduroy road had to be laid down and the growth either side of the track cleared back to allow the sun to dry the track out. The roads were useless without the jeeps that were used to bring up supplies and take out the wounded. As the report made clear, 'These vehicles performed most astonishing tasks.'[37]

Due to the development of the Buna base and the improvements at Oro Bay, the supplies required by 7th Division could be delivered by sea to these two ports in the vicinity of the airfield complex at Dobodura. Air transport squadrons could therefore be based at Dobodura and fly in supplies to Nadzab without having to cross the main Owen Stanley Range, which was all too often blocked by cloud cover. With efficient aircraft loading a key consideration, the Australian 2nd Air Maintenance Company was established at Port Moresby on 28 July 1943. The company moved to Dobodura on 1 August, a month prior to Operation Postern, and obtained invaluable experience working on air supply to Wau, the Bulolo Valley and forward drop zones in support of the Australian advance on Salamaua during August. Air supply to the Salamaua front finished on 2 September, giving the unit five days to prepare loads for the supply operation to Nadzab. Between 7 September and 10 October the company delivered 570,000 kilograms of military rations, 113,000 kilograms of native rations, 53,500 kilograms of petrol, oil and lubricants and 230 kilograms of hospital supplies, all net figures. Fresh bread was also sent forward from Dobodura daily.[38]

The 7th Division had prepared a balanced ration scale which allowed for 900 such rations to be sent per aircraft; however, this involved 36 separate commodities, a very time-consuming task that was only carried out for daily maintenance requirements. To build up a four-week supply reserve, it was found more efficient to send the rations across in bulk with only four to six separate commodities having to be handled per aircraft. The rations were then balanced by the receiving units at Nadzab.[39]

The US First Air Task Force also operated from Dobodura to control transport operations to Nadzab and beyond. There were 36 transport aircraft operating daily from Dobodura for maintenance while troop movements were still carried out from Port Moresby where 54 aircraft were available. In the first twenty days of Nadzab's operation, 2015 aircraft landed at the airfield, an average of over 100 per day.[40]

•

On the Markham Road west of Lae there was a terrific rain storm on the morning of 16 September which cut communications between Colonel Marson's 2/25th Battalion and Brigadier Eather. Following the fall of Edwards' Plantation, further enemy resistance was expected at Jacobsen's, where aerial photos showed that extensive defensive positions had been built. Marson's battalion was to advance along the road while the other two battalions cleaned out the Japanese pocket in the hills to the north. Meanwhile a 2/25th fighting patrol led by Sergeant Claude Turner was sent out from Emery's and entered Lae at 1100 that morning. To the astonishment of all, Turner reported that the town was deserted except for stragglers.

At that point a scheduled air attack began, with strafing runs along the road from Emery's to Lae, the road Turner's patrol had

'Fix bayonets'

just traversed. The troops from Captain Gilbert Gow's company were now on the road and hurriedly found a level spot to mark out an X on the ground to indicate forward friendly troops. However, the strafing along the road continued, followed by the dropping of parachute-retarded bombs and two men were hit. Turner's patrol was also bombed but by waving their hats madly they finally managed to get the overly enthusiastic American airmen to desist.[41]

Another 2/25th patrol under Lieutenant John Anderson headed to Mount Lunamun, which overlooked Lae. There the men found a red signal flag flying over a wooden platform, manned by two straw dummies, complete with uniforms and helmets. Then, as Anderson's patrol prepared to move down into town, artillery fire from the 9th Division began to fall. After it stopped the men moved off, killing four Japanese stragglers on the way to the waterfront where they met up with surprised 9th Division troops who had approached in attack formation.[42]

Once word came back that Lae was deserted and the shelling by the 9th Division had ceased, the 2/31st Battalion and Brigadier Eather's brigade headquarters immediately moved forward, Eather right up at the front in his jeep badgering the forward company commander to hurry up. Meanwhile Eather's driver had found two abandoned cars in the scrub by the road and, investigating further, he found two Japanese soldiers in one, 'enjoying a hurried meal'. Seeing him approach, one of the Japanese tried to attack him with a fork but was soon subdued and captured.[43] Further on, an enemy sergeant was found face down by the road refusing to move. Suspicious of a hidden grenade, Eather ordered a rope be tied to the prisoner's legs but when the rope touched him, he sprung up and cried out in pidgin that all the Japanese had left Lae.[44] Eather then headed up to Mount Lunamun to replace the Japanese flag with an Australian one. Brigadier Evans, the 24th Brigade commander, met Eather on the outskirts of Lae. 'I was covered in mud and had all my belongings on my back,' Evans later wrote, 'Eather was smart and trim and riding in a jeep.'[45] 'We came over the hill from Chinatown with fixed bayonets,' Sergeant Dave Richardson wrote of the Australians, 'and what happens but up comes the brigadier of the first brigade of the 7th—and in a jeep!'[46] Major Keith Mollard later noted, 'In the mighty final assault on this great Lae fortress, I think I am correct in saying that we shot one sick Jap and one old Chinaman, in Chinatown, this later being a case of mistaken identity.'[47]

The 9th Division troops had been hampered by having to wait for the air strike and then the artillery bombardment before advancing into Lae.[48] They didn't know that it was unnecessary but what it did mean was that the 7th Division reached Lae first, though only to find the town empty and 'blasted to the ground—just an evil smelling rubbish heap'. The Japanese had gone.[49]

Chapter 12

'A PRECARIOUS RETREAT'

On 11 September, while the infantry brigades of the 9th Division were held up on the east bank of the lower Busu River, the 2/4th Independent Company had moved up to the east bank of the river further upstream above the Sankwep River junction. 'We were to be flank cover and explorer to find where the Japs were,' Ralph Coyne noted.[1] Lieutenant Gordon Hart, the commander of B Platoon, was more specific as to the role of the commandos. The company 'had explicit orders not to cross the Busu and not to go beyond Musum 2,' he wrote.[2] After crossing the Sankwep River via a fallen tree, Lieutenant 'Sam' Cox's A Platoon reached the Busu River about midday on 11 September. Like Hart, Cox was under orders not to cross the river and the platoon dug in along the east bank overlooking a flimsy kunda (cane) bridge some 30 to 40 metres long which spanned the torrent. As the commando's padre, Arthur Bottrell, later wrote, it was 'not much more than a decorated tightrope'.[3]

About two hours after reaching the Busu, the commandos allowed a Chinese carrier and two natives to cross the bridge unmolested before they were stopped by some native policemen accompanying the commandos. An hour later a larger party of about a dozen Japanese soldiers approached with twenty native carriers and the first two men started across. One of them was a Japanese naval officer resplendent in white gloves with his sword hanging by his side and he would not be allowed to cross. 'They got in the centre of the bridge, this big captain and we had to shoot him,' Norm Miles said. Miles was somewhat disappointed because 'I wanted him on our side because he was full of medals, swords and whatnot.' The commandos then turned their fire onto the Japanese 'lined up on the beach waiting to come across' and they lost a lot more men before they could dig in. 'We all had machine guns,' Norm Miles said, 'and they just fell down like flies.'[4] However, once they were under cover the Japanese troops replied with mortar and machine-gun fire. On the next morning of 12 September, twenty more Japanese troops arrived but were unable to cross the river while Cox's platoon remained in place. With the Japanese garrison in Lae cut off from the east and west by the Australian advance, the 2/4th commandos had effectively blocked the only alternative Japanese escape route.

Early the next day, 13 September, a section of men from Hart's platoon tried to wade across the river upstream of the bridge under covering fire from another section on the east bank. However, the current proved too strong in the narrow river channel and most of the men were carried away downstream past the Kunda bridge.

'A precarious retreat'

The section commander, Lieutenant Wally Staples, managed to drag himself ashore but was shot and wounded during the subsequent fighting. It was then decided to use the Kunda bridge to get Hart's platoon across to the west bank.[5]

Lieutenant David Trevaldwyn's 18-man section went across the bridge first with six men from the scout group leading, each man about 3 metres apart. The Bren-gun group followed, with Alan Haly carrying the Bren and Brian Jaggar in support. 'The river was running very fast with turbulent wave action, creating a loud roaring noise,' Jaggar noted. The first men had almost got across when a sharp metallic clang from the equipment of one of the men on the bridge alerted the Japanese troops who opened fire with two machine guns, one aimed at each end of the bridge. Ken Markham was about to get onto the bridge 'when the machine-gun fire struck its main supports and it partially collapsed into the water'. Halfway across the bridge, Brian Jaggar 'was first aware that we were under fire when I saw my comrades falling in front of me'. Of the ten men on the precarious bridge, seven managed to reach the west bank as the weight of fire collapsed the bridge into the river. Three of the commandos were killed on the bridge: Bruce Veitch, Dudley Sheldrick and Doug Sidney. While Jaggar and Haly struggled with the Bren gun up towards the A-frame support on the far bank of the river, David Trevaldwyn was thrown off the bridge when his rifle butt was hit and he was washed downstream for about 300 metres. Back on the east bank, one of the Bren gunners, Norm Miles, was hit across the scalp by a bullet as he raised his head, 'neatly parting his hair and belting him down into his foxhole'.[6]

Meanwhile, Jaggar and Haly had got across the bridge and found shelter with the other five men in low scrub about 10 metres from the river bank. The Japanese positions were further upstream where the river came closer to the bank and Jaggar threw two grenades as the seven commandos continued the attack. Out in front with the Bren gun, Haly was hit and badly wounded by a nearby machine gun hidden in the thick scrub but Jaggar took over the weapon and soon silenced the enemy post. The Australian attack, helped by covering fire from Cox's platoon on the eastern bank, drove the rest of the Japanese off, abandoning their weapons.[7]

Crouched behind the river bank, Jaggar did what he could for the badly wounded Haly, binding his broken leg with driftwood and ammunition belts and giving him morphine. In the mid-afternoon a grenade launcher on the eastern bank fired across an empty grenade with a message attached telling the seven men they should recross the river, so the men decided to try to swim back across as soon as it got dark. The three best swimmers—Brian Jaggar, Bill Hunter and Bob Timmins—helped Alan Haly but all were swept off their feet by the current. However, the lion-hearted Jaggar, an experienced surf swimmer, had bound himself to Haly and, despite the battering he took against the rocks, was able to progress by diving down to the bed of the river and pushing off with his feet. He somehow managed to get Haly to the other side where Billy Hanlon saw that Haly's leg 'was absolutely shattered—but not a murmur out of him'. Meanwhile, Bob Timmins had grabbed onto the cane vines from the fallen bridge to drag himself across and, despite having his trousers and leggings torn away by the current, also made it back. Bill Hunter also lost his clothes but was thrown out of the current onto the safety of the east bank further downstream. Meanwhile a gallant Jim Pitos had draped the weapons of Jaggar and Haly around his neck but that only added to the difficulties he already had in

'A precarious retreat'

being a poor swimmer, and once the current grabbed him he was never seen again.[8]

Andrew Hamersley and a wounded Frank Mannion were the last to enter the Busu and the current soon swept both off their feet. Hamersley was pulled under and never seen again but Mannion managed to stay afloat and got ashore a kilometre downstream, although still on the western bank. Next morning his mates on the east bank spotted him but he had to hide to avoid a large group of enemy troops. He then went further upstream above the Sankwep junction before drifting down to where a human chain had been set up out into the river from where he could be grabbed and brought ashore.[9]

•

On 7 September, with the situation in Lae desperate for the Japanese, General Nakano sent for Masamichi Kitamoto, the engineering officer who had pioneered the route across the Saruwaged Range from the north coast. When Kitamoto entered Nakano's headquarters he saw the Lae commander was in conference with his key officers poring over a map that was spread out across the table. Under orders from General Adachi, Nakano had decided that there would be no *Gyokusai* or final battle to the death for Lae, and had ordered a retreat. Civilian employees had already left, beginning their trek west to Madang carrying twenty days of rations on the day of the landing, 4 September.[10] Nakano saw two options for the retreat of the Lae garrison, either across the Saruwaged Range to the north coast or through the foothills of the Finisterre Ranges heading west parallel to the Markham Valley. Kitamoto, who had the best knowledge of both routes, was asked for his opinion. 'It was a responsibility too heavy for just a Lieutenant to decide,' Kitamoto thought, but, well aware that Allied aircraft could easily interdict the route through the open kunai of the Markham Valley foothills, he told Nakano that 'the second plan is impossible'. He then added that 'The first plan is difficult but there is still some chance of success.' Kitamoto said he 'would choose plan one. However, the sacrifice will be great.' Nakano agreed and issued the retreat order, which was drawn up and distributed to all Japanese units on the following day, 8 September. 'We should ready our packs as we would retreat over the mountains from 10th to 15th of September,' Kitamoto wrote.[11]

The orders for the Japanese withdrawal specified there would be four retreating groups totalling about 8650 men. The naval forces would travel in the first and fourth echelons, the army forces in the second and third groups. Standard infantry equipment was to be carried including 120 rounds of ammunition, two grenades and provisions for ten days. Infantrymen also had to carry their machine guns and small mortars while the artillery unit had to manhandle their 75 mm mountain guns, and the machine-cannon company their 20 mm guns, across the daunting ranges. The signals units were required to take their wireless and the medical units their surgical gear. Valuable installations, including the airfield and nearby roads, were to be destroyed and military equipment smashed, burned or thrown into the sea.[12]

With supplies no longer being sent to the Salamaua front, there were provisions available for the retreat.[13] The chief of staff of the 18th Army, Lieutenant General Kane Yoshihara, later wrote that the generally healthy men from the Lae-based naval units were able to carry enough provisions for fourteen or fifteen days but the army units, most of whom had been fighting at Salamaua for months, were 'in an extreme of exhaustion' and only able to carry half that amount. 'With these meagre supplies they set off for [Saruwaged] Peak,' Yoshihara added.[14]

Lae field hospital would be closed on 12 September with some patients to be evacuated by submarine but the majority 'sent back as speedily as possible overland'. The first food dump would be set up near Bungalumba, the second at Iloko village and the third at Melanpipi or Ulap, on the northern side of the range. The 1st Field Hospital would be set up near Bungalumba, part of the 3rd Field Hospital at Iloko and the 2nd Field Hospital at Kiari on the north coast. A water purification section was sent to Boana. All medical facilities would later be moved across the ranges to Sio with the rearguard.[15]

The naval medic Kamesaku Iwata had been attached to a scratch infantry unit comprising slightly injured or sick men and deployed to guard the Busu River. Around 12 September he was summoned to headquarters where a commander's aide told him the unit would soon commence a withdrawal from Lae. 'How many men are seriously injured or sick in your squad?' the aide asked. After Iwata told him there were about 200, he was handed a bottle of about 500 disinfectant tablets. 'Give two tablets of this medicine to each man unable to move, saying they are for malaria,' a shocked Iwata was told. 'Killing by poison. All men,' Iwata wrote. 'To think that they are to be poisoned because they would encumber the living.' He decided to bury the bottle and ran to the hospital telling the patients to assemble to leave immediately. 'Those who are unable to walk must follow even if crawling,' Iwata told them.[16] Fortunately there was another way out for some of them.

Masamichi Kitamoto also had concerns about the sick and wounded after being told that there were 500 hospital patients unable to walk. He wanted to carry them out on stretchers, though that would require 2000 men and there were no native carriers left in Lae. Kitamoto reported the problem to the divisional logistics staff officer Lieutenant Colonel Motoaki Suzuki, who responded angrily, 'Your duty is to guide the 10,000 men. Any other problems including the patients at Salamaua is none of your business.'[17]

It was obvious to Colonel Suzuki that the sick would die in the mountains but would also die if they remained. 'There was nothing for them to wait for but death,' Kane Yoshihara wrote. Suzuki thought that the shipping engineers may be able to do something as the Allied navy may have grown a little careless and would not expect an incursion past their blockade off the coast. In the ten days since the Allied landing, the Japanese MLCs had been used to bring most of the troops from Salamaua to Lae and the boats were now available for other tasks. The 5th Shipping Unit (three large landing barges, and one small barge) and the 8th Shipping Unit (two large landing barges and one raft) loaded up the wounded and, under a full moon on the night of 14 September, 'daringly went straight into the heart of the enemy'. Under the command of Captain Sadaichi Teramura and Lieutenant Ishihara, the seven MLCs headed east along the coast between the shore and the Allied ships and, although one barge was lost, the others safely reached Finschhafen before dawn, saving some 300 men. That was Iwata's version of the story but an engineering sergeant who was later captured said that, of the ten barges that were involved, 'eight were destroyed by enemy action and nothing was ever heard of the other two'. Whatever happened

'A precarious retreat'

to the barges, one thing was clear: for any sick or wounded who remained in Lae 'there was nothing left for them but an extreme measure,' Yoshihara wrote.[18]

Although it was thought that all the patients had been loaded onto the MLCs that night, thirteen patients including Lieutenant Masayoshi Yoshikawa had been left stranded on the beaches. These men had already come across from Salamaua and, with nothing to wear but their loincloths, they waited for days for the barges to return but they never did. 'I never felt so angry at the army at that time,' Yoshikawa thought, 'I wanted to die but I could not.' He decided he had no choice but to walk out if he wanted to live, so the wounded men began their death trek. 'Near naked half dead men marching,' as Yoshikawa saw it. At one point a well-educated soldier, a graduate of Takasaki Technical School, accompanied them for a few days before moving on. 'If I stay with you I will die,' he told the struggling group of men, 'I must return to Japan because there are so many things I must do.' Yoshikawa's group took heart from that and pushed on. Yoshikawa later pondered how 'If we didn't meet up with him, we may not be alive today.'[19]

There was a saying in the Japanese armed forces that 'Java is heaven, Burma is hell, but you never come back alive from New Guinea.'[20] Defying that saying, Kamesaku Iwata came back alive from New Guinea and in June 1946 another Japanese veteran, who had recently been repatriated home from Australia, visited him. The returned veteran told Iwata that he had been captured while lying unconscious in a critical condition in the Lae field hospital in September 1943. 'He thanked me for what I did in Lae in those days,' Iwata wrote of his refusal to administer the poison to the hospital patients. 'I am convinced that because I did not carry out the order, several dozens of men are alive today.'[21]

•

The original plan for the retreating Japanese echelons was for the first and third groups to cross the Busu River at the Kunda bridge and then travel via Gawan and Bungalumba to the summit of the Saruwaged Range. This was the route pioneered from the north by Kitamoto during his journey across the Saruwaged Range five months previously. The second and fourth groups were also to cross the Busu at the Kunda bridge but then head to Kemen, Hanobmain, Bainduang and Avin before following the Sanem River valley up across the main range further west. However, the plan was thrown into disarray once the Kunda bridge crossing was blocked by the Australian commandos on 11 September. This action was not lost on the Japanese command in Lae and it was noted how the Australian advance 'seems to have cut off the retreat route of the Division'.[22] In the end all four echelons would have to find another way across the Busu further upstream from the Kunda bridge and then take the second route across the mountains.

The first echelon comprised the 7th Base Force headquarters, the 85th Communications unit, the 23rd Anti-Aircraft unit and part of the Sasebo 5th SNLP, 1054 men in all.[23] This echelon was under the command of the recently arrived Rear Admiral Kunizo Mori and left Lae at dusk on 12 September carrying rifles, ammunition and ten days' supply of food. Lieutenant Kitamoto's engineers led the way, setting up sign posts and repairing the track as they went. With the planned route across the Busu River

'A precarious retreat'

to Musom now blocked at the Kunda bridge, the echelon left Lae further west and headed up the Butibum River valley north of the rugged Atzera Range, looking for a way out between the advancing Australian pincers. On the morning of 13 September the leading troops came under attack from a patrol of the 1/503rd Parachute Battalion that had been operating east of Nadzab and this forced the echelon to divert through the jungle towards Yalu.

•

A clever Australian ploy had led to considerable information being obtained from captured Japanese documents and equipment at Lae. The soldier finding any such items could put his name and address on the captured equipment label and the item would be returned to him as a souvenir after intelligence had had a look at it, and this led to excellent cooperation from the troops. When the 2/25th Battalion captured Heath's Plantation on the morning of 14 September, considerable equipment was found, some of it unused and still packed in grease. As the Australians looked over the abandoned site, a member of Lieutenant Don Macrae's platoon took a satchel from a dead soldier of the 15th Anti-Aircraft Machine Cannon Unit. The unit, equipped with 20 mm anti-aircraft guns, had been based at Heath's Plantation and the satchel, which was handed to the battalion commander Lieutenant Colonel Marson, contained a number of papers and maps. Among the maps was one showing enemy dispositions around the Markham River and Lae, and 'Judging the documents to be important' Marson sent them off to 25th Brigade headquarters. From there Vasey's divisional headquarters was advised that the orders were on their way for translation.[24]

There were three US Army interpreters attached to 7th Division headquarters, all of Japanese descent. They were Sergeant Yoshikazu Yamada, Master Sergeant Arthur Ushiro and Sergeant Munnekawa.[25] All prisoners, captured documents and captured material came to these interpreters for assessment. The divisional intelligence officer was present at any POW interrogations and a copy of all reports was forwarded to each brigade as well as to I Corps and New Guinea Force headquarters. By mid-afternoon the translations had been made. Marson was later told that 'a most uninteresting paper in appearance', the last one to be translated, was the Lae evacuation order.[26] The intelligence officer at Vasey's headquarters considered the paper important enough to immediately send a copy across to Port Moresby.[27]

It was about 1545 on that afternoon of 14 September when Flying Officer Alex Miller-Randle was ordered to fly one of his squadron's Wirraways from Tsili Tsili down to Nadzab to pick up an army intelligence officer. Miller-Randle was told that this officer carried documents 'which must be taken to Port Moresby as quickly as possible'. Miller-Randle was confused by the order and even more so when he reached Nadzab and met the intelligence officer, Captain Andrew McLay. McLay was excited about something and emphatic that he needed to get to Port Moresby urgently but it was now after 1600 and the idea of crossing the Owen Stanley Range was a daunting prospect. Miller-Randle was unsure whether his plane had sufficient fuel for the flight and did not know what the cloud cover was like over Port Moresby. Any landing would also be at night and Miller-Randle did not have a radio operator to organise the landing or even a compass bearing to guide him to an airfield. He could also see

'A precarious retreat'

that the weather over the mountains was building into something ominous and he was only dressed in shorts and tropical shirt, hardly the ideal wear for the high-level flight across the range. For all these reasons and despite strong objections from McLay, Miller-Randle only flew the intelligence officer back to Tsili Tsili.[28]

Nonetheless, somebody still had to fly McLay to Moresby and Flight Lieutenant Eric 'Bob' Staley volunteered to make the flight. Staley made the trip in patchy moonlight, firstly heading down the coast to Dobodura, before crossing the range to Port Moresby. General Berryman was at the outdoor cinema in Moresby when Colonel Ken Wills, his intelligence officer, notified him of the captured evacuation order. Berryman left Port Moresby at 0750 the next morning on a Wirraway, landing at Tsili Tsili before proceeding to Nadzab. He then returned to Port Moresby that afternoon where he met with General Blamey and General Herring to explain the situation at Lae.[29]

•

Following the translation of the Japanese order, General Vasey was given permission to use Lieutenant Colonel Tolson's 3/503rd Parachute Battalion to try to intercept the enemy withdrawal. On 15 September the parachute battalion 'moved out in single file along a narrow path covered with thick vines that had to be hacked away with machetes'. It was a gruelling trek into the Atzera Range to a log crossing of the Butibum (also known as the Bumbu) River where Captain John Davis's lead company came under machine-gun fire from the west bank of the river. The position was soon silenced but, when Lieutenant Lyle Murphy's platoon 'collided headlong' with the Japanese force, Tolson called up the rest of the battalion and heavy fighting ensued. That night the Japanese broke off the fight and headed off in a new direction to the north-west.[30]

Tolson's paratroopers had clashed with the 34 men from the advanced guard of the first echelon, which had lost contact with the main group.[31] Tolson advised that the enemy strength was greater than first realised and fighting had continued into the next day, 16 September. 'Believe this to be the main route of withdrawal', a perceptive Colonel Ken Kinsler advised General Vasey. Vasey, aware of General MacArthur's directive that parachute troops were not to be used in infantry roles, ordered that the newly arrived 2/16th Battalion move to the area accompanied by the headquarters of 21st Brigade. The Australians would take over from the paratroopers who were to return to Port Moresby.[32]

Aware that it was vital to maintain the secrecy of the withdrawal route and not get engaged in a fixed battle, the first-echelon commander, Rear Admiral Mori, once again changed the course of the retreat. Instead of trying to reach Boana he would take his men north across the Atzera Range to Kemen.[33] By the time the first 21st Brigade units reached the Bumbu River crossing on 17 September, they could only confirm that the Japanese had bypassed the area and were indeed now heading north.[34] On that same day Mori's first echelon, after blazing a trail through the jungle on a compass bearing to the north, had reached the Busu River.[35] 'After three days, we were finally able to escape from the enclosure of the enemy,' Masamichi Kitamoto wrote. 'With the enemy on our back, it was a precarious retreat.'[36] Kitamoto had good reason to think that the enemy was on the

'A precarious retreat'

back of the Japanese first echelon but the lack of urgency from the Australian side was staggering.

•

The first two battalions of the second of General Vasey's brigades, Brigadier Ivan Dougherty's 21st Brigade, had landed at Nadzab on 15 September. The next morning a company from the 2/16th Battalion, accompanied by battalion headquarters, was sent up to the Bumbu River crossing where the paratroops had contacted the Japanese. Following the rough creek bed, with the men's boots heavy with water, by the time the company reached the Bumbu log crossing on the following day, 17 September, the Japanese had gone. Orders were then issued to try to intercept the Japanese force, now thought to be headed to Boana, but that night the men were suddenly ordered back to Nadzab.

Meanwhile the first units of the 2/14th Battalion, which had landed at Nadzab on the morning of 15 September, were immediately ordered to Boana to secure the village and use it as a base to destroy any Japanese forces to the north and east. On 17 September the battalion crossed the Atzera Range after a five-hour climb to the top. 'Very steep and hard going,' as Sergeant James Milbourne wrote, but 'Going down was worse than going up.'[37] There were signs that the track had been used but it was not by the retreating Japanese force. However, there were Japanese troops in the area and, when the Australians reached the upper reaches of the Busu River south of Boana, they were held up by an enemy covering-force dug in on the other side of a flooded tributary. On 20 September a dilapidated wire bridge was found, but only three hours after the battalion began crossing the rebuilt bridge orders were received to withdraw to Nadzab.[38] The reason for the sudden change of role for the 2/14th and 2/16th Battalions was a stunning coup by Captain Gordon King's 2/6th Independent Company further west up the Markham Valley.

•

On 16 September General Vasey had flown into Port Moresby to discuss further operations in the Markham Valley with General Herring and General Berryman. Vasey had told Herring that he wanted the Nadzab paratroop drop replicated at Dumpu, 160 kilometres north-west of Lae in the Ramu Valley.[39] Herring agreed despite the plan being for Kaiapit, 93 kilometres north-west of Lae in the Markham Valley, to be the next objective. General Berryman, who had a poor opinion of Herring, informed General Blamey of Herring's idea and had Kaiapit confirmed as the next objective. Of Herring's proposed change of plan, Berryman noted that Blamey 'was a bit sharp with him and he richly deserved it for not following chief's policy instead of trying his own'. That evening General MacArthur's senior operations officer, Brigadier General Stephen Chamberlin, told Berryman that Colonel David Hutchinson had landed his Piper Cub aircraft on the Leron River flats, 18 kilometres from Kaiapit and that the 5th Air Force was prepared to fly an Australian company there on the next day in order to capture Kaiapit. Blamey readily agreed to the plan and Vasey was ordered to organise the troops. Captain Gordon King's 2/6th Independent Company was already standing by, ready to go.[40]

On 17 September King's company was flown from Port Moresby and landed on the river flats on the western bank of the

'A precarious retreat'

Leron River. General Vasey flew in soon thereafter and gave King his final orders which were to 'go to Kaiapit as quickly as you can, destroy any enemy resistance there, occupy Kaiapit and prepare a landing strip 1200 yards long as soon as possible'.[41] King then led his company from Sangan to the Japanese occupied village of Kaiapit, reaching it on the afternoon of 19 September. The commandos stormed and captured the village, killing some twenty defenders from the Takano platoon, part of Captain Teruyuki Morisada's reconnaissance force from the 80th Regiment. As King's men set up a defensive perimeter for the night, little did they know that a much stronger Japanese force of over 300 men was also headed to Kaiapit and would arrive on the following morning.

This was the advance force of Major General Masutaro Nakai's 78th Regiment which had been ordered to secure Kaiapit as quickly as possible to protect the withdrawal of the 51st Division from Lae, at that stage thought likely to be via the Markham Valley. The main force, which would include a battalion from the 26th Field Artillery Regiment, was to follow in order to attack the Allied airbase at Nadzab.[42] There were some 400 men in the advance party under the command of Major Tsuneo Yonekura, made up of the two infantry companies from the 3rd Battalion with attached headquarters, machine-gun and engineer units. Carrying ten days' rations, Yonekura's force had left Kankiryo on 12 September facing a forced march of seven nights to reach Kaiapit. The force would travel only by night to avoid being spotted from the air during daylight hours. While King's men were attacking Kaiapit on 19 September, Yonekura's force was held up crossing the Umi River, 12 kilometres to the west. Yonekura didn't begin the move to Kaiapit until dusk and, with about one-third of his men dropping behind as stragglers, this meant he was leading about 270 men towards Kaiapit.[43]

Expecting Kaiapit to be Japanese occupied, Yonekura's men were totally confused and disorganised as they came under fire in the dull light of dawn that morning. Gordon King was also confused but quickest to react. Reorganising his perimeter to free Lieutenant Derrick Watson's platoon, King had them counter-attack the Japanese column. Watson 'blew his whistle, which was the signal, and off they went and killed over a hundred Japanese in the first hundred yards,' King later recounted.[44]

Captain Morisada later stated that the first 100 men of the advance force reached Kaiapit at 0300 on 18 September determined to attack the Australians at dawn. Morisada, who was probably not present at the battle, had his date out by two days and Yonekura was not attacking Kaiapit but was instead caught unaware with his troops spread out in a column of march. Nonetheless he got two things right: it was a sudden encounter in kunai grass and the enemy had superior firepower. As Morisada stated, the battalion headquarters personnel 'was annihilated in the disorder'.[45] Following this defeat, the rest of Nakai's force withdrew to the mountain strongholds above the Ramu Valley. After the war Nakai confirmed to Australian interrogators that Yonekura's advanced force was almost wiped out at Kaiapit.[46]

Late on the afternoon of 21 September the first units of the 2/16th Battalion landed at Kaiapit. On the morning of 23 September the first units of 2/27th Battalion joined them, followed by the first units of 2/14th Battalion the following afternoon. General Vasey now had a fresh brigade in position to advance deep into the Markham and Ramu valleys. General Vasey had an exciting new campaign to run and was keen to wipe his hands of the failure to stop the Japanese evacuation from Lae. 'I have no desire to chase a retreating Jap towards Sio,' he wrote to General Herring, 'I am sure to do so would be good experience for 9 Div!!'[47]

•

Back at Lae, word had reached 9th Division headquarters during the night of 14–15 September that the Japanese order to evacuate Lae had been found and translated. In response, the 2/24th Battalion was ordered back across the Busu River and north along the east bank to Musom and Gawan to block the supposed line of withdrawal. The first warning order to move was not received by the battalion until 1100 on 15 September, and recrossing the Busu and changing the direction of the battalion's advance took another 24 hours. An extra 640 personnel also had to be organised to maintain a new supply line into the mountains.[48] It was not until 18 September that patrols from the 2/24th Battalion reached Gawan and Musom, but due to the blocking of the Kunda bridge crossing the Japanese evacuation route had now moved further west. A Japanese prisoner captured at Gawan on 19 September said that 50 Japanese troops had been at the village but had now moved on.[49]

With the 2/24th Battalion now available to take over control of the Kunda bridge crossing, the commandos from the 2/4th Independent Company were able to patrol along the Busu River further upstream to try to intersect the new Japanese evacuation route. Having lost over 40 men before it had even reached Lae, the company was well under strength for the task at hand. Nonetheless, a section patrol had reached Musom 2 as early as

10 September, but not Musom 1 on the other side of the valley. Although Gordon Hart later said 'It turned out that was where the Jap get-away line went, through Musom 1', that was not now the case. There were relatively few Japanese troops that had already crossed the Kunda bridge to 'plod unmolested on their long journey over the high ranges to Sio'.[50] Most of them were still trapped on the wrong side of the Busu further upstream.

Chapter 13

'LIKE BEGGARS IN A PROCESSION'

After reaching the Busu River some 9 kilometres upstream of the fallen Kunda bridge on 17 September, it was obvious to the retreating Japanese that 'our troops could not wade across this river' and a crossing would be required. Therefore the two accompanying engineer regiments were ordered to construct a bridge.[1] Sergeant Shogo Kagayama was serving with the 51st Field Engineer Regiment, which had been building a road from the Markham Valley road near Heath's Plantation down to the Markham River when the Allied attack on Lae had begun. Kagayama's company had then switched to building defence positions for the Japanese marines around Heath's until the night of 13–14 September when the company moved back to Edwards' Plantation and began its withdrawal from Lae. These engineers were part of the second of the four echelons, which included General Nakano, who had soon found the going too harsh and now had to be carried by four soldiers. Carrying his rifle and spade, with a pick strapped to his rifle and his tools in his pack, Kagayama moved north-west from Edwards' Plantation along a steep and rough track between the east side of the Atzera Range and the Busu River. Upon reaching the river, Kagayama's engineering company helped to build the new crossing.[2]

The first and second echelons were held up for three days while the engineers worked on a makeshift bridge. Taking a different route out of Lae, likely following the track along the south bank of the Busu River, the third and fourth echelons also arrived in the area before the new crossing was completed.[3] The fourth echelon, mainly naval troops but including some army personnel, had left Lae on 15 September.[4] Able Seaman Kiichi Wada, who was in that fourth echelon, had experienced a change in outlook following the retreat order. 'When fight to death changed to retreat there arose a change in the psychology of fighting men,' he wrote, 'from the weakness of a losing battle, all becoming timid and wanting to survive.' Wada was told that the destination was Kiari on the northern coast across the range, a journey of ten days (see Map 16). With orders to leave Lae, the men of Wada's gun battery had fired off the remaining 230 shells, disassembled the gun and left their base after dark, each man equipped with a backpack of his own making. 'We fled as if in a night runaway,' Wada wrote. 'It was as though there lurked tigers in the back, wolves on both sides, and serpents in front.' Wada's unit silently marched out of Lae behind the rest of the 82nd Naval Garrison and on 18 September, their third day out of Lae, the men rested with some 8500 other men as they all waited to cross the Busu.[5]

'Like beggars in a procession'

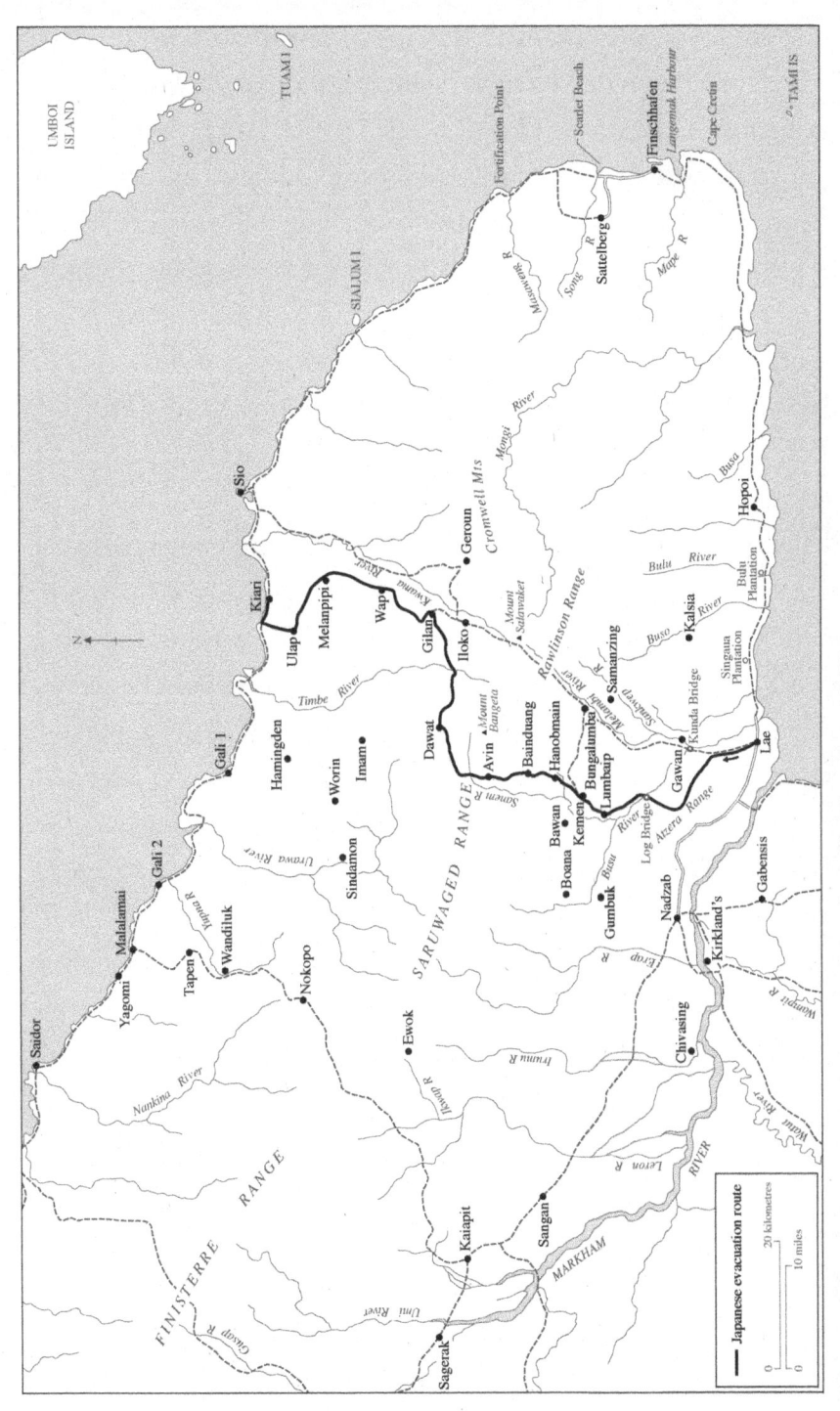

Map 16: Japanese evacuation route from Lae, September 1943

Hiromasu Sato had been serving at Salamaua with an anti-aircraft machine-gun company when the order to retreat from Salamaua to Lae came. Down to just 70 men 'after our damaged guns had been hastily dismantled, we withdrew, hiding under the night shadow, to Lae, with only one gun and very dispirited, heavy of heart,' Sato wrote. On reaching Lae, another company from Sato's unit 'was ordered to become a shield and sally out against the Australian force in order to buy some time . . . Two days later, the sound of their firing had stopped and was never heard again; all dead.' Sato's group survived and the men were able to gather up 'rice and packets of dried bread, which had been delivered by our submarine . . . We each collected one bootful of rice, three packets of dried bread, to last seven days.' Sato also searched desperately for salt. 'There they were, wrapped in strong waxed papers like a toffee: 50 compressed salt cubes,' he wrote. 'We joined the last artillery and edged our way into the jungle.' Sato's unit reached the Busu River 'after skirting around US paratroopers under our noses and discarding our field guns, in the dark untrodden jungle'. The men then had to wait three days to cross the river.[6]

At the new crossing point a large rock stood out from the river about two-thirds of the way across to the north bank. Although the first eight logs used to bridge the gap from the south bank to the rock failed, washed away by the relentless Busu torrent, the phenomenal persistence and belief of the Japanese engineers shone through. All of them knew that the fate of the Lae garrison rested on their skills and endurance and somehow the ninth log held. The new bridge was of two spans. The longest span of about 30 metres was that log from the west bank which rested on the midstream boulder. From there it was joined to the eastern

'Like beggars in a procession'

bank by a shorter log, about 8 metres long. Each log span was 45 centimetres wide with smaller 15-centimetre logs attached on either side, fixed in place by bayonets hammered into the wood like huge nails. The two logs were joined at the rock using more bayonets and vines. There was no handrail. 'The effort expended to span the bridge was enormous,' Wada later wrote.[7]

When it came Kiichi Wada's turn to approach the crossing, he could hear 'a torrent flowing with deep, booming noise, which gripped us by fright'. To Wada it was 'an entrance to the Hell'. Army troops were crossing when he arrived, one man at a time with no assistance. As each man crossed over, an officer would yell 'next . . . go across, quickly'. Wada watched as a 'sick man had to cross crawling on all fours' and another 'toppling midway, plunging into the rapids and vanishing downstream in no time'. Wada pitied the stragglers, 'the injured and sick who were left behind, but nothing could be done'.[8]

The first echelon finally crossed the Busu River on 20 September and the other three echelons had crossed by 22 September. The retreating Japanese echelons then moved north through a precipitous mountain area on a compass bearing to Lumbaip and on to Kemen.[9] Of the move north through these ranges, 18th Army headquarters observed that 'The division had to cross these ravines more than six times a day advancing by compass through the narrow native roads.'[10]

Meanwhile the Australians had finally begun to patrol the Busu River upstream of the Kunda bridge. 'The track on the river bank on the west side rose to high cliffs and then dropped sharply to river level, passing through an area which had all the signs of a recent Jap camp,' Alf McDonald wrote. To McDonald, the river 'sounded like an express train'. On 23 September a Japanese encampment was found on the west side of the Busu near the Kunda bridge. It was estimated that more than 1000 troops had passed through the encampment over the previous two weeks. There were also stragglers about, eighteen of whom were killed. The Japanese 'had a callous disregard for their wounded or sick. They just left them behind to fend for themselves,' one of the Australian commandos, Ian Hampel observed.[11] On 25 September the Australians finally found the new Busu River crossing point, 9 kilometres further upstream from the fallen Kunda bridge. By then the main Japanese force was three days ahead of its pursuers.

Some native carriers were also captured, having deserted on 22 September once the Japanese had ceased to feed them. They said the Japanese had passed through a week earlier, heading 'over a mountain to more water'.[12] On 26 September the Australians destroyed the log bridge and a 2/24th Battalion patrol which had moved along the east bank began following the Japanese retreat route north from the crossing.

•

The 14th Field Artillery Regiment was part of the second echelon. The unit commander, Lieutenant Colonel Sukenobu Watanabe, considered that artillery troops were of no use 'if they could not fire a shot on the battlefield'. For his tired and weakened unit, 'one cannon would be enough' but 'they must also carry some shells'. His men sacrificed carrying sufficient food as he led them up into the Saruwaged carrying mountain-gun components that weighed up to 50 kilograms each.[13]

Hiromasu Sato's anti-aircraft unit had already abandoned their guns in the Atzera Range and the overriding concern was

'Like beggars in a procession'

food. Sato and his comrades only had enough for four days and were now told it would take twenty days to reach the north coast. 'We were stricken with apprehension,' he wrote, but 'the effect of salt worked wondrously . . . those of us without salt became weakened . . . I used my salt sparingly and never drank unboiled water'.[14] Having only arrived in Lae a week before the Australian landing, 22-year-old Shigeru Horiuchi had gone through 'two weeks of hell' under constant bombing attack when 'even the officers were trembling in funk holes and had no taste for fighting'. His company left Lae on 17 September but, as he carried a leg wound, Horiuchi soon dropped out and was captured a few days later.[15]

After Kemen the track became increasingly difficult and, for the Japanese, 'casualties began to mount from this point'.[16] It was reported that 'The road between Kemen and Ave is very precipitous but still in good condition' but there was only enough native food around Avin for the leading units.[17] A Papuan Infantry Battalion patrol in mid-October found that many Japanese had died from sickness around Kemen and there were obvious signs that 'The enemy are suffering severely from dysentery.' Those that remained alive 'are in most cases very weak', the report noted, although 'Some parties are armed and prepared to fight.'[18] Masamichi Kitamoto thought that about 200 men had died even before reaching Kemen and that 'the mountains were only 500 metres high and this much casualties'. 'How many will die before we clear Mt. Sarawaket?' he added. Kitamoto knew that 'The sharp precipices rising before us will take many victims.' As the track began to rise, 'At the beginning the soldiers helped each other along,' he wrote, but soon all anyone could do was try to survive. In the first 1500 metres of the climb after leaving Kemen, another 500 men had died.[19]

As the climb progressed, the men became weaker and soon discarded their rifles, shovels and blankets, only keeping a grenade for suicide. Shogo Kagayama, one of the heroic engineers who had helped span the Busu, had fallen out with malaria and was captured on 23 October near Bainduang. Well treated by his captors, and able to speak English, he persuaded three others to also surrender.[20]

Kiichi Wada watched as the men progressively discarded their equipment. Rifle ammunition was the first to go, then helmets followed by the rifles themselves. Masamichi Kitamoto ordered his engineers to gather as many abandoned rifles as they could and use their files to erase the chrysanthemum insignia, the symbol of the emperor, to mitigate the disgrace. Wada also watched men dispose of rice then their personal belongings, the back cloth of their hat and the lower half of their pants. In the end all that was left was their life. 'From about ten days in the retreat, weak soldiers started to drop behind,' Wada observed. As the men got weaker, the cold and rain led to an increase in malaria recurrence, causing more and more men to drop out.[21]

Not all the men discarded their weapons. Major Shintani's 1st Battalion of the 80th Regiment apparently carried all their weapons across the Saruwaged, including four machine guns. Shintani had told his men, 'the soldier who abandons his arms will be shot to death'. Although Shintani died during the crossing, his men carried on to Kiari with their arms and then supposedly set off for Finschhafen to continue the fight.[22]

The men of Colonel Watanabe's 14th Field Artillery Regiment continued the retreat high up into the range carrying their single mountain gun. Kane Yoshihara noted that the officers and men 'clung on to the rocks with truly formidable spirit'. General Nakano 'was deeply stirred by their sense of responsibility but could not overlook their suffering'. He finally ordered that the last of the regiment's guns should be abandoned. The gunners, 'with tears in their eyes, bade a formal farewell' as they did so. Colonel Watanabe would survive the Saruwaged crossing along with 280 of his men.[23]

The track deteriorated as it followed the upper reaches of the Sanem River along a primitive track cut into the precipitous side of the river valley (see Map 17). 'After we escaped the clutches of the enemy we were confronted by nature,' Kitamoto wrote. Here the living had to walk across the dead to stay on the track. 'Using the dead bodies as stepping stones and clinging to the slippery lichen covered rocks, the men made their way up the mountain. Fresh red blood ran from the mouth of the dead when they were stepped on and their glassy eyes stared us in the face.' Approaching 4000 metres, the cold bit hard into the light summer uniforms the soldiers wore but the exhausted men could not stop to sleep or they would freeze to death. Kitamoto remembered the sound of 'The screaming voices of the men who slipped from the log bridges to their death in the canyons below', and 'the wailing cries of the men who could move no more and were asking for help'. 'It was a sense of hell,' he wrote, 'something quite out of this world.'[24]

As food ran out, the men took to raiding the native gardens. Kiichi Wada heard of some army personnel who 'were chased by the poisonous arrows of the native who got angry at our ransacking the gardens'. However, Wada only found ruined gardens with nothing left to eat by the time he passed through. Even if men had rice left, there was rarely wood available for fire and any

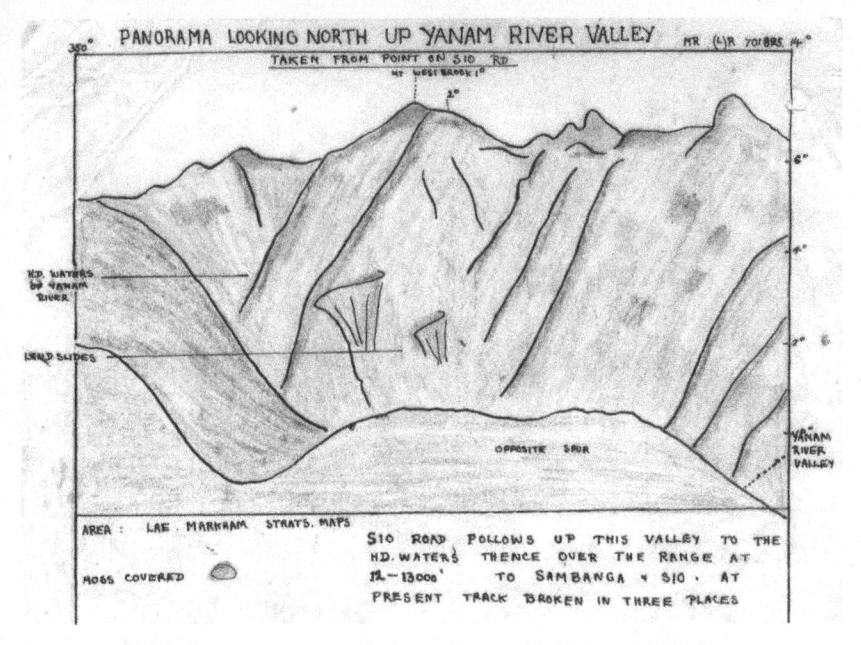

Map 17: Sketch of the upper Yanam (Sanem) River valley (from 24th Battalion War Diary, AWM52, 8/3/62/55, p. 99, Copyright Australian War Memorial)

that was found did not burn easily. The men took to burning the rubber of their rain coats despite them being 'the only anti-cold or water-proof equipment to guard our lives,' Wada wrote. The men would slice the coat edge into small strips to burn until the raw wood caught fire.[25]

Eating anything to stay alive, the men were soon afflicted with diarrhoea, further weakening them and forcing them to drop behind. Wada observed that while navy units would leave any straggler behind, at least in some army units 'a straggler was also assigned with an attending soldier' to either help him recover or report his death. 'I had seen dead straggling soldiers holding on to rifles,' Wada wrote, 'the majority of the bodies stripped naked, eyes open, with clothes and possessions taken away by the men who followed.' Wada kept going, part of an Imperial Japanese Navy that had been reduced to men who 'were like beggars in a procession'.[26]

The way forward looked impossibly steep but Kiichi Wada's group 'advanced trusting that . . . if men had walked ahead, there should be no place that we could not'. They now came to a sheer cliff and they had to 'traverse the precipice horizontally for about ten metres like *itagumo*'. *Itagumo* were spiders and the men mimicked them by hanging on to tree roots and rocks as they crossed the cliff face. With constant use, some rocks loosened and on one a note reading 'This rock moves' was attached. 'We perspired in cold sweat at moments of extreme tension,' Wada wrote. His tension heightened as a soldier 'ahead of me slipped and fell into the valley trailing a scream'.[27]

As the altitude passed 3000 metres, the temperature fell below 10 degrees. Any fire from the moss-covered wood was weak, so the men 'heated the gun powder from rifles, setting it alight in a big flame'. On the next morning, all the group's rifles were missing but the commander said it was not a problem. Wada and his companions were puzzled until they saw the remains of their rifles in the fire, the wooden parts burned away.[28] A month later an Australian patrol in this same area found weapons 'stripped of their wood evidently in an endeavour to make fires. No food in this area or beyond.'[29]

With the rations gone, in some cases the starving men turned to the dead and even the living. Approaching the summit of the Saruwaged Range, Masamichi Kitamoto saw that 'three soldiers had pinned a trooper to the ground while one of them stabbed him in the heart with his bayonet'. A shocked Kitamoto watched as 'The remaining three soldiers cut slices of the dead trooper's thigh and began to devour the human flesh.' Kitamoto shouted at them 'as flies swarmed about their faces . . . They had become mad with hunger and fatigue.' Kitamoto covered the corpse and moved on.[30]

Beyond Avin the track deteriorated and was 'only passable on bare feet without any heavy packs' and some simple scaffolding had been set up by the engineers to help the troops pass. The cold increased as the group climbed higher and the 'Precipitous cliffs continued, one after another.' More men began to die from the cold and from losing their footing.[31] This was at the head of the Sanem River valley where there was a sheer drop on one side of the track and a sheer rock face about 90 metres high on the other.[32]

The final climb to the summit was made over a muddy one-man track where the line came to a stop and the men sat with their legs dangling over the edge of the track. 'There was a precipice ahead, jamming the troops,' Wada wrote. 'Regardless of night or day, they were climbing.' Next day Wada's group moved forward to confront a 10-metre cliff with a vine ladder hanging down with rungs 'wildly misplaced'. Wada 'waited, looking up to the sky', watching others take the five- to eight-minute climb. When he climbed up he found an extensive grassland at the top where 'cold wind blew against us without mercy'. Two men lay dead in an embrace in a nearby tent. About 1 kilometre on, Wada came to another cliff, one that he had to descend. Below that there were tiers of steep rock covered in mud, very treacherous ground. 'The soldiers who fell to death onto this rocky flat would have counted more than 100. I walked striding over the bodies.' He had never seen so many dead before.[33]

Wada's group walked for another three days, the men steadily descending until they reached a plateau. 'Far in distance, I could see the blue horizon between mountains,' he wrote, 'Kiari is near!' The fourth echelon reached Kiari on 18 October, 33 days after it had left Lae. Kiichi Wada stated that the journey took him 35 days, so he may have been two days behind the main group. For him, reaching Kiari gave great joy, but 'going back to Japan was nothing but a dream'.[34]

'For ten days on end,' Hiromasu Sato wrote, 'mountain and valley reappeared again and again in front us.' He watched as 'the bodies of those who simply could not go on started to pile up on both side of the path', just before his unit reached the foot of the range. A command orderly came down from the mountain and told Sato and his companions that 'There is snow on the top of the mountain. You must go over without a stop . . . If you must, kill yourself away from the path.'[35]

'We must reach the top before the sun disappears,' Sato's commander told his men before the final climb. 'Then we began to tackle wisteria vines clinging over an almost vertical cliff . . . There were already a few who gave up at the foot of cliff,' Sato wrote. Seven hours later he reached the summit, 'crawling with my legs as thin as my arms'. At the top he found a vast swamp and 'Soon I was left behind . . . I knew that if I stopped, the place would be my grave.' He passed a dead infantryman still holding the rifle he had carried to the summit in his arms. As night fell and the cold came, Sato still had not commenced the descent so he used the shavings from a tree and a photo he had of his mother to try to light a fire. 'I watched fire ignite the photo,' he wrote, 'burning slowly up from mother's feet to her smiling face.' Whispering 'Help me, Mother', he watched as the small fire came alive to give him warmth. Another man from Sato's unit, Gorô Kobayashi, soon joined him and helped build up the fire. With only their 'short-sleeved summer shirts and shorts', they 'held each other close to share the warmth'. Later in the night as he drowsed, Sato saw stragglers walking past in the moonlight and he told Kobayashi, 'This is no good. Let's walk, otherwise we'll freeze to death.' After some hours passed and the morning light began to pierce the darkness, Sato looked out across 'a sea of thick cloud, shrouding the world far below. We were standing on the edge of a precipice.'[36]

On the north coast steps were being taken to supply the Japanese evacuees once they had got over the range. Local natives were enlisted to carry the food and medical supplies that had been landed at Kiari up to the troops moving down to the coast. It had been planned to have more food available, but the twenty landing craft allocated to bring food from Madang were being used for troop transport following the Australian landing at Finschhafen on 22 September. A series of food caches were set up in the villages on the north side of the range with three and a half tonnes of rice carried up from Kiari to Ulap, 4 tonnes to Melanpipi, 4 tonnes to Wap and three and a half tonnes to Gilan. This meant that any troops that could get across the top of the Saruwaged Range and down to Gilan could be fed and this became the route out of the mountains.[37] 'They wept for joy when they met the units who were crossing from the other side,' Kane Yoshihara wrote.[38]

Although Masamichi Kitamoto had made it across, his strength had finally given out and he had to be carried to the coast on a stretcher, reaching Kiari twenty days after leaving Lae, about a week ahead of the rest of the first echelon. Here he met Colonel Shigeru Sugiyama, the operations officer for 18th Army, who told him, 'I wish to bow my head in gratitude for your strong legs . . . They say a man's special skill helps him in life but your

'Like beggars in a procession'

special skill has saved the lives of thousands of men.' Once he recovered, Kitamoto headed back to the top of the range to help the stragglers reach the coast. He saw that the survivors 'were a group of invalids . . . in no condition to fight'.[39]

The first troops from Lae had reached Kiari on 23 September. They would have been those that had left before the Kunda bridge route was cut by the Australian commandos on 11 September. The first retreating echelon did not reach Kiari until 9 October and, after four days of rest, the men went on to Sio on 14 October. On arrival the men 'presented a very pathetic picture'.[40]

Map 18: Sketch of Japanese evacuation route, September–October 1943 (*Japanese monograph 38*, p. 214, US Army)

Some 8650 men had left Lae, 6600 army troops and 2050 from naval units.[41] An 18th Army intelligence report dated 5 November 1943 stated that 5001 of the 6600 army troops (75.8 per cent) had reached Kiari by late October.[42] A post-war Japanese naval assessment stated that 1543 naval troops reached Kiari of the 2054 that had left Lae (75.1 per cent).[43] General Blamey's assessment that few of the enemy remnant 'will escape the hardship of the mountain tracks' was clearly wrong.[44]

•

From General Blamey down, the eyes of the Australian commanders were on the new offensives into the Ramu Valley and at Finschhafen. This had allowed the main body of the retreating Japanese army from Lae to reach the north coast almost untouched by Allied action. The unit that was ideally suited to the task of identifying the Japanese line of retreat was the Papuan Infantry Battalion. A PIB company had been operating in the Markham Valley as a screen for the 7th Division since the landing at Nadzab but the PIB company allocated to 9th Division, which had landed at Red Beach on 6 September, was not used in a similar screening role. A PIB platoon had supported the commandos at the Kunda bridge across the Busu River since 9 September but it was not until 30 September that this platoon had contacted Japanese stragglers on the track to Kemen, killing 23 of them over two days.[45]

On 12 October another PIB patrol surrounded Kemen and killed another eight enemy stragglers, all of whom had initially been found asleep. Although they only had one rifle between them, the stragglers all had hand grenades. The Japanese had been exchanging their weapons for food, one rifle getting the starving men one taro root. Another four Japanese stragglers, all weak and dying, were killed on the track down to Lumbaip and three more in Lumbaip itself. 'The Japs in this area are weak and dying as well as ill armed,' the PIB report noted. On 13 October, in response to a request for a live enemy prisoner, Private Kazuo Hanazawa was captured near Kemen and handed over to ANGAU personnel. Hanazawa was from the 15th Independent Machine Cannon Company and was one of the forlorn evacuees from Lae hospital, afflicted with malaria and beri beri and too weak to move. As with most of the other sick, the climb above Kemen was beyond him. Hanazawa didn't want to return to Japan as he considered himself a disgrace to his family and his country.[46]

Meanwhile natives working for Warrant Officer Charlie Blake from ANGAU, who was stationed at Gumbuk, reported that Japanese troops were in the area east and north-east of Boana. On 7 October two platoons from Captain Sydney Whitelaw's company of the 24th Battalion, which had crossed the Markham River, were ordered into the Boana area.[47] On 9 October it was reported that the head man at Bawan had said 'that the Japs were very sick and he could not bury them all'. There were also plenty of Japanese looking after the sick, most of them around Bainduang.[48] On 12 October Lieutenant Jeffrey Thomas led a sixteen-man patrol to Bawan, a village high up on a plateau and unapproachable during daylight without being seen. Climbing hand over hand for the final pinch in the pre-dawn darkness, Thomas's men reached Bawan without being seen and then split up to cover the two tracks leading out of the village. One group attacked the village at dawn and, although one of the enemy soldiers fought back with rifle fire and two grenades were thrown, fifteen Japanese were killed, including a medical officer. The capture of Bawan was a fine feat of arms by the Australians as the village was atop a 'rocky pimple with sheer sides which would be impossible to take by day'.[49]

One of the Japanese who tried to escape was captured. He was a medical orderly from the 238th Infantry Regiment who spoke a little English. He had left Salamaua with the last 30 men of his company on 9 September, reaching Lae three days later and leaving again on 14 September for the trek north. Suffering from malaria and weak legs he had dropped behind and it had been one of his jobs to give a grenade to wounded or sick men with little hope of recovery. He thought that being a prisoner was worse than death and, like many others in the same predicament, he didn't want to return to Japan as he considered that he had let his country down.[50]

On 12 October a 24th Battalion patrol reached the Sanem River north of Kemen. The retreating Japanese had come into the area some weeks earlier from Lumbaip, many of them unarmed, in poor condition and with no food. They later cut the bridge over the 50-metre-wide river, took food from the native population and headed north. The Australian patrol moved along the valley and on 19 October reported small groups of Japanese stragglers hiding along the Sanem River valley. 'Enemy dispersed by day but gather by night to sleep in out of way huts or encampment lean-tos,' the report noted.[51]

On 23 October a Japanese soldier and a Chinese carrier were captured on the track north of Bainduang. Two more Chinese carriers were captured nearby. The three Chinese, all brothers, had originally been taken from Hong Kong and shipped south to Salamaua. They had seen the Australians approaching Bainduang but had not warned the Japanese troops who were sheltering there. While most of the Japanese troops were killed, the three Chinese managed to surrender. Sores on their feet and legs indicated where they had been kicked by Japanese soldiers during the retreat from Lae and they had also been forced to live on grass. They were openly hostile to the Japanese prisoner. On 26 October they reached Boana and that night the three Chinese brothers tied the Japanese prisoner to a tree with signal wire around his neck. He survived, but when later interrogated in Lae the Chinese expressed a desire to finish the job by cutting his throat.[52]

On 16 October the 42nd Battalion, which had moved from Salamaua to Lae, took over from the 2/24th Battalion in the Busu River area. On 31 October patrols from the battalion reported 38 Japanese bodies and graves had been found in Lumbaip, Kemen and along the track between the two villages. The patrols also found evidence that not more than 110 Japanese had escaped via the Kunda bridge route before it had been cut on 11 September.[53] During October the 24th Battalion reported that 155 Japanese had been killed, 13 taken prisoner and 115 found dead along the evacuation route.[54]

Staff Sergeant Bob Emery, who had served with the NGVR on the outskirts of Lae following the Japanese landing in March 1942, was now back in the same area working with ANGAU. He followed the evacuation route along the Sanem Valley from Avin north to the headwaters below Mount Bangeta. The natives stated that no white man had ever travelled this track, but after the Japanese echelons had used it the track was now impassable. After the main force had passed through, the Japanese had apparently destroyed all the vine ropes, bridges and rails along the route.[55] On 3 November a 24th Battalion patrol confirmed

Emery's report, finding the track blocked in two places by landslides at the head of the Sanem River valley. This is where there was a vertical drop on one side of the track and a sheer rock face about 90 metres high on the other, the place where the retreating Japanese had scrambled like spiders across the rock face. A camp for 1000 men was found nearby containing at least 52 Japanese dead from cold or starvation or both. Five Japanese who were still alive were killed by the patrol.[56]

On 5 November a patrol to Samanzing reported that only six Japanese had been seen there since the start of the war, confirming that it was clearly not on the evacuation route. When two PIB sergeants, Robert MacIlwain and Cyril Duncan, climbed the range from Bungalumba up to Mount Salawaket in mid-November they found the track overgrown; it had played a minimal role in the Japanese evacuation. Local natives said it had not been used for twenty years and this confirmed that what had been one of the two planned Japanese evacuation routes had only been used during the withdrawal by one well-organised party of about 30 Japanese evacuees.[57]

•

It seemed quite extraordinary that an operation that had been so intricately planned and so well carried out by the Allies as Operation Postern had been unable to prevent the Japanese from evacuating Lae. The overriding failure on the Allied side was that of underestimating the enemy. This was the same mindset that had allowed Japanese successes at Pearl Harbor and in Malaya in the early days of the war and facilitated the advances across the Kokoda Track and to the outskirts of Wau during the war in

'Like beggars in a procession'

Papua and New Guinea. In all of the Operation Postern planning documents there was an overriding assumption that the Japanese forces at Lae would do nothing but fight to the death to hold the town. Once that assumption had been made it was only compounded by the lack of urgency to block the Japanese evacuation.

A failure to coordinate operations between the three separate ground forces once Operation Postern started had much to do with that. The I Corps commander, Lieutenant General Edmund Herring, needs to take most of the responsibility. He had shown during the campaign for the Papuan beachheads, and also in this campaign, that he was capable of working with the American allies, but in both campaigns he had shown much less ability in coordinating the Australian ground troops. Any thought that it may be prudent to at least strongly patrol the gap between the 7th and 9th Division was absent from the planning process. Knowing that the 7th Division had reached Yalu, Gordon Hart later wrote that 'from the 10th September onwards we were chaffing at the bit' at having to stay put at the Kunda bridge; 'we were expecting orders every day to make a contact'.[58] Hart's unit actually had an important role to play in holding the Kunda bridge crossing point, but this task could just as easily have been carried out by an infantry company, freeing up the independent company to patrol the east bank of the Busu River further upstream and thus prevent the 8650 Japanese evacuees from building a new crossing and evacuating Lae. Instead most of the 9th Division infantry battalions spent considerable time twiddling their thumbs on the east bank of the Busu River while they waited for their own bridge to be built.

On 20 September General Berryman noted in his diary that General Herring had shown 'reluctance and slowness in getting a 9 Div Bn en route to Muson [*sic*] when ordered by us to block enemy escape. He did not realise there was very little in front of 9 Div & to support his action he says 9 Div were strongly opposed.'[59] It is true that there was some delay in getting the 2/24th Battalion to Musom, but it was not significant as the main escape route was at the new Busu River crossing further upstream. The 2/24th Battalion didn't reach the site until three days after the last Japanese echelon had crossed. Properly used, the 2/4th Independent Company could have reached it a week earlier and blocked any Japanese attempt to cross.

Chapter 14

BEYOND LAE

When the Australians entered Lae they found only ruins. 'The whole place echoed with the shriek of galvanised iron as working parties pulled the tangled wreckage of houses into neat, salvageable heaps,' Peter Hemery observed. The ruins extended into the water. 'Rusted sheets of torn metal thrust from the cool, green water showed the last resting place of dozens of barges. One large invasion barge . . . looked as though a great cat, mad with fury, had torn the thing to pieces with its claws.'[1]

'The bristling fortress of Lae was undoubtedly an empty eggshell,' Bill Robertson observed.[2] Although the Allied forces had used a sledgehammer to smash that eggshell, it now meant that a significant Australian ground force as well as naval and air support was now available for subsequent operations using Lae as a forward base. Plans to deploy the 7th Division north-west into the Markham Valley and the 9th Division east to Finschhafen were now brought forward.

After the Allied strategy meeting on 16 September that had given the go ahead for the Markham Valley advance, General Chamberlin had told General Berryman that 'they wanted us to take on Finsch as quickly as possible'. A landing at Finschhafen, using 9th Division troops, was to go ahead as soon as Rear Admiral Barbey had enough shipping ready. The following day Barbey said he could get four APDs, six LSTs and fifteen LCIs into Lae within 48 hours, enough shipping to lift 5000 men. The first assault waves could be landed at Finschhafen 24 hours later. Berryman noted that this was a 'volte face', an about-face from the previous estimate of ten days for such an operation.[3] The success of the Lae operation and the opportunities that it had created had clearly galvanised General MacArthur's key commanders.

Even while the planning for the Lae operation had been underway, General Wootten had told Brigadier Victor Windeyer, the 20th Brigade commander, to 'cock your eye at Finsch—may have to do it'.[4] On 22 September, only six days after Lae had fallen, the men of Windeyer's brigade boarded Barbey's promised landing craft just east of Lae. As Wootten had earlier intimated, they were heading for Finschhafen, the next stepping stone on the long road to Tokyo. The 22nd Battalion, which had been landed at Yellow Beach, was already advancing east along the coast towards the same objective. It was only now that the detailed planning that had gone into the Lae operation, and the patience shown in building up an army, navy and air force that was strong enough to complete the capture of New Guinea, was reaping the greatest benefit.

Beyond Lae

The capture of Finschhafen had not been part of the original Postern plan, and although some planning had taken place, no orders could be issued until the course of the Lae operation was clear.[5] But it was now obvious that the rest of the Huon Peninsula was there for the taking and MacArthur finally had the resources to take advantage of that opportunity (see Map 19). Unfortunately his intelligence staff would underestimate the strength of the Japanese at Finschhafen and the final stronghold at Sattelberg would not fall until late November. With this key base secured, MacArthur would follow up with landings by US troops at Arawe and Cape Gloucester on West New Britain in December to secure the Vitiaz Strait. Another unopposed landing at Saidor on the north coast west of Sio would follow in January 1944, consigning all Japanese forces on the Huon Peninsula, including those who had crossed the Saruwaged Range in the retreat from Lae, to another perilous trek through the Finisterre Ranges to reach Madang.[6] However, Madang and even Wewak would soon be isolated by General MacArthur's bold drive west along the northern New Guinea coast which would culminate in the landings at Aitape and Hollandia on 22 April 1944.[7]

As a result of the victory at Kaiapit, the Markham and Ramu valleys were now open to General Vasey's 7th Division and by 25 September the three battalions of Brigadier Dougherty's 21st Brigade had been flown from Nadzab into Kaiapit. By early October General Vasey would have two brigades advancing west into the Ramu Valley against minimal opposition, capturing Dumpu on 4 October. A major airbase developed around Gusap would pave the way for Allied air superiority extending as far as the Japanese airfields at Hollandia in Dutch New Guinea. General Kenney's air force was then able to neutralise the Japanese

D-DAY NEW GUINEA

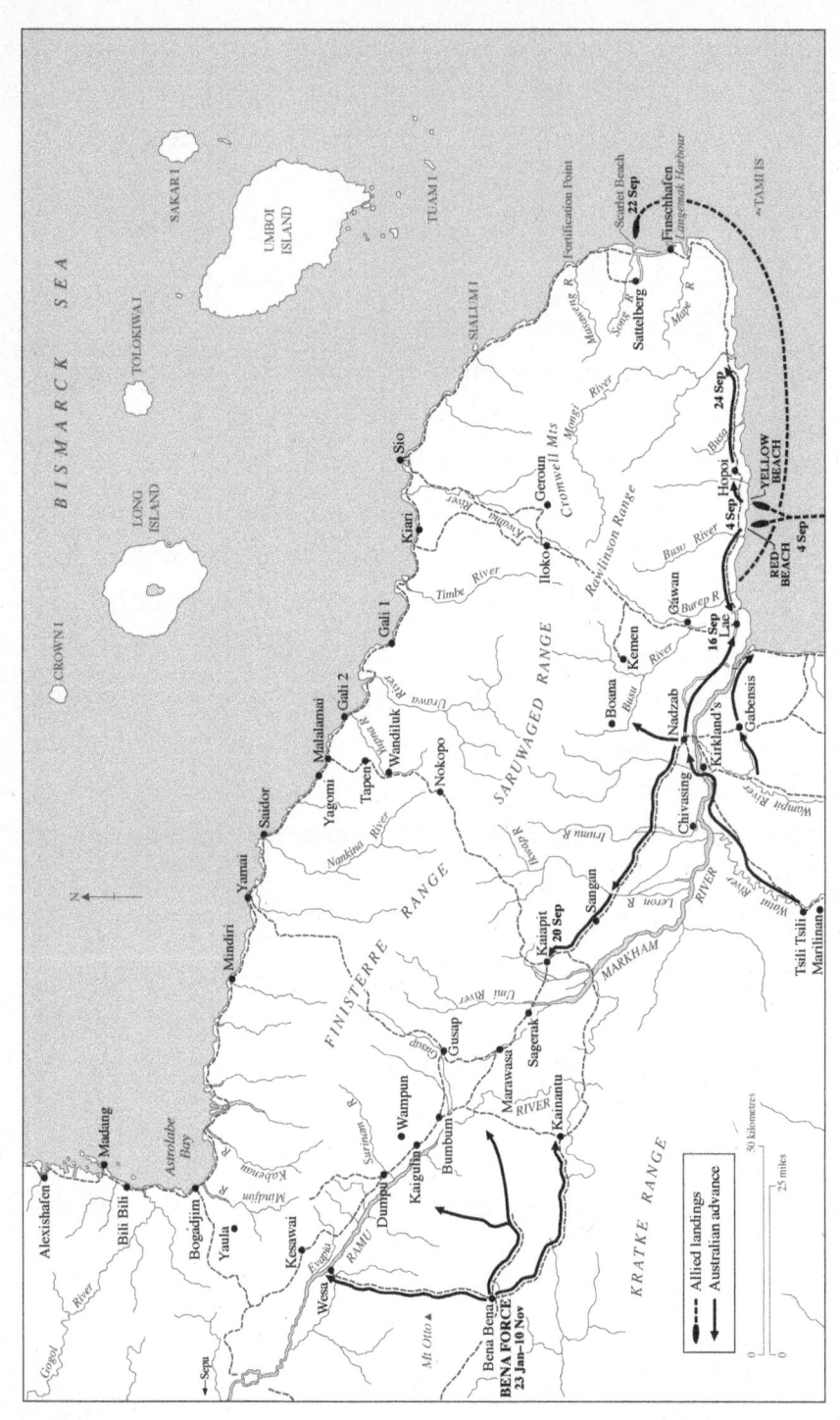

Map 19: Huon Peninsula–Ramu Valley operations, September 1943

air threat in New Guinea, enabling MacArthur to make his bold leap west to Hollandia.

The success of Operation Postern had opened the way for Allied victory in New Guinea.

•

Two major diversions contributed to the success of Operation Postern. The use of a small independent force at Bena Bena to divert Japanese attention from the main threats at Tsili Tsili and Nadzab had been particularly beneficial. Had those Japanese air and land units deployed against Bena Bena been used to defend Nadzab and attack the Tsili Tsili airbase, the Allied operation against Lae would have been a much more difficult and costly proposition. This was a good example of how the use of special forces, in this case Australian independent companies, could influence the course of a military campaign at a strategic level.

In a similar way, the stubborn Japanese defence of Salamaua, considered the shield of Lae, diverted attention from Lae's vulnerability to amphibious and air landing assaults that could bypass Salamaua. At a time when the Japanese command needed to take into account Allied amphibious and air transport capability, they had turned a blind eye to it. The warnings had been there: Allied air transport capability had denied Wau to the Japanese while the amphibious landing at Nassau Bay had helped to unhinge the defence of Salamaua. The threat of an Allied attack across the Markham River had been partially recognised with the deployment of a garrison at Markham Point, but this did not go nearly far enough. The Markham River crossings needed to be controlled at least as far as Nadzab and the Leron River junction. A ground force also needed to be in place around Nadzab to protect against any air landing east of the Leron River. Instead of being sent to Salamaua or being allocated to the Bena Bena operation, either the 80th or 78th infantry regiments should have been deployed at Nadzab. Defending the shorelines east of Lae was a more difficult proposition, but one of the greatest potential threats to such a landing, Japanese submarine patrols of the Huon Gulf, were non-existent due to all available submarines being pressed into transport service. The other major threat, that of air attack, was partly neutralised by Kenney's strikes against Wewak, and, although there remained a major air threat from Rabaul, this was mitigated by the heavy bombing of the intermediate airfields at Gasmata and Cape Gloucester.

•

Operation Postern, particularly the successful landing of the 503rd Parachute Infantry Regiment at Nadzab, also had a major impact on the war beyond New Guinea shores. The successful drop at Nadzab directly impacted the planning for the greatest D-Day of all, Operation Overlord, the Allied invasion of France on 6 June 1944.

The first American airborne operation of the war had taken place in North Africa as part of Operation Torch on 8 November 1942, also in concert with an amphibious landing. It had been a small scale, one battalion affair, and had taken place after an eight-hour flight from England. The operation had been a complete failure after the 39 aircraft failed to maintain contact, leading to considerable losses in aircraft and men for no effect. The next American airborne operation was made in support of Operation Husky, the Allied amphibious landings on Sicily in July 1943.

Two American air drops were made alongside two British operations. The first American drop was of an airborne regiment carried from North Africa by 226 troop transports. Only some 12 per cent of the paratroopers landed on the drop zone and even they were scattered by strong winds. However, the mere presence of airborne troops in the area disrupted the German response to the amphibious landings. Two days after the initial operation a second American regiment was dropped, this time onto an Allied-controlled airfield. Unfortunately Allied anti-aircraft fire, both over sea and over land, targeted the 144 transport aircraft, hitting 60 of them. Casualties were heavy: 229 paratroopers and 60 aircrew. Those paratroopers that managed to get down were widely scattered. Both American airborne operations on Sicily, as well as the two British drops, had to be considered failures.[8]

With five American airborne divisions being formed, and considerable air transport resources allocated to the airborne concept, these operational failures raised considerable doubts about the future of Allied airborne operations. General Dwight D. Eisenhower, the supreme commander of Operation Overlord and who was one of those doubters, appointed Major General Joseph Swing to form a board to review the airborne concept in light of the debacle over Sicily. Swing thought that the concept could still work if more joint training took place between the troop carrier squadrons and the parachute regiments; however, the Army Ground Forces Commander, Lieutenant General Lesley McNair, thought airborne operations could only work on a smaller scale. This was an opinion shared by Eisenhower.[9]

It was under this cloud over the future of the American airborne arm that the 503rd Parachute Infantry Regiment's successful drop at Nadzab took place. The Swing Board was meeting at that very time and the contrast of the success at Nadzab with the two recent debacles on Sicily was stark and certainly had an impact on the board. When the Swing Board made its final recommendations at the end of September 1943, large-scale airborne operations were supported. To have made such a recommendation, and for it to be adopted, an example of a successful operation was vital. The drop at Nadzab was that example.[10]

It is now history that a key component of Operation Overlord was the dropping of three Allied airborne divisions behind the German lines on the night prior to the D-Day landings. The presence of these units had a significant effect on the ability of German troops and armour to reinforce the D-Day beaches in time to stop the landings, and thus paved the way for the successful invasion of France.

•

There were also vital lessons learned from the amphibious phase of Operation Postern, the first operation by Rear Admiral Barbey's 7th Amphibious Force against an enemy-occupied coastline. Although much had been learned from the unopposed landings of Operation Chronicle, so much more experience had been gained from the Lae landings, including a costly lesson in how air cover had to be organised. With the success of the amphibious operation at Lae, Barbey was able to carry out another major landing at Finschhafen only eighteen days later. By the end of the war in the Pacific, Barbey's 7th Amphibious Force had carried out over 25 successful assault landing operations.[11]

The battle for Lae also stands as a great example of the capability of the Australian army. General Blamey noted that success 'was due to the skilful planning of the staff and the bold and able leadership of the commanders of all grades'.[12] As Chief of Army Lieutenant General Peter Leahy observed in 2003, 'As a successful exercise in complex operational planning, it is difficult to think of a better example than Lae.'[13]

ACKNOWLEDGEMENTS

To Professor David Horner and Doctor Mark Johnston, who supported my two research grant applications, and to the Australian Army for approving them.

To the staff at the research centre and the copyright section at the Australian War Memorial in Canberra. Also to the staff at the National Archives of Australia at Chester Hill in Sydney.

To Rick Dunn for his generosity in providing accommodation and sage advice during my trips to Washington. To Justin Taylan and Edward Rogers for their help and camaraderie researching at the US National Archives and US Naval Records in Washington. To Jim Zobel for his help at the MacArthur Archives in Norfolk, Virginia, and to the staff at the Office of Naval Records and Library in Washington for their assistance, including having some records declassified for me.

To Ian and Irene Priestley for their hospitality in Lae and to James Collins for getting me to some pretty remote spots around Lae. To John Douglas for his hospitality and assistance in Port Moresby.

A special thanks to Harumi Sakaguchi for access to Japanese accounts from Lae and for his skilful translation work. Thanks also to Steve Bullard for his translations and help with Japanese records from the AJRP. A big thanks to Keith Mitchell for his fine cartography and patience with my map changes.

To Rebecca Kaiser at Allen & Unwin for her support in getting the book proposal over the line. To my editor Angela Handley for again ensuring that every piece of this complex jigsaw was in the right place and to the copyeditor John Mahony for his diligent work. To Luke Causby for his outstanding design work.

NOTES

PROLOGUE
1 Kitamoto, *A Record of Marathon Adventures,* pp. 80–2. Wada, *The Lae Naval Guard Unit,* pp. 235–8.

CHAPTER 1: THE OBSERVATION GAME
1 NGVR WD, AWM52, 8/4/18, 21 January 1942.
2 Downs, *NGVR 1939–1943: A History,* p. 283.
3 NGVR WD, AWM52, 8/4/18, 21 Jan 1942.
4 Gilchrist interview, AWM67, 2/41, p. 11.
5 NGVR WD, AWM52, 8/4/18, 22–23 Jan and 2 Feb 1942.
6 Ibid., 5 Feb 1942. Burton interview with Bob Collins, *Harim Tok Tok,* vol. 74.
7 NGVR WD, AWM52, 8/4/18, 13 and 23 Feb 1942.
8 Bōeichō, *Senshi Sōsho: Port Moresby–Guadalcanal Campaigns,* ch. 2. The Japanese referred to Gasmata airfield as Surumi.
9 Ibid.
10 Ibid.
11 Ibid.
12 Ibid.
13 NGVR WD, AWM52, 8/4/18, 8 March 1942. Burton interview, *Harim Tok Tok,* vol. 74.
14 Morison, *History of United States Naval Operations in World War II, Vol. 3,* p. 388.
15 Nesmith, *No Higher Honor,* pp. 66–8.
16 AWM54, 589/7/32.
17 Bullard, *Japanese Army Operations in the South Pacific Area,* p. 41.

18 Burton interview, *Harim Tok Tok,* vol. 74.
19 Bōeichō, *Senshi Sōsho: Port Moresby–Guadalcanal Campaigns,* ch. 2.
20 Gillison, *Royal Australian Air Force: 1939–1942,* p. 460. 75 Sqn WD, NAA A9186 /95, pp. 007–9.
21 Bōeichō, *Senshi Sōsho: Port Moresby–Guadalcanal Campaigns,* ch. 2.
22 75 Sqn WD, NAA A9186 /95. pp. 009–11 and 019–20.
23 Bōeichō, *Senshi Sōsho: Port Moresby–Guadalcanal Campaigns,* ch. 2. Sakai, *Samurai,* p. 113.
24 Bōeichō, *Senshi Sōsho: Port Moresby–Guadalcanal Campaigns,* ch. 2.
25 Sakai, *Samurai,* p. 113.
26 AWM54, 589/7/20.
27 Ibid.
28 Ibid.
29 Burton interview, *Harim Tok Tok,* vol. 74.
30 Mollard notes, AWM93, 50/2/23/512.
31 AWM54, 589/7/20.
32 Bob Emery interview, AWM, MSA S0727, pp. 11–14.
33 Ibid., pp. 39–40.
34 Edwards interview, AWM67, 2/76.
35 White interview, AWM67, 2/117.
36 Downs, *NGVR 1938–1943: A History,* p. 285. Burton interview, *Harim Tok Tok,* vol. 74.
37 Emery interview, AWM, MSA S0727, pp. 42–3. Burton interview, *Harim Tok Tok,* vol. 74.
38 AWM54, 589/7/20.
39 Emery interview, AWM, MSA S0727, pp. 41–2. Lyon interview, AWM 67, 2/33. Downs, *NGVR 1938–1943: A History,* p. 177.
40 Downs, *NGVR 1938–1943: A History,* p. 284.
41 Emery interview, AWM, MSA S0727, pp. 43–4.
42 Ibid., pp. 46–9. NGF HQ WD, AWM52, 1/5/51, June 42, pp. 22–3.
43 McCarthy, *South-West Pacific Area First Year,* p. 87.
44 Burton interview, *Harim Tok Tok,* vol. 74.
45 Downs, *NGVR 1938–1943: A History,* p. 285.
46 Bullard, *Japanese Army Operations in the South Pacific Area,* p. 119.

CHAPTER 2: 'SUCH A DANGEROUS LOOKING MOB'
1 MacArthur interview, AWM67, 1/7, p. 19a.
2 Murray-Smith memoir, AWM67, 3/283.
3 Emery interview, AWM, MSA S0727, p. 50.
4 Pirie, *Commando Double Black,* p. 62.
5 Hamilton interview notes, AWM67, 3/154.
6 Wylie report, AWM54, 589/7/20.
7 Pirie, *Commando Double Black,* p. 85.
8 Wylie report, AWM54, 589/7/20. Murray-Smith memoirs, AWM67, 3/283.

Notes

9 For details, see Bradley, *Hell's Battlefield*, pp. 32–8.
10 Pirie, *Commando Double Black*, p. 86.
11 Wylie report, AWM54, 589/7/20. Murray-Smith memoirs, AWM67, 3/283, p. 17. Hamilton interview notes, AWM67, 3/154.
12 Murray-Smith memoirs, AWM67, 3/283, pp. 15–17.
13 Wylie report, AWM54, 589/7/20. See Photo 2 for an aerial view of Heath's Plantation.
14 Pirie, *Commando Double Black*, pp. 90–1. Murray-Smith memoirs, AWM67, 3/283, p. 18.
15 Pirie, *Commando Double Black*, p. 91.
16 Pirie, *Commando Double Black*, pp. 91–2. Hamilton interview, AWM67, 3/154.
17 Wylie report, AWM54, 589/7/20.
18 Murray-Smith memoirs, AWM67, 3/283, p. 19.
19 Pirie, *Commando Double Black*, p. 93. Wylie report, AWM54, 589/7/20. Hamilton interview notes, AWM67, 3/154.
20 Wylie report, AWM54, 589/7/20.
21 Pirie, *Commando Double Black*, pp. 92–3.
22 Wylie report, AWM54, 589/7/20.
23 Murray-Smith memoirs, AWM67, 3/283, p. 20.
24 Pirie, *Commando Double Black*, p. 88.
25 Murray-Smith memoirs, AWM67, 3/283, p. 21.
26 Hamilton interview notes, AWM67, 3/154.
27 Wylie report, AWM54, 589/7/20.
28 Bullard, *Japanese Army Operations in the South Pacific Area*, p. 119.
29 Murray-Smith memoirs, AWM67, 3/283, p. 21.
30 Pirie, *Commando Double Black*, pp. 98–9.
31 Ibid., p. 101.
32 Downs, *NGVR 1939–1943: A History*, p. 212. Pirie, *Commando Double Black*, pp. 101–2.
33 NGF HQ WD, AWM52, 1/5/51/155, 076–7. Whittaker interview, AWM67, 2/33, pp. 59–60.
34 Boxall, *A Story of the 2/5 Australian Commando Squadron AIF*, Foreword. 2/5th Ind Coy WD, AWM52, 25/3/5/1, 008.
35 Kenney diary, MMLA, RG54, 18/8/42.
36 Ibid., 8/9/42.
37 Ibid., 18/9/42.
38 Ibid., 23/9/42.
39 Blamey papers, AWM 3DRL6643, 2/47.
40 Ibid.
41 Letter to Kenney, 24/10/42. MMLA, RG54.
42 AWM54, 583/6/4. AWM54, 589/7/27.
43 Ford, *My New Guinea Diary*, pp. 33–4.
44 Ibid., p. 39.
45 Ibid., p. 81.

CHAPTER 3: 'WE WILL DIE FIGHTING'
1 AWM54, 589/7/14.
2 US Army, *Japanese monograph 45*, pp. 124–6.
3 For a detailed account, see Bradley, *Hell's Battlefield*, pp. 183–203.
4 Dunshea interview with author.
5 Graham, *None Shall Survive*, p. 63.
6 Brazenor and Fred Anderson interviews with author.
7 AWM55, 6/2, IR059, 6/3, IR091, IR098.
8 Cook and Cook, *Japan at War*, p. 301.
9 Wada, *The Lae Naval Guard Unit*, pp. 219–20.
10 AWM54, 643/6/8.
11 US Army, *Japanese monograph 37*, p. 124.
12 AWM55, 3/18, ATIS 140.
13 For a detailed account, see Bradley, *Hell's Battlefield*, pp. 204–13.
14 AWM54, 643/6/5. Saramoa is Salamaua.
15 Orita & Harrington, *I-Boat Captain*, pp. 142–3.
16 AWM55, 6–5, IR 220.
17 Kitamoto, *A Record of Marathon Adventures*, p. 50.
18 AWM54, 589/7/14.
19 51st Engineering Regt Field Diary, AWM55, 5/14, EP-159.
20 Bradley, *To Salamaua*, pp. 78–88.
21 AWM55, 6/5, IR231.
22 Yoshihara, *Southern Cross*, ch. 10.
23 Shinoda, *The 66th Infantry Regiment*.
24 US Army, *Japanese monograph 38*, p. 39.
25 Ibid., p. 140.
26 AWM55, 6/5, IR 220.
27 US Army, *Japanese monograph 38*, p. 49.
28 64th LOC Unit Field Diary, AWM55, 5/13, EP-146, p. 24.
29 Bruning, *Jungle Ace*, p. 110.
30 Army Air Forces, *The Fifth Air Force in the Huon Peninsula Campaign*, p. 193.
31 US Army, *Japanese monograph 38*, pp. 79–80.
32 Ibid., p. 59.
33 Yoshihara, *Southern Cross*, ch. 10.
34 US Army, *Japanese monograph 38*, p. 48.
35 Hashimoto, *Sunk*, p. 97.
36 Orita & Harrington, *I-Boat Captain*, pp. 143–5. Hashimoto, *Sunk*, pp. 68–77. Kenney diary, 19 March 1943, MMLA, RG54. Henebry, *The Grim Reapers*, pp. 78–81. Henebry gives the wrong date in his account.
37 Orita & Harrington, *I-Boat Captain*, pp. 145–7. Hashimoto, *Sunk*, pp. 77–83.
38 Hashimoto, *Sunk*, p. 83–5. NAA, A9186, 21, pp. 223 and 226.
39 AWM55, 3/13, ATIS 1205.
40 AWM55, 6/5, IR212.

Notes

41 AWM54, 589/7/14.
42 AWM55, 6/5, IR202 and IR226.
43 51st Division Intel Report, AWM55, 5/4, EP-44, 12 June 1943.
44 Orita & Harrington, *I-Boat Captain*, pp. 138–9. AWM 55, 6/5, IR212. AWM 54, 423/4/16, AE416.
45 Miller, *Cartwheel: The Reduction of Rabaul*, pp. 194–5.
46 AWM54, 779/3/22, AE82. Hashimoto, *Sunk*, p. 68.
47 51st Division Tactical Plan, AWM55, 5/5, EP-53.
48 Wada, *The Lae Naval Guard Unit*, pp. 217–18.
49 Ibid., pp. 218–19.
50 Register of aviation stores, Captured doc B 484-5893, Courtesy of Rick Dunn.
51 Hiroyuki Shindo, 'The Japanese Army's Strategy', in Dean (ed.), *Australia 1943*, pp. 74–84.
52 US Army, *Japanese monograph 38*, pp. 17–18.
53 AWM54, 589/4/13.
54 AWM55, 3/8, ATIS 891. AWM55, 6/5, IR220.
55 AWM54, 589/7/14.
56 US Army, *Japanese monograph 38*, p. 37.
57 51st Div Intel Report, AWM55, 5–4, EP-44, 25 July 1943.
58 Ibid., 21 August 1943.
59 AWM54, 589/4/12.
60 AWM54, 589/4/13.
61 AWM54, 589/3/12.
62 AWM52, 8/3/24/31, p. 72.
63 AWM54, 589/7/26. Only one 155 mm was spotted by Allied intelligence but two were later captured.
64 US Army, *Japanese monograph 38*, p. 21.
65 AWM54, 423/6/8.

CHAPTER 4: MOUNTAINS TO CLIMB

1 NGF HQ WD, AWM52, 1/5/51/032, 093.
2 AWM54, 519/6/58.
3 Kenney diary, MMLA, RG54, 19 August 1942.
4 Ibid., 29 May and 8 June 1943.
5 Berryman diary, 3 and 7 June 1943, AWM PR84/370, Item 3.
6 Kenney diary, MMLA, RG54, 6 June 1943.
7 Army Air Forces, *The Fifth Air Force in the Huon Peninsula Campaign*, p. 173.
8 US Army, *Japanese monograph 38*, pp. 4–9 and 26.
9 Ibid., p. 6.
10 ANGAU WD, AWM52, 1/10/1/008, pp. 88–90. US Army, *Japanese monograph 37*, pp. 160–2.
11 3rd Division HQ WD, AWM52, 1/5/4/039, p. 6.
12 ANGAU WD, AWM52, 1/10/1/009, 063.
13 Ryan, *Fear Drive My Feet*, p. 108.

14 Ibid., pp. 55–66.
15 Ibid., pp. 114–15.
16 ANGAU WD, AWM52, 1/10/1/007, pp. 131–3. Ryan interview with author. Ryan, *Fear Drive My Feet*, pp. 115–18.
17 Ryan, *Fear Drive My Feet*, p. 117–19. Four months later Ryan was told that Peter Ah Tun had been shot by the Japanese for collaboration, but, as Ryan discovered when he met Ah Tun again many years later in Lae, this was not the case.
18 Kitamoto, *A Record of Marathon Adventures*, pp. 3, 6, 9. Today called the Sarawaget Range.
19 AWM55, 5/5, EP-55, 20th Engineering Regt orders, 24 February 1943. Kitamoto, *A Record of Marathon Adventures*, pp. 1–4.
20 AWM55, 5/5, EP-55, 20th Engineering Regt orders, 24 April 1943. Kitamoto, *A Record of Marathon Adventures*, p. 10. In his account, Kitamoto confirms his orders came from Lieutenant Colonel Murai and this is important in establishing the date of Kitamoto's mission.
21 Kitamoto, *A Record of Marathon Adventures*, pp. 10–15. In a 1969 interview Kitamoto said he arrived in Lae on 3 April 1943 after a three-week journey from Teliata Point. However, Kitamoto's unit did not even reach Tuluvu until 8 April. Cross-checking of Japanese and Australian records shows that the three-week journey took place from 24 April, when Murai's official order was issued, to 18 May when the arrival of Kitamoto in Lae was recorded at 51st Division headquarters. AWM54, 741/5/14 also confirms the presence of Kitamoto's detachment near Bawan on 15 May. In the same 1969 interview Kitamoto said his unit reached Teliata Point by flying boat, contradicting his written account.
22 Ibid., pp. 17, 27, 30–3. Kitamoto refers to Dawat as Dagawat. It is today known as Dowat.
23 Ibid., pp. 37–9.
24 Ibid., pp. 40–4. Tukaget is also known as Tukwambet.
25 Ibid., pp. 52–4. Holmes, *Smiles of Fortune*, p. 66. 20th Division Intel Report, AWM55, 5/13, EP-145, 13 May 1943.
26 Kitamoto, *A Record of Marathon Adventures*, p. 54.
27 20th Division Intel Report, AWM55, 5/13, EP-145, 20 May 1943.
28 Ibid., 18 May 1943. Kitamoto, *A Record of Marathon Adventures*, pp. 48–50.
29 AWM55, 5/4, EP-44, 51st Division Intel Report, 27 April 1943.
30 Ibid., 28 April 1943.
31 Kitamoto, *A Record of Marathon Adventures*, pp. 54–5.
32 AWM54, 741/5/14. Ryan, *Brief Lives*, p. 76. Ryan, *Fear Drive My Feet*, pp. 141 and 153.
33 AWM54, 741/5/14.
34 20th Division Intel Report, AWM55, 5/13, EP-145, 13 May 1943.
35 AWM54, 741/5/14. Ryan, *Fear Drive My Feet*, pp. 177–8.
36 Kitamoto, *A Record of Marathon Adventures*, p. 45.

Notes

37 AWM54, 741/5/14. Ryan, *Fear Drive My Feet*, pp. 179–82. Kitamoto, *A Record of Marathon Adventures*, p. 45.
38 Kitamoto, *A Record of Marathon Adventures*, pp. 45 and 54.
39 'Honour where due', *Australian*, 25 April 2006.
40 US Army, *Japanese monograph 37*, pp. 163–6.
41 AWM55, 3/13, ATIS 1167.
42 US Army, *Japanese monograph 37*, pp. 171–4.
43 Kitamoto, *A Record of Marathon Adventures*, pp. 56–7.
44 Ibid., pp. 57–9.
45 20th Division Intel report and map, AWM55, 5/13, EP-145, 22 June. Also referred to as Ofmalakan, Wafmaragen or Orforfragen.
46 Kitamoto, *A Record of Marathon Adventures*, pp. 60–1.
47 ANGAU WD, AWM52, 1/10/1/012, pp. 74–5. AWM55, 3/10, ATIS 940.
48 51st Division Intel Report, AWM55, 5/4, EP-44, 25 June 1943.
49 ANGAU WD, AWM52, 1/10/1/012, p. 29. Kitamoto, *A Record of Marathon Adventures*, pp. 63–4.
50 51st Division Intel Report, AWM55, 5/4, EP-44, 10 August 1943.
51 AWM54, 741/5/4.
52 Ryan, *Fear Drive My Feet*, pp. 197 and 205. Ryan interview with author.
53 AWM54, 741/5/4.
54 Ibid.
55 ANGAU WD, AWM52, 1/10/1, June 43, p. 134. Ryan, *Fear Drive My Feet*, pp. 232–3.
56 ANGAU WD, AWM52, 1/10/1, June 43, p. 134. Ryan, *Fear Drive My Feet*, pp. 233–7.
57 Ryan interview with author. Ryan refers to the former Australian prime minister, who was found disoriented in a US hotel without his trousers.
58 51st Division Intel Reports, AWM55, 5/4, EP-44, 23, 24 and 27 June 43. Chivasing is also referred to as Jidishigu, Jibshingu and Jibushingu in these reports.
59 Advanced HQ WD, AWM52, 1/2/2/009, 092.
60 20th Division Intel report, AWM55, 5/13, EP-145, ATIS documents 5496 and 6022.
61 Kenney diary, MMLA, RG54, 6 June 1943.
62 ANGAU WD, AWM52, 1/10/1/013, pp. 70–6.
63 Whitehead letter, 20 July 1943, MMLA, RG54. Army Air Forces, *The Fifth Air Force in the Huon Peninsula Campaign*, p. 183.
64 AWM55, 3/13, ATIS 1167.
65 Byrne and Dunshea interviews with author.
66 Hawker letter, AWM67, 3/164.
67 Dunshea interview with author.
68 Kalamsei citation, AWM119, 048.
69 Byrne interview with author.
70 Foster notes, AWM67, 3/131.

71 Ibid.
72 Dexter, *The New Guinea Offensives*, p. 247. Hawker letter, AWM67, 3/164.

CHAPTER 5: THE SECRET AIRBASE
1 Leggett, 'Interview with General GC Kenney', NAA, SP300/3, 578.
2 Kenney diary, MMLA, RG54, 31 August 1942. Tokyo Rose was the nickname for an English-speaking Japanese broadcaster.
3 Ibid., 25 November 1942. Kenney refers to Faurot as Ferrault.
4 Ibid., 4 and 6 February 1943.
5 Ibid., 14 February 1943.
6 Yoshihara, *Southern Cross*, ch. 8.
7 Kenney diary, MMLA, RG54, 14 February 1943.
8 Ibid., 23 February 1943.
9 Ibid., 10 June 1943. Blamey to Herring, 15 June 1943, AWM54, 591/7/21.
10 Kenney diary, MMLA, RG54, 20 June 1943.
11 Blamey to Herring, 15 June 1943, AWM54, 591/7/21.
12 Kenney diary, MMLA, RG54, 1 September 1943.
13 Smith notes, AWM93, 50/2/23/387. Beattie notes, AWM93, 50/2/23/619.
14 Kenney diary, 29 May and 1 June 1943, MMLA, RG54.
15 Smith notes, AWM93, 50/2/23/387.
16 Ryan, *Fear Drive My Feet*, p. 290.
17 Frazier, *Tsili Tsili Sting, Vol. 2*, pp. 44–5, 48.
18 Ryan interview with author.
19 Frazier, *Tsili Tsili Sting, Vol. 2*, p. 70.
20 Kenney diary, MMLA, RG54, 8 June 1943.
21 Ibid., 7 June 1943.
22 Berryman diary, 12 June 1943, AWM PR 84/370, Item 3.
23 Kenney diary, MMLA, RG54, 13 June 1943.
24 Herring interview with Dexter. AWM172/6.
25 AWM54, 589/7/27.
26 Corfield, *Hold Hard, Cobbers Vol. 2*, p. 77.
27 Marston notes, AWM93, 50/2/23/176.
28 Savige notes on Official History, AWM 3DRL2529, Item 126.
29 3rd Division HQ WD, AWM52, 1/5/4/557, p. 2.
30 871st Engineer Aviation Battalion History, NARA, RG407, Box 15277.
31 Seale memoir emailed to author.
32 Kenney diary, MMLA, RG54, 10 July 1943.
33 Kenney, *General Kenney Reports*, pp. 269–70.
34 Herring interview with Dexter, AWM172/6.
35 Marston notes, AWM93, 50/2/23/176.
36 Ibid.
37 Seale memoir emailed to author.
38 Kenney, *General Kenney Reports*, p. 270.

Notes

39 Vern Tuskin interview, http://australiansatwarfilmarchive.unsw.edu.au/archive/250.
40 871st Engineer Aviation Battalion History, NARA, RG407, Box 15277.
41 Dunn, '4 *Kokugan* takes charge', p. 9.
42 51st Div Intel Report, AWM55, 5–4, EP-44, 21 August 1943.
43 Ryan, *Fear Drive My Feet*, p. 289.
44 AWM55, 6/4, IR 164.
45 Dunn, '4 *Kokugan* takes charge', p. 9.
46 AWM55, 6/4, IR 164. AWM55, 3/8, ATIS 881.
47 Ford, *My New Guinea Diary*, pp. 302–5. www.pacificwrecks.com/airfields/png/tsili-tsili.
48 Park, *Angels Twenty*, p. 89.
49 Dunn, '4 *Kokugan* takes charge', p. 10.
50 Corfield, *Hold Hard, Cobbers Vol. 2*, p. 87.
51 Ibid., pp. 89–90. 871st Engineer Aviation Battalion History, NARA, RG407. Doney lived to the age of 72.
52 Bullard and Tamura, *From a Hostile Shore*, pp. 66–8. Odgers, *Air War against Japan 1943–1945*, p. 70.
53 AWM55, 6/4, IR 164.
54 Odgers, *Air War against Japan 1943–1945*, p. 70.
55 Army Air Forces, *The Fifth Air Force in the Huon Peninsula Campaign*, pp. 59–60 and 160.
56 Henebry, *The Grim Reapers*, pp. 84–6.
57 Army Air Forces, *The Fifth Air Force in the Huon Peninsula Campaign*, pp. 62–3.
58 Ibid., p. 195.
59 Ibid., p. 196.
60 Ibid., p. 197.
61 Middlebrook, *Air Combat at Twenty Feet*, pp. 427–8.
62 Craven & Cate, *The Army Air Forces in WW2*, p. 179.
63 Henebry, *The Grim Reapers*, pp. 82–91. Craven & Cate, *The Army Air Forces in WW2*, p. 179.
64 US Army, *Japanese monograph 38*, p. 29.
65 Craven & Cate, *The Army Air Forces in WW2*, pp. 179–80.
66 Ibid., p. 180.
67 George Greene, 57/60th Bn, in Corfield, *Hold Hard, Cobbers Vol. 2*, p. 90.
68 Craven & Cate, *The Army Air Forces in WW2*, pp. 171–3.
69 Corfield, *Hold Hard, Cobbers Vol. 2*, p. 92.
70 Gray diary, 29 August 1943, AWM PR00433.

CHAPTER 6: MACARTHUR'S NAVY

1 Miller, *Cartwheel: The Reduction of Rabaul*, p. 19. AWM54, 589/3/11.
2 Kenney diary, 28 March 1943, MMLA, RG54.
3 AWM54, 519/6/58.

4   Ibid., AWM54, 589/7/1.
5   For more background on Berryman, see Dean, *The Architect of Victory*.
6   AWM54, 213/3/20.
7   Barbey, *MacArthur's Amphibious Navy*, p. 20.
8   Ibid., p. 9.
9   Ibid., p. 22.
10 Ambrose, *D-Day*, p. 45.
11 Barbey, *MacArthur's Amphibious Navy*, pp. 62–4.
12 Ibid., p. 44.
13 US Army, *History of the Second Engineer Special Brigade*, ch. 3.
14 Baldwin, 'Aviation and Amphibian Engineers in the Southwest Pacific', in Fowle (ed.), *Builders and Fighters: U.S. Army Engineers in World War II*, p. 357.
15 US Army, *History of the Second Engineer Special Brigade*, ch. 3.
16 AWM54, 213/3/20.
17 AWM54, 589/4/8.
18 Stephens, 'Rendezvous at Nassau Bay', *Khaki and Green*, pp. 149–52.
19 US Army, *History of the Second Engineer Special Brigade*, pp. 43–5.
20 AWM54, 213/3/20.
21 Berryman diary, 28 July 1943, AWM PR 84/370, Item 3.
22 AWM54, 589/7/27.
23 AWM54, 589/3/8.
24 Operation Chronicle Report, Barbey papers, ONR, Box 14, Item 210.
25 Barbey, *MacArthur's Amphibious Navy*, p. 66.
26 Task Force 76 WD, NARA, RG38, Box 250.
27 AWM54, 589/3/10.
28 AWM54, 213/3/20.
29 Berryman diary, 23 July 1943, AWM PR 84/370, Item 3.
30 Kenney diary, MMLA, RG54, 1 and 3 Sept 43.
31 Robertson notes, AWM93, 50/2/23/358.
32 Johnston & Stanley, *Alamein*, p. 265.
33 AWM54, 589/7/26.
34 Whitehead notes, AWM93, 50/2/23/476.
35 Australian Military Forces, *Jungle Warfare*, p. 43.
36 AWM54, 589/7/26.
37 Wells, *B Company Second Seventeenth Infantry*, p. 150.
38 Australian Military Forces, *Jungle Warfare*, p. 43.
39 2/13th Bn WD, AWM52, 8/3/13/001, p. 15.
40 AWM54, 589/3/9.
41 2/13th Bn WD, AWM52, 8/3/13/001, p. 19.
42 AWM54, 589/7/8. AWM54, 213/3/20.
43 AWM54, 589/7/1. AWM54, 213/3/20.
44 AWM54, 589/7/26.
45 AWM54, 213/3/20.
46 Ibid.

47 US Army, *History of the Second Engineer Special Brigade*, p. 44.
48 AWM54, 589/7/3.
49 AWM54, 591/7/5.
50 AWM54, 589/7/2. AWM54, 589/7/3.
51 2/13th Bn WD, AWM52, 3/3/13/001, p. 25.
52 AWM54, 589/7/3.
53 Task Force 76 WD, NARA, RG38, Box 251.
54 AWM54, 589/7/26.
55 AWM54, 589/3/2. AWM54, 589/6/7.
56 AWM54, 589/7/26.
57 AWM54, 213/3/20.
58 AWM54, 589/7/26.
59 AWM54, 589/7/2.
60 AWM54, 213/3/20.
61 Task Force 76 WD, NARA, RG38, Box 250.
62 AWM54, 589/7/2.
63 Gill, *Royal Australian Navy 1942–1945*, pp. 328–9.
64 US Army, *History of the Second Engineer Special Brigade*, p. 45.
65 Gill, *Royal Australian Navy 1942–1945*, pp. 328–9.
66 Morison, *Breaking the Bismarcks Barrier*, pp. 159–60.
67 AWM54, 589/4/3.
68 2/13th Bn WD, AWM52, 3/3/13/001, p. 28.

CHAPTER 7: AIRBORNE INFANTRY
1 AWM54, 589/7/27.
2 AWM54, 589/5/3.
3 AWM54, 213/3/20. For a detailed account of the Bulldog Road, see Bradley, *To Salamaua*, pp. 94–100.
4 AWM54, 589/3/9.
5 AWM54, 213/3/20.
6 Berryman diary, 15 July 43, AWM PR84/370, Item 3.
7 Kenney diary, MMLA, RG54, 1 September 43.
8 AWM54, 213/3/20.
9 AWM54, 589/5/3.
10 AWM54, 213/3/20.
11 Kenney diary, MMLA, RG54, 20 June 43.
12 AWM54, 589/7/27.
13 AWM54, 589/3/8.
14 AWM54, 591/7/5.
15 AWM54, 589/4/5.
16 AWM54, 589/7/27.
17 AWM54, 589/3/9.
18 AWM54, 213/3/20.

19 AWM54, 589/3/10, Part 2. Robertson letter, AWM93, 50/2/23/358. Herring letter, 23 July 1956, AWM 67/3, 167.
20 Ennis Whitehead letter, MMLA, RG54, 31 July 1943.
21 Robertson letter, AWM93, 50/2/23/358.
22 AWM54, 589/3/11.
23 Dougherty interview, AWM172/13.
24 AWM54, 589/7/2 Part 3.
25 Ibid.
26 Robertson letter, AWM93, 50/2/23/358.
27 AWM54, 589/7/2 Part 3.
28 AWM54, 589/7/23.
29 AWM54, 589/3/10 Part 2.
30 AWM54, 589/7/23.
31 Campbell, *The Operations of the 503 PIR*, pp. 6–7.
32 AWM54, 589/7/23.
33 Ibid.
34 AWM54, 589/7/2 Part 3.
35 Campbell, *The Operations of the 503 PIR*, pp. 9–10.
36 AWM54, 589/4/12.
37 AWM54, 589/4/13.
38 Campbell, *The Operations of the 503 PIR*, pp. 9–10.
39 AWM54, 589/4/12.
40 AWM54, 589/4/13. Robertson letter, AWM93, 50/2/23/358.
41 Dexter, *The New Guinea Offensives*, p. 338.
42 Norm Anderson interview with author.
43 Parsons, *Gunfire*, p. 162. Warby, *The 25 Pounders*, p. 303.
44 2/4th Field Regt WD, AWM52, 4/2/4, 31 August 1943.
45 AWM54, 589/7/1.
46 AWM54, 589/7/2 Part 3. Campbell, *The Operations of the 503 PIR*, p. 7.
47 AWM54, 589/7/2 Part 3.
48 AWM54, 589/7/23.
49 Campbell, *The Operations of the 503 PIR*, pp. 23–5.
50 AWM54, 589/7/23.
51 Campbell, *The Operations of the 503 PIR*, p. 11. AWM54, 589/4/12.
52 AWM54, 589/7/23. Campbell, *The Operations of the 503 PIR*, p. 14.
53 AWM54, 589/3/10 Part 2.
54 AWM54, 589/4/13.
55 AWM54, 589/7/1.
56 Robertson letter, AWM93, 50/2/23/358.
57 AWM54, 589/7/2 Part 3.
58 Milbourne memoir, AWM PR87/221, p. 36.
59 AWM54, 589/7/2 Part 3.
60 Ibid.
61 AWM54, 213/3/20.

Notes

62 AWM54, 589/7/2 Part 3.
63 AWM54, 213/3/20.
64 Berryman diary, AWM PR84/370, Item 3, 11 August 1943.
65 Ibid., 18 August 1943.
66 Dexter, *The New Guinea Offensives*, p. 279.
67 Berryman diary, AWM PR84/370, Item 3, 28 August 1943.
68 Chamberlin memo, 28 August 1943, AWM54, 589/3/9.
69 Herring notes on Official History, AWM67, 3/167.
70 Berryman papers, AWM PR84/370, Item 37.

CHAPTER 8: D-DAY DAWNS

1 Holmes memoir, AWM67, 3/169. AWM54, 589/3/5.
2 Australian Military Forces, *Jungle Warfare*, p. 43.
3 AWM54, 589/3/5.
4 20th Bde WD, AWM52, 8/2/20/100, 005.
5 AWM54, 589/3/5. AWM54, 589/3/10 Pt 2. AWM54, 589/7/3. Task Force 76 WD, NARA, RG38, 2553-M.
6 Hemery, 'Lae landing', NAA, SP300/3, 419.
7 2/23rd Bn WD, AWM52, 8/3/23/42, p. 4.
8 Carty, *Flickers of History*, pp. 70 and 90.
9 AWM54, 591/7/5.
10 2/13th Bn WD, AWM52, 8/3/13/001, pp. 30–1.
11 Holmes memoir, AWM67/3/169.
12 AWM54, 591/7/5.
13 Australian Military Forces, *Jungle Warfare*, p. 44.
14 Hemery, 'Lae landing', NAA, SP300/3, 419.
15 Wells, *B Company Second Seventeenth Infantry*, p. 152.
16 Wada, *The Lae Naval Guard Unit*, p. 228.
17 Holmes memoir, AWM67/3/169.
18 2/13th Bn WD, AWM52, 8/3/13/001, p. 33.
19 Ibid., p. 35.
20 Ibid., p. 36.
21 Clothier diary, 4 Sept 1943, AWM PR00588.
22 Tuckerman notes, AWM67, 3/405.
23 Wells, *B Company Second Seventeenth Infantry*, p. 152.
24 Hemery, 'Australians attack Lae', NAA, SP300/3, 398.
25 Windeyer interview, AWM93, 50/2/23/250.
26 US Army, *Japanese monograph 32*, p. 12B.
27 www.j-aircraft.com/research/rdunn/tuluvu/tuluvu_6. US Army, *Japanese monograph 38*, p. 27.
28 Yoshihara, *Southern Cross*, ch. 11. ATIS captured documents, Bulletin 768. Morison, *Breaking the Bismarcks Barrier*, p. 262. Morison confirms the presence of the nine aircraft at Lae and Adachi's citation confirms the three bombers were Sonias.

29 Wada, *The Lae Naval Guard Unit*, p. 228.
30 AWM54, 589/7/7.
31 Hemery, 'Australians attack Lae', NAA, SP300/3, 398.
32 Wells, *B Company Second Seventeenth Infantry*, p. 152.
33 Australian Military Forces, *Jungle Warfare*, p. 44. LCI 338 WD & AAR, NARA, RG38, 370-46-5-7, 370-45-6-5. LCI 338 was alongside LCI 339.
34 Clothier diary, 4 Sept 1943, AWM PR00588. Oscars were often misidentified as Zeros.
35 LCI 341 AAR, NARA, RG38, 370-45-6-5.
36 Share, *Mud and Blood*, pp. 259–60.
37 Carty, *Flickers of History*, p. 90.
38 Wada, *The Lae Naval Guard Unit*, p. 228.
39 Allan Dawes, 'We beat the Japs at their own game', *The News* (Adelaide), 7 September 1943.
40 Guard and Tring, *The Pacific War Uncensored*, pp. 174 and 177–8.
41 Fielder interview, http://4osailor.com/Sea%20Stories.htm. LCI 339 was towed off the beach and sunk 300 metres out to sea on 10 September. LCI 341 was recovered on 11 October and towed to Milne Bay.
42 ATIS captured documents, Bulletin 768, Item 9492.
43 Dickson, *Flying for the Army*, p. 53.
44 AWM54, 589/7/5.
45 US Army, *Japanese monograph 99*, p. 64.
46 AWM54, 589/6/8.
47 AWM54, 589/7/9.
48 AWM54, 589/7/2.
49 AWM54, 589/7/9.
50 AWM54, 589/5/1.
51 Allan Dawes, 'We beat the Japs at their own game', *The News* (Adelaide), 7 September 1943.
52 Weston, 'Landing at Lae', *Western Mail*, 16 September 1943.
53 AWM54, 589/7/3. AWM54, 589/7/9.
54 Whitehead interview, AWM93, 50/2/23/476.
55 Windeyer interview, AWM93, 50/2/23/250.
56 Army Air Forces, *The Fifth Air Force in the Huon Peninsula Campaign*, pp. 210–11.
57 www.j-aircraft.com/research/rdunn/tuluvu/tuluvu_7.
58 AWM54, 589/6/8. *USS Reid* War Diary, NARA RG38, 370-45-11-7.
59 LST 471 AAR, NARA, RG38, 370/45/8/2. AWM54, 589/7/7. Lambert, *Commando: From Tidal River to Tarakan*, pp. 269–71.
60 2/2nd MG Bn WD, AWM52, 8/5/2, Sept 43, p. 27.
61 Lambert, *Commando: From Tidal River to Tarakan*, p. 272.
62 Ibid., p. 271. 2/2nd MG Bn WD, AWM52, 8/5/2, Sept 43, p. 28. LST 473 is the USN number; it was also designated LST 143.
63 LST 473 WD and AAR, NARA, RG38, 370/46/8/1 and 370/45/8/2. Morison, *Breaking the Bismarcks Barrier*, p. 265.

Notes

64 Lambert, *From Tidal River to Tarakan*, p. 271.
65 2/2nd MG Bn WD, AWM52, 8/5/2, Sept 43, p. 28. LST 471 is referred to as LST 141.
66 Lambert, *From Tidal River to Tarakan*, p. 270.
67 Coyne manuscript, AWM MSS1928, p. 50.
68 LST 471 AAR, NARA, RG38, 370/45/8/2. Dexter, *The New Guinea Offensives*, p. 335.
69 AWM54, 589/6/8.
70 LST 471 WD, NARA, RG38, 370/46/8/1. Fielder interview, http://4osailor.com/Sea%20Stories.htm.
71 Fielder interview, http://4osailor.com/Sea%20Stories.htm.
72 AWM54, 589/6/8.
73 Rick Dunn notes for author.
74 2/13th Bn WD, AWM52, 8/3/13/001, pp. 36–7.
75 Odgers, *Air War against Japan 1943–1945*, pp. 74–5. King, *Song of the Beauforts*, p. 108. 22 Sqn WD, 4 September 1943, NAA, A9186/45.
76 Odgers, *Air War against Japan 1943–1945*, pp. 75–6. 22 Sqn WD, 5 September 1943, NAA, A9186/45.
77 Yoshihara, *Southern Cross*, ch. 11.
78 Bōeichō, *Senshi Sōsho, South Pacific Area operations (3) Munda-Salamaua*, pp. 367–70.
79 Iwata, *Hellish Battlefield*, p. 55.
80 Bōeichō, *Senshi Sōsho, South Pacific Area operations (3) Munda-Salamaua*, pp. 370–2.

CHAPTER 9: 'THE WOLF AT THE BACK GATE'

1 Robertson letter, AWM93, 50/2/23/358.
2 AWM54, 589/4/13. AWM54, 589/7/2.
3 Kenney, *General Kenney Reports*, p. 289.
4 Vasey papers, NLA MS3782, Box 20.
5 Breuer, *Geronimo*, p. 107.
6 Miller, *Cartwheel: The Reduction of Rabaul*, pp. 208–9. General Kenney said it only took one minute and ten seconds for the 1700 men to drop.
7 Campbell, *The Operations of the 503 PIR*, p. 17.
8 Weston, 'The story of the Lae campaign', *The Australasian*, 1 January 1944.
9 Miller-Randle, 'Invictus Asbestos', p. 112.
10 Kenney letter to Arnold, MMLA, RG54, 7 September 43.
11 AWM54, 589/4/13. 2/4th Field Regt WD, AWM52, 4/2/4, 5 Sept 1943.
12 Leggett, 'Australian artillery parachute to fame', NAA SP300/3, 556.
13 Norm Anderson interview with author. Henry, *The Story of the 2/4th Field Regiment*, pp. 210–11. AWM54, 589/7/2. Part 3.
14 Yoshihara, *Southern Cross*, ch. 11.
15 AWM54, 589/4/13. AWM54, 589/7/2. Peck, *Sappers of the Silent Seventh*, p. 314. McNicoll, *The Royal Australian Engineers 1919 to 1945, Vol. 3*, p. 191.

16 Peck, *Sappers of the Silent Seventh*, p. 315.
17 2/6th Field Coy WD, AWM52, 5/13/6, 5 Sept 1943. AWM54, 589/6/1. Peck, *Sappers of the Silent Seventh*, p. 313.
18 McInnes interview with author. AWM54, 589/7/2, Part 3.
19 AWM54, 589/7/2, Part 3.
20 5th Air Force Operations Report, NARA, RG18, Box 5658. AWM54, 589/4/13. 2/2nd Pioneer Bn WD, AWM52, 8/6/2, 6 Sept 1943.
21 5th Air Force Operations Report, NARA, RG18, Box 5658. AWM54, 589/4/13.
22 AWM54, 229/21/1.
23 Ibid.
24 Neil Wilson, 'Australia's secret tragedy', *Herald Sun*, 9 April 2004. Crooks, *The Footsoldiers*, p. 268.
25 Neil Wilson, 'Australia's secret tragedy', *Herald Sun*, 9 April 2004.
26 Crooks, *The Footsoldiers*, p. 268.
27 Neil Wilson, 'Australia's secret tragedy', *Herald Sun*, 9 April 2004.
28 2/33rd Bn WD, AWM52, 8/3/33/12, p. 83.
29 AWM54, 229/21/1.
30 Ibid.
31 Marshall notes, AWM93, 50/2/23/749.
32 Neil Wilson, 'Australia's secret tragedy', *Herald Sun*, 9 April 2004.
33 Bergerud, *Touched with Fire*, p. 103.
34 Crooks interview with author.
35 Ibid.
36 Crooks, *The Footsoldiers*, p. 272. Bergerud, *Touched with Fire*, p. 104. AWM54, 229/21/1.
37 Balfour-Ogilvy notes. Crooks, *The Footsoldiers*, p. 271.
38 Bergerud, *Touched with Fire*, p. 104.
39 MacDougal interview with author. MacDougal notes for author.
40 Crooks interview with author.
41 Balfour-Ogilvy notes.
42 AWM54, 229/21/1. The Official History lists 59 Australians killed and 92 injured but does not take into account that Private Mannix Daniel, Private Jack Ling and Private Edwin Cafe, all initially listed as injured, died from their injuries on 19 September 1943.
43 MacDougal notes for author.
44 871st Engineer Aviation Battalion History, NARA, RG407, Box 15277.
45 5th Air Force Operations Report, NARA, RG18, Box 5658.
46 Australian Military Forces, *Jungle Warfare*, pp. 21–3.
47 Yoshihara, *Southern Cross*, ch. 11.
48 Berryman diary, 5 September 1943, AWM PR 84/370, Item 3.
49 US Army, *Japanese monograph 99*, pp. 66–7.
50 Christensen, *That's the Way it Was*, p. 105.
51 AWM54, 779/3/22, AE106.

Notes

52 Dexter, *The New Guinea Offensives*, p. 341. Bunbury notes, AWM93, 50/2/23/818. Bunsell notes, AWM93, 50/2/23/181.
53 24th Bn WD, AWM52, 8/3/62/50, p. 22.
54 Bunbury notes, AWM93, 50/2/23/818.
55 24th Bn WD, AWM52, 8/3/62/50, p. 22.
56 Ibid.
57 Christensen, *That's the Way it Was*, pp. 109–10.
58 Bunsell notes, AWM93, 50/2/23/181. 24th Bn WD, AWM52, 8/3/62/50, pp. 07-12 and 22.
59 24th Bn WD, AWM52, 8/3/62/50, pp. 22–4.
60 Ibid.
61 Duell notes, AWM93, 50/2/23/814. Dexter, *The New Guinea Offensives*, p. 343.
62 Dexter, *The New Guinea Offensives*, p. 343. AWM52, 8/3/62/050, 007-8.
63 Christensen, *That's the Way it Was*, p. 108.
64 Betson, DeLacy, Hellens and Young are listed on MIA plaques at Lae cemetery.

CHAPTER 10: 'A TERRIFYING BUT MAGNIFICENT SPECTACLE'

1 Lawrie notes, AWM93, 50/2/23/657. Share, *Mud and Blood*, pp. 266–7.
2 US Army, *Japanese monograph 38*, pp. 45–6.
3 AWM54, 589/7/34. Lawrie notes, AWM93, 50/2/23/657. Fairlie and Schram citations, AWM119/33. Share, *Mud and Blood*, pp. 267–8. McRae notes, AWM93, 50/2/23/579.
4 Share, *Mud and Blood*, pp. 271–4.
5 AWM54, 589/7/34.
6 Share, *Mud and Blood*, pp. 275–6. AWM119/32. Lawrie notes, AWM93, 50/2/23/657.
7 AWM54, 589/7/34.
8 AWM54, 589/7/26. RAAF 4 Sqn WD, NAA, A9186, 170.
9 Miller-Randle, 'Invictus Asbestos', p. 115.
10 AWM54, 589/7/3. AWM54, 589/7/9.
11 Windeyer notes, AWM93, 50/2/23/250.
12 Weston, 'Landing at Lae', *Western Mail*, 16 September 1943.
13 AWM54, 589/6/2.
14 Ibid.
15 Wells, *B Company Second Seventeenth Infantry*, p. 154.
16 AWM54, 589/6/2.
17 AWM54, 589/7/34.
18 Ainslie letter, AWM93, 50/2/23/172.
19 Coates, *Bravery above Blunder*, p. 273.
20 Whitehead notes, AWM93, 50/2/23/476.
21 AWM54, 589/6/2.
22 Whitehead notes, AWM93, 50/2/23/476.
23 Evans letter, AWM93, 50/2/23/475.
24 2/28th Battalion Association DVD.

25 Mollard notes, AWM93, 50/2/23/512.
26 2/28th Battalion Association DVD.
27 Ibid., Mollard notes, AWM93, 50/2/23/512. AWM54, 589/7/36.
28 2/28th Battalion Association DVD.
29 Ibid., May citation, AWM119, 034.
30 Norman notes, AWM93, 50/2/23/578. Mollard notes, AWM93, 50/2/23/512.
31 Masel, *The Second 28th*, p. 165.
32 Mollard notes, AWM93, 50/2/23/512.
33 US Army, *Japanese monograph 38*, p. 46.
34 Herring to Vasey, 12 Sept 43, Vasey papers, NLA MS3782, Box 2, Folder 13.
35 Norman notes, AWM93, 50/2/23/578. 2/28th Battalion Association DVD.
36 2/28th Battalion Association DVD.
37 Ibid.
38 Ibid.
39 Evans letter, AWM93, 50/2/23/475.
40 US Army, *History of the Second Engineer Special Brigade*, p. 49.
41 AWM54, 589/7/24. AWM52, 8/3/24/031, p. 39.
42 AWM54, 589/7/24.
43 2/24th Bn WD, AWM52, 8/3/24/31, pp. 39–40.
44 Ibid., pp. 41–2. Gillespie notes, AWM93, 50/2/23/595.
45 2/24th Bn WD, AWM52, 8/3/24/31, pp. 42–3. AWM54, 589/7/9.
46 Whitehead notes, AWM93, 50/2/23/476.
47 AWM54, 589/7/27.
48 Wootten notes, AWM93, 50/2/23/330.
49 AWM54, 589/7/9.
50 AWM54, 589/7/26. US Army, *Japanese monograph 99*, p. 65.
51 AWM54, 589/7/26 and 589/7/34.
52 AWM54, 589/7/9. Horner, *The Gunners*, p. 363.
53 AWM54, 589/7/34.
54 Ibid.
55 Share, *Mud and Blood*, p. 283.
56 Whitehead notes, AWM93, 50/2/23/476.
57 2/23rd Bn WD, AWM52, 8/3/23/42, 217.
58 Lovell, *I Carried my Sketchbook*.
59 AWM54, 589/6/2.
60 Whitehead notes, AWM93, 50/2/23/476.
61 Ibid.
62 AWM54, 589/7/2.
63 AWM54, 589/6/2.

CHAPTER 11: 'FIX BAYONETS'
1 2/25th Bn WD, AWM52, 8/3/25/024, p. 96.
2 Gilbert notes, AWM93, 50/2/23/575.
3 Yoshihara, *Southern Cross*, ch. 11.

Notes

4 US Army, *Japanese monograph 38*, p. 46.
5 Henry, *The Story of the 2/4th Field Regiment*, pp. 220–1. AWM54, 589/7/33.
6 AWM54, 589/7/2, Part 3. 5th Air Force Operations Report, NARA, RG18, Box 5658.
7 AWM54, 589/7/33.
8 Ibid.
9 AWM54, 589/4/13.
10 AWM54, 589/7/33.
11 Gilbert notes, AWM93, 50/2/23/575.
12 Ibid.
13 Ibid.
14 Dexter, *The New Guinea Offensives*, pp. 373–5.
15 Bickle interview notes, AWM67, 3/31.
16 AWM54, 981/2/1.
17 Australian Army, *Reconquest*, pp. 49–50.
18 Dexter, 'VC winner wants to visit mother in Ireland', *The Argus*, 3 Jan 1944.
19 Bickle interview notes, AWM67, 3/31.
20 Gilbert notes, AWM93, 50/2/23/575.
21 Ibid.
22 2/31st Bn WD, AWM52, 8/3/31/14, p. 82. AWM54, 779/3/22, IR60. US Army, *Japanese monograph 99*, p. 66.
23 Weston, 'Australian airborne forces victory', *The Advertiser*, 17 September 1943.
24 Gilbert notes, AWM93, 50/2/23/575.
25 AWM54, 589/7/33. Fletcher interview with author.
26 MacDougal notes to author.
27 Crooks, *The Footsoldiers*, pp. 293–4.
28 Ibid., pp. 297–8.
29 Ibid., pp. 299–301.
30 Hall letter, AWM93, 50/2/23/664.
31 Scott citation, AWM119/34.
32 Laffin, *Forever Forward*, p. 122.
33 Crooks, *The Footsoldiers*, pp. 301–2.
34 Laffin, *Forever Forward*, pp. 119–20. 2/31st Bn WD, AWM52, 8/3/31/14, p. 7.
35 Laffin, *Forever Forward*, p. 120.
36 Marien, 'The Australian Soldier', NAA, SP300/656.
37 AWM54, 589/7/33.
38 AWM54, 589/7/1.
39 Ibid.
40 Ibid.
41 Gilbert notes, AWM93, 50/2/23/575.
42 Ibid.
43 Eather notes, AWM93, 50/2/23/269.

44   AWM54, 589/6/1.
45   Evans notes, AWM93, 50/2/23/475.
46   Richardson, 'The Australians who captured Lae', *Yank*, 12 November 1943.
47   Mollard notes, AWM93, 50/2/23/512.
48   Ibid.
49   AWM54, 589/6/1.

CHAPTER 12: 'A PRECARIOUS RETREAT'

1   Coyne manuscript, AWM, MSS1928, p. 53.
2   Hart letter, AWM93, 50/2/23/169.
3   Bottrell, *Cameos of Commandos*, p. 6.
4   2/4th Ind Coy WD, AWM52, 25/3/4, Sept 43. Miles interview with author.
5   Hart letter, AWM93, 50/2/23/169.
6   2/4th Ind Coy WD, AWM52, 25/3/4, Sept 43. Hart letter, AWM93, 50/2/23/169. Lambert, *Commando*, pp. 280–3. Miles interview with author.
7   Lambert, *Commando*, pp. 281–2.
8   Hart letter, AWM93, 50/2/23/169. Jaggar citation, AWM119, 033. Lambert, *Commando*, pp. 281–4.
9   Hart letter, AWM93, 50/2/23/169. Jaggar citation, AWM119, 033. Lambert, *Commando*, p. 284.
10 AWM55, 6/4, IR194.
11 Kitamoto, *A Record of Marathon Adventures*, pp. 75–6.
12 AWM54, 589/7/2, Part 3.
13 25th Bde WD, AWM52, 8/2/25/024, p. 17.
14 Yoshihara, *Southern Cross*, ch. 11.
15 AWM54, 589/7/2, Part 3.
16 Iwata, *Hellish Battlefield*, p. 55.
17 Kitamoto, *A Record of Marathon Adventures*, pp. 76–7.
18 Yoshihara, *Southern Cross*, ch. 11. Iwata, *Hellish Battlefield*, p. 55. AWM55, 6/5, IR206.
19 Kitamoto, *A Record of Marathon Adventures*, pp. 77–8.
20 Watanabe, *The Naval Land Unit that Vanished in the Jungle*, p. 20.
21 Iwata, *Hellish Battlefield*, p. 55.
22 US Army, *Japanese monograph 38*, p. 81. Avin also spelt Ave or Amyen.
23 US Army, *Japanese monograph 99*, p. 66.
24 AWM54, 589/7/2, Part 3. Gilbert notes, AWM93, 50/2/23/575.
25 7th Div HQ WD, AWM52, 1/5/14/59, p. 138.
26 25th Bde WD, AWM52, 8/2/25/24, pp. 10–11. Gilbert notes, AWM93, 50/2/23/575.
27 Robertson notes, AWM93, 50/2/23/358.
28 Miller-Randle, 'Invictus Asbestos', pp. 113–14.
29 Berryman diary, 15 September 1943, AWM PR84/370, Item 3.
30 Breuer, *Geronimo*, pp. 108–9.
31 US Army, *Japanese monograph 99*, p. 68.

Notes

32 7th Div HQ WD, AWM52, 1/5/14/50, p. 18. AWM54, 589/7/23.
33 US Army, *Japanese monograph 38*, p. 76.
34 7th Div HQ WD, AWM52, 1/5/14/50, p. 21.
35 US Army, *Japanese monograph 38*, p. 76.
36 Kitamoto, *A Record of Marathon Adventures*, p. 79.
37 Milbourne memoir, AWM PR87/221, p. 36.
38 AWM54, 589/7/2, Part 3. 2/14th Bn WD, AWM52, 8/3/14, Sept 43, p. 6.
39 Vasey to Herring, 16 Sept 1943, Vasey papers, NLA MS3782, Box 2, Folder 13.
40 Berryman diary, 16 September 1943, AWM PR84/370, Item 3.
41 King interview with author.
42 US Army, *Japanese monograph 38*, pp. 151–2.
43 AWM55, 6/4, IR 189. AWM54, 423/4/33.
44 King interview with author.
45 US Army, *Japanese monograph 38*, p. 153.
46 Nakai interview notes, AWM67, 10/12.
47 Vasey to Herring, 16 Sept 1943, Vasey papers, NLA MS3782, Box 2, Folder 13.
48 AWM54, 589/7/3, 589/7/8. 2/24th Bn WD, AWM52, 8/3/24/31, pp. 46–7.
49 2/24th Bn WD, AWM52, 8/3/24/31, pp. 48–9.
50 Lambert, *Commando*, p. 290.

CHAPTER 13: 'LIKE BEGGARS IN A PROCESSION'
1 US Army, *Japanese monograph 38*, p. 76.
2 24th Bn WD, AWM52, 8-3-62-53, p. 106. AWM55, 6/5, IR206. Dexter, *The New Guinea Offensives*, pp. 407–8.
3 US Army, *Japanese monograph 99*, p. 66.
4 AWM54, 779/3/22, AE105.
5 Wada, *The Lae Naval Guard Unit*, p. 231.
6 Sato, 'My survival: Five *sen* coin', www.awm.gov.au/ajrp.
7 2/24th Bn WD, AWM52, 8/3/24/31, p. 53. Wada, *The Lae Naval Guard Unit*, p. 232.
8 Wada, *The Lae Naval Guard Unit*, p. 232.
9 US Army, *Japanese monograph 38*, p. 81.
10 Ibid., p. 73.
11 Lambert, *Commando*, pp. 291–2.
12 2/24th Bn WD, AWM52, 8/3/24/31, p. 53.
13 Yoshihara, *Southern Cross*, ch. 11.
14 Sato, 'My survival: Five *sen* coin', http://www.awm.gov.au/ajrp.
15 AWM54, 779/3/22, AE81.
16 Kitamoto, *A Record of Marathon Adventures*, p. 79.
17 US Army, *Japanese monograph 38*, p. 73. Avin and Ave are the same village.
18 2/24th Bn WD, AWM52, 8/3/24/31, p. 100.
19 Kitamoto, *A Record of Marathon Adventures*, p. 80.

20 24th Bn WD, AWM52, 8/3/62/51, pp. 129–31 and 8/3/62/53, p. 106.
21 Wada, *The Lae Naval Guard Unit*, pp. 231–2, 235. Kitamoto, *A Record of Marathon Adventures*, p. 80.
22 US Army, *Japanese monograph 38*, p. 77.
23 Yoshihara, *Southern Cross*, ch. 11.
24 Kitamoto, *A Record of Marathon Adventures*, pp. 80–2.
25 Wada, *The Lae Naval Guard Unit*, pp. 233–4.
26 Ibid., pp. 235–6.
27 Ibid., p. 237.
28 Ibid., pp. 237–8.
29 24th Bn WD, AWM52, 8-3-62-56, pp. 84–6.
30 Kitamoto, *A Record of Marathon Adventures*, pp. 83–5.
31 US Army, *Japanese monograph 99*, pp. 67–8.
32 24th Bn WD, AWM52, 8-3-62-56, pp. 84–6.
33 Wada, *The Lae Naval Guard Unit*, pp. 238–40.
34 Ibid., p. 241.
35 Sato, 'My survival: Five *sen* coin', http://www.awm.gov.au/ajrp.
36 Ibid.
37 US Army, *Japanese monograph 99*, pp. 82 and 94.
38 Yoshihara, *Southern Cross*, ch. 11.
39 Kitamoto, *A Record of Marathon Adventures*, pp. 87–90.
40 Tanaka, *Operations of the Imperial Japanese Armed Forces*, p. 62. US Army, *Japanese monograph 99*, pp. 67–8.
41 Hattori notes, AWM67, 10/12.
42 AWM54, 589/7/14.
43 US Army, *Japanese monograph 99*, p. 67.
44 Berryman notes, AWM PR84/370.
45 PIB WD, AWM52, 8/4/4, October 1943. Sinclair, *To Find a Path*, pp. 177–8.
46 PIB WD, AWM52, 8/4/4, October 1943. AWM54, 779/3/22, AE96. AWM55, 6/5, IR228.
47 24th Bn WD, AWM52, 8/3/62/53, p. 5.
48 Ibid., p. 7.
49 Ibid., pp. 11, 164–6.
50 AWM55, 6/5, IR 220.
51 24th Bn WD, AWM52, 8/3/62/53, pp. 82, 98.
52 Ibid., p. 109.
53 42nd Bn WD, AWM52, 8/3/81/16, pp. 18, 54.
54 24th Bn WD, AWM52, 8/3/62/53, p. 44.
55 Ibid., p. 24.
56 24th Bn WD, AWM52, 8/3/62/56, pp. 84–6.
57 PIB WD, AWM52, 8/4/4, Nov 1943. Dexter, *The New Guinea Offensives*, p. 409.
58 Hart letter, AWM93, 50/2/23/169.
59 Berryman diary, 20 September 1943, AWM PR84/370, Item 3.

Notes

CHAPTER 14: BEYOND LAE
1. Hemery, 'The morning after', NAA, SP300/3, 425.
2. Bill Robertson notes, AWM93, 50/2/23/358.
3. Berryman diary, 16 September 1943, AWM PR 84/370, Item 3.
4. Windeyer interview, AWM93, 50/2/23/250.
5. AWM54, 589/7/27.
6. For more detail, see Bradley, *Hell's Battlefield*, pp. 334–42.
7. Ibid., pp. 378–86.
8. Lowe, *Nadzab (1943)*, pp. 12–17.
9. Ibid., pp. 20–1.
10. Ibid., pp. 61–5.
11. Barbey, *Seventh Amphibious Force*, Annex (C).
12. Berryman notes, AWM PR84/370.
13. Dennis & Grey (eds), *The Foundations of Victory*, p. xv.

BIBLIOGRAPHY

Records and archives

1) NATIONAL ARCHIVES OF AUSTRALIA:
A9186, RAAF Squadron Operational Records
B883, Second Australian Imperial Forces Personnel Dossiers, 1939–1947
SP300/3, ABC Radio Transcripts, 1939–1945
    398   Peter Hemery, 'Australians attack Lae'
    419   Peter Hemery, 'Lae landing'
    425   Peter Hemery, 'The morning after'
    556   Dudley Leggett, 'Australian artillery parachute to fame'
    578   Dudley Leggett, 'Interview with General GC Kenney'
    656   Bill Marien, 'The Australian Soldier'

2) AUSTRALIAN WAR MEMORIAL, CANBERRA:
AWM52, Unit histories, 1939–1945 War
AWM54, Written records, 1939–1945 War
AWM55, ATIS records of POW Interrogations and Captured Documents
AWM67, Gavin Long, papers of the Official Historian
  Interviews:
    1/07   Douglas MacArthur, SWPA HQ: 2/12/44
    2/33   Hugh Lyon, NGVR: 6/12/43
    2/33   George Whittaker, NGVR: 6/12/43
    2/41   Victor Gilchrist, NGVR: c. 1/12/43
    2/76   Bill Edwards, NGVR: 5/3/45
    2/117 Francis White, NGVR: 9/12/44

Documents:
　3/31　　Johnson Bickle, 2/25th Battalion, interview notes
　3/131　 Tom Foster, 2/2nd Independent Company, notes
　3/154　 Jim Hamilton, 2/5th Independent Company, interview notes
　3/164　 Bill Hawker, 2/7th Independent Company, letter
　3/167　 Edmund Herring, New Guinea Force, records
　3/169　 John Holmes, 2/13th Battalion, memoir
　3/283　 Stephen Murray-Smith, 2/5th Independent Company, memoir
　3/405　 Vic Tuckerman, 24th Battalion, notes
　10/12　 Takushiro Hattori, Imperial Japanese Army, notes
　10/12　 Masutaro Nakai, Imperial Japanese Army 78th Regiment, interview notes

AWM93, AWM registry files—First Series
　50/2/23/169　Gordon Hart, 2/4th Independent Company, letter
　50/2/23/172　Robert Ainslie, 2/48th Battalion, letter
　50/2/23/176　Robert Marston, 57/60th Battalion, notes
　50/2/23/181　Aylmer Bunsell, 24th Battalion, notes
　50/2/23/250　Victor Windeyer, 20th Brigade, interview notes
　50/2/23/269　Ken Eather, 25th Brigade, notes
　50/2/23/330　George Wootten, 9th Division, notes
　50/2/23/358　Bill Robertson, 7th Division, letter
　50/2/23/387　George Smith, 24th Battalion, notes
　50/2/23/475　Bernard Evans, 24th Brigade, letter
　50/2/23/476　David Whitehead, 26th Brigade, interview notes
　50/2/23/512　Keith Mollard, 2/32nd Battalion, notes
　50/2/23/575　Les Gilbert, 2/25th Battalion, notes
　50/2/23/578　Colin Norman, 2/28th Battalion, notes
　50/2/23/579　Eric McRae, 2/23rd Battalion, notes
　50/2/23/595　Andrew Gillespie, 2/24th Battalion, notes
　50/2/23/619　Adrian Beattie, 24th Battalion, notes
　50/2/23/657　Don Lawrie, 2/23rd Battalion, notes
　50/2/23/664　Ken Hall, 2/31st Battalion, letter
　50/2/23/814　Arthur Reginald Duell, 24th Battalion, notes
　50/2/23/818　Clyde Bunbury, 24th Battalion, notes

AWM119, Office of Military Secretary, Army honours and awards: confidential working files

AWM172, Official History, 1939–45 War, Series 1 (Army) Volume VI: Records of David Dexter
　06　Edmund Herring, New Guinea Force, interview: 6/4/51
　13　Ivan Dougherty, 21st Brigade, interview

AWM218, Card Index to interrogation reports of captured Japanese personnel

Murdoch Sound Archive:
　S0727　Bob Emery, NGVR: 13/3/90

Bibliography

Private records:
- 3DRL/0514   Stephen Murray-Smith journal
- 3DRL/2529   Stan Savige papers
- 3DRL/6643   Thomas Blamey papers
- MSS1928   Ralph Coyne manuscript
- PR00433   Alan Gray diary
- PR00588   Les Clothier diary
- PR84/370   Frank Berryman diary and papers
- PR87/211   James Milbourne memoirs

3) NATIONAL LIBRARY OF AUSTRALIA, CANBERRA:
MS3782 George Vasey papers

4) NATIONAL ARCHIVES AND RECORDS ADMINISTRATION, COLLEGE PARK, MARYLAND, USA:
- RG 18   Records of the Army Air Forces
- RG 38   US Navy records
- RG 82   US Navy photographs
- RG 111   US Army Signal Corps photographs
- RG 342   USAAF photographs
- RG 373   USAAF aerial reconnaissance films
- RG 407   US Army War Diaries

5) MACARTHUR MEMORIAL LIBRARY AND ARCHIVES, NORFOLK, VIRGINIA, USA:
- RG03   Papers of General Douglas MacArthur
- RG 54   George C. Kenney diary and papers

6) OFFICE OF NAVAL RECORDS AND LIBRARY, WASHINGTON DC, USA:
Papers of Rear Admiral Daniel E. Barbey

Published references

BOOKS AND MONOGRAPHS

Ambrose, Stephen E., *D-Day June 6, 1944: The climactic battle of World War II*, Touchstone, New York, 1994

Army Air Forces Historical Office, *The Fifth Air Force in the Huon Peninsula Campaign: January to October 1943*, 1946

Australian Army, *Reconquest*, Director General of Public Relations, 1944

Australian Military Forces, *Jungle Warfare*, Australian War Memorial, Canberra, 1944

Australian Military Forces, *Khaki and Green*, Australian War Memorial, Canberra, 1943

Barbey, Daniel, *MacArthur's Amphibious Navy*, US Naval Institute, Annapolis, 1969
Barbey, Daniel, *Seventh Amphibious Force Command History*, US Navy, 1945
Bergerud, Eric, *Touched with Fire*, Penguin Books, New York, 1996
Bōeichō Bōei Kenshūjo Senshishitsu (ed.), *Senshi Sōsho (War history series: South Pacific Area Army Operations. (1) Port Moresby–Guadalcanal Campaigns)*, Asagumo Shinbunsha, Tokyo, 1968
——, *Senshi Sōsho (War history series: South Pacific Area Army Operations. (3) Munda–Salamaua Campaigns)*, Asagumo Shinbunsha, Tokyo, 1970
Bottrell, Arthur, *Cameos of Commandos*, self published, 1971
Boxall, Jack, *A Story of the 2/5 Australian Commando Squadron AIF*, self published, 1960
Bradley, Phillip, *To Salamaua*, Cambridge University Press, Melbourne, 2010
——, *Hell's Battlefield*, Allen & Unwin, Crows Nest, 2012
Breuer, William B., *Geronimo*, St Martin's Press, New York, 1992
Bruning, John R., *Jungle Ace*, Brassey's Inc., Dulles VA, 2001
Bullard, Steven (translator), *Japanese Army Operations in the South Pacific Area: New Britain and Papua campaigns 1942–43*, Australian War Memorial, Canberra, 2007
Bullard, Steven and Tamura, Keiko, *From a Hostile Shore*, Australian War Memorial, Canberra, 2004
Campbell, Elden C., *The Operations of the 503 PIR*, The Infantry School, Fort Benning GA, 1949
Carty, William, *Flickers of History*, Harper Collins, Sydney, 1999
Christensen, George, *That's the Way it Was*, 24th Battalion (AIF) Association, 1982
Coates, John, *Bravery above Blunder*, Oxford University Press, South Melbourne, 1999
Cook, Haruko & Cook, Theodore, *Japan at War*, New Press, New York, 1992
Corfield, Robin S., *Hold Hard, Cobbers, Volume 2*, 57/60th Battalion (AIF) Association, Glenhuntly Victoria, 1991
Craven, Wesley & Cate, James, *The Army Air Forces in World War II, Vol. IV*, University of Chicago Press, Chicago, 1950
Crooks, Bill, *The Footsoldiers*, 2/33rd Battalion Association, Brookvale, 1971
Dean, Peter J., *The Architect of Victory*, Cambridge University Press, Melbourne, 2011
Dean, Peter J. (ed.), *Australia 1943*, Cambridge University Press, Melbourne, 2014
Dennis, Peter & Grey, Jeffrey (eds), *The Foundations of Victory: The Pacific War 1943–1944: The Chief of Army's History Conference 2003*, Army History Unit, Canberra, 2004
Dexter, David, *Australia in the War of 1939–1945, Series 1, Vol. VI: The New Guinea Offensives*, Australian War Memorial, Canberra, 1961
Downs, Ian, *The New Guinea Volunteer Rifles, 1939–1943: A History*, Pacific Press, Broadbeach Waters Queensland, 1999
Ford, Ernest C., *My New Guinea Diary*, White Stag Press, Roseville CA, 2010

Bibliography

Fowle, Barry W. (ed.), *Builders and Fighters: U.S. Army Engineers in World War II*, US Army Corps of Engineers, Fort Belvoir Virginia, 1992

Frazier, Everette E., *Tsili Tsili Sting, Volume 2*, Desk Top Production, San Antonio TX, 1992

Gill, George Hermon, *Australia in the War of 1939–1945, Series 2, Vol. II: Royal Australian Navy 1942–1945*, Australian War Memorial, Canberra, 1968

Gillison, Douglas, *Australia in the War of 1939–1945, Series 3, Vol. I: Royal Australian Air Force 1939–1942*, Australian War Memorial, Canberra, 1962

Graham, Burton, *None Shall Survive*, F.H. Johnston Publishing, Sydney, 1946

Guard, Harold & Tring, John, *The Pacific War Uncensored*, Casemate, Havertown PA, 2011

Hashimoto, Mochitsura, *Sunk: The story of the Japanese submarine fleet 1942–1945*, Cassell and Company Ltd, London, 1954

Henebry, John, *The Grim Reapers*, Pictorial Histories Publishing, Montana, 2002

Henry, Russell, *The Story of the 2/4th Field Regiment*, Merrion Press, Melbourne, 1950

Holmes, John, *Smiles of Fortune*, Kangaroo Press, East Roseville NSW, 2001

Horner, David, *The Gunners*, Allen & Unwin, St Leonards, 1995

Iwata, Kamesaku, *Hellish Battlefield*, Jyomo Newspaper Publication Bureau, 1989

Johnston, Mark, *That Magnificent 9th*, Allen & Unwin, Crows Nest, 2002

Johnston, Mark & Stanley, Peter, *Alamein: The Australian Story*, Oxford University Press, South Melbourne, 2002

Kenney, George, *General Kenney Reports*, Duell, Sloan and Pearce, New York, 1949

King, Colin, *Song of the Beauforts*, Air Power Development Centre, Tuggeranong ACT, 2008

Kitamoto, Masamichi, *A Record of Marathon Adventures in the New Guinea War*, Australian War Memorial, Canberra, 1968

Laffin, John, *Forever Forward*, 2/31st Australian Infantry Battalion Association, Newport NSW, 1991

Lambert, George, *Commando: From Tidal River to Tarakan*, 2/4th Commando Association, 1994

Lovell, Ken, *I Carried my Sketchbook*, John Sissons, Hughesdale Victoria, 1984

Lowe, James P., *Nadzab (1943)*, Louisiana State University, 2004

McCarthy, Dudley, *Australia in the War of 1939–1945, Series 1, Vol. V: South-West Pacific Area—First Year*, Australian War Memorial, Canberra, 1959

McNicoll, Ronald, *The Royal Australian Engineers, 1919 to 1945, Volume 3: Teeth & Tail*, Corps Committee of RAE, Canberra, 1982

Masel, Philip, *The Second 28th*, 2/28th Battalion and 24th Anti-Tank Company Association, Perth, 1961

Middlebrook, Garrett, *Air Combat at 20 Feet*, Author House, Indiana, 2004

Miller, John, *Cartwheel: The Reduction of Rabaul*, United States Army, Washington, 1990

Morison, Samuel E., *History of United States Naval Operations in World War II: Volume 3, The Rising Sun in the Pacific*, Little, Brown & Co., Boston, 1953
——, *History of United States Naval Operations in World War II: Volume 6, Breaking the Bismarcks Barrier*, Naval Institute Press, Annapolis, 2010
Nesmith, Jeff, *No Higher Honor*, Longstreet, Atlanta, 1999
Odgers, George, *Australia in the War of 1939–1945, Series 3, Vol. II: Air War against Japan 1943–1945*, Australian War Memorial, Canberra, 1957
Orita, Zenji & Harrington, Joseph D., *I-Boat Captain*, Major Books, Canoga Park CA, 1976
Park, Ted, *Angels Twenty*, University of Queensland Press, St Lucia Queensland, 1994
Parsons, Max, *Gunfire: A History of the 2/12 Australian Field Regiment 1940–1946*, Globe Press, Melbourne, 1991
Peck, Lindsay, *Sappers of the Silent Seventh*, 7th Division Engineers Association, Sydney, c. 1989
Pirie, Andy, *Commando Double Black*, 2/5th Commando Trust, Sydney, 1993
Ryan, Peter, *Fear Drive My Feet*, Angus and Robertson, Sydney, 1959
——, *Brief Lives*, Duffy & Snellgrove, Sydney, 2004
Sakai, Saburo, *Samurai*, ibooks, New York, 1957
Share, Pat (ed.), *Mud and Blood*, Heritage Book Publications, Braeside, 1978
Shinoda, Masuo, *The 66th Infantry Regiment at Salamaua*, Maru supplement no. 2, Ushio Shobō, Tokyo, 1986
Sinclair, James, *To Find a Path, Vol. 1*, Crawford House Press, Bathurst NSW, 1990
Tanaka, Kengoro, *Operations of the Imperial Japanese Armed Forces in the Papua New Guinea Theatre during WWII*, Japan Papua New Guinea Goodwill Society, Tokyo, 1980
Tann, Lloyd, *2/5th Australian Field Ambulance*, self published, 1987
United States Army, *History of the Second Engineer Special Brigade*, The Telegraph Press, Harrisburg PA, 1946
——, *Japanese monograph 32: Southeast Area Air Operations Record, Nov 1942 – Apr 1944*, Department of the Army, 1958
——, *Japanese monograph 37: 18th Army Operations Vol. I*, Department of the Army, 1958
——, *Japanese monograph 38: 18th Army Operations Vol. II*, Department of the Army, 1958
——, *Japanese monograph 99: Southeast Area Naval Operations Part II, Feb–Oct 1943*, Department of the Army, 1947
Wada, Kiichi, *The Lae Naval Guard Unit that Crossed Saruwaged Range*, Maru supplement no. 2, Ushio Shobō, Tokyo, 1986
Warby, John, *The 25-Pounders*, 2/6th Field Regiment Association, Pymble, 1995
Watanabe, Tetsuo, *The Naval Land Unit that Vanished in the Jungle*, Tabletop Press, Canberra, 1995
Wells, Harry, *B Company Second Seventeenth Infantry*, self published, 1984
Yoshihara, Kane, *Southern Cross*, Doris Heath translation, Australian War Memorial, Canberra

Bibliography

NEWSLETTERS
Harim Tok Tok, Newsletter of the NGVR and PNGVR Ex-Members Association Inc, vol. 74, April 2011

NEWSPAPER, JOURNAL AND MAGAZINE ARTICLES
Dawes, Allan, 'We beat the Japs at their own game', *The News* (Adelaide), 7 September 1943
Dexter, Frank, 'VC winner wants to visit mother in Ireland', *The Argus*, 3 January 1944
Richardson, Dave, 'The Australians who captured Lae', *Yank*, 12 November 1943
Ryan, Peter, 'Honour where due', *The Australian*, 25 April 2008
Weston, Mervyn, 'Australian airborne forces victory', *The Advertiser*, 17 September 1943
Weston, Mervyn, 'Landing at Lae', *The Western Mail*, 16 September 1943
Weston, Mervyn, 'The story of the Lae campaign', *The Australasian*, 1 January 1944
Wilson, Neil, 'Australia's secret tragedy', *The Herald Sun*, 9 April 2004

Unpublished references
2/28th Battalion Association, DVD of interviews supplied to author
Bain, Don, 3rd Division HQ, Photographs supplied to author
Balfour-Ogilvy, John, 2/33rd Battalion, Notes (22 July 1969) supplied to author
Dickson, Ron, No. 4 Squadron RAAF, 'Flying for the Army', Memoirs supplied to author
Dunn, Richard, '4 *Kokugan* takes charge', Article supplied to author
Dunshea, Pat, 2/7th Independent Company, Records supplied to author
MacDougal, Dave, 2/33rd Battalion, Notes supplied to author
Miller-Randle, Alec, No. 4 Squadron RAAF, 'Invictus Asbestos', Memoir supplied to author
Sato, Hiromasa (translated by Ms Kaoru Kikuchi), 'My survival: Five *sen* coin', Article supplied to author
Seale, Walter, US 871st Engineer Aviation Battalion, Memoir supplied to author

Interviews and private communication
Anderson, Fred, RAAF No. 30 Squadron, interview: 28/3/04, letter: 30/3/04
Anderson, Norm, 2/4th Field Regiment, interview: 11/4/13
Brazenor, Bob, RAAF No. 30 Squadron, interview: 27/3/04
Byrne, Ted, 2/7th Independent Company, interviews: 6/1/05, 4/5/05, 6/5/11
Dunshea, Pat, 2/7th Independent Company, interviews: 29/11/04, 13/12/04, 15/12/04, 22/7/09, 10/8/09
King, Gordon, 2/6th Independent Company, interviews: 13/4/02, 21/7/02
Loffman, Phil, 2/28th Battalion, letter: 10/8/09
MacDougal, Dave, 2/33rd Battalion, interview: 4/10/02, letter: 8/7/03
McInnes, Alan, 2/2nd Pioneer Battalion, interview: 29/9/01

Miles, Norm, 2/4th Independent Company, interview: 25/4/08
Miller-Randle, Alex, RAAF No. 4 Squadron, interview: 11/2/03, letter: 7/3/03
Roberts, Merv, 2/33rd Battalion, interviews: 3/2/02, 5/6/03
Ryan, Peter, ANGAU, interview: 5/1/06

Online sources
4-0 sailor, http://4osailor.com
Australian War Memorial, www.awm.gov.au
Australians at War Film Archive, http://australiansatwarfilmarchive.unsw.edu.au/
Commonwealth War Graves Commission, www.cwgc.org
Department of Veterans' Affairs, www.ww2roll.gov.au
Hyperwar archive, www.ibiblio.org/hyperwar
j-aircraft.com, www.j-aircraft.com
National Archives of Australia, www.naa.gov.au
National Library of Australia, www.trove.nla.gov.au
Pacific Wreck Database, www.pacificwrecks.com

INDEX

Adachi, Lt Gen Hatazo 50-1, 58, 150, 154, 233
Ah Tun, Peter 61
Ainslie, Lt Col Robert 193
Alexishafen 98, 150
Allanson, FO Tom 163
Aluki 190-1
Anderson, FO Bruce 9
Anderson, L Cpl Frank 17-18
Anderson, Sgt Fred 37
Anderson, Lt John 217, 227
Anderson, Pte Norm 134, 168-9
Angus, Capt William 144
Anthony, Lt Colin 16
Apo 157, 191-2
Araki, Lt Asakichi 43-4
Arawe 46, 273
Arnold, Gen Henry 99, 168
Atkinson, Lt Jack 189
Atzera Range 212-4, 239-43, 250, 254
Australian Army
    Kanga Force 28, 31-2
    New Guinea Force 14, 56, 84, 102, 130, 141, 181, 240
    Wampit Force 140, 181, 224
    field companies
    2/3rd Fld Coy 205

2/5th Fld Coy 211
2/6th Fld Coy 140, 169-70
2/7th Fld Coy 154
2/8th Fld Coy 90
field regiments
14th Fld Regt 205
2/4th Fld Regt 133, 172, 211
2/6th Fld Regt 204
2/12th Fld Regt 204-5
independent companies
1st Ind Coy 14
2/2nd Ind Coy 57, 78
2/4th Ind Coy 158-61, 229-30, 247, 270
2/5th Ind Coy 20, 30
2/6th Ind Coy 244
2/7th Ind Coy 54, 57, 78
infantry battalions
24th Bn 85, 167, 181, 224, 265-7
57/60th Bn 87
2/13th Bn 115-17, 121, 143-9, 188
2/14th Bn 138, 243-4, 246
2/15th Bn 121, 144
2/16th Bn 242-4, 246
2/17th Bn 121, 144, 154
2/23rd Bn 121, 149-52, 188, 206
2/24th Bn 192-3, 201-2, 247, 270
2/25th Bn 172, 209-18, 226-7, 239

Index

2/27th Bn 246
2/28th Bn 194–5, 200
2/31st Bn 178, 212, 221, 223, 227
2/33rd Bn 173, 178, 211–14, 219–22
2/43rd Bn 200
2/48th Bn 192–3
infantry brigades
17th Bde 31–3
18th Bde 104, 114, 203
20th Bde 121–2, 144, 149, 272
21st Bde 32–3, 128, 224, 242–3, 273
24th Bde 155, 192, 194, 202, 228
25th Bde 124, 130, 209, 225, 239
26th Bde 122, 191–3, 201–2
other units
2/2nd MG Bn 122, 158–9
2/2nd Pnr Bn 132, 140, 169–71, 214, 223
2/3rd Pnr Bn 114, 143
2/4th Lt AA Regt 120, 154, 204
7th Cavalry Regt 32–3
ANGAU 58–9, 85, 129, 265, 267
NGVR 2–5, 8, 11–12, 15–18, 20
PIB 87, 166, 264, 268
Avin 238, 255, 260, 267

Baker, FO John 163
Bainduang 238, 256, 265–6
Balfour-Ogilvy, Capt John 176–7
Barbey, Rear Adm Daniel 104–11, 116–17, 120, 141, 272, 278
Bawan 66, 68, 265–6
Beal, Sgt Paul 29
Bena Bena 54–8, 77–8, 86–7, 275–6
Benness, Lt Edwin 196–7, 200
Beros, Sapper Bert 170
Berryman, Maj Gen Frank 102, 272
  and Blamey 57, 86, 113, 128, 244
  and Herring 241, 244, 269
  and Kenney 56–7, 86, 125
  and Vasey 128, 141
Betson, L Cpl Allan 185
Beveridge, Lt Andrew 80
Bewapi Creek 21–2
Bickle, Pte Johnson 215
Bismarck Sea 36, 39, 61–2, 69, 164
Blake, WO Charles 265

Blamey, Gen Sir Thomas 19, 86, 112, 128, 140, 264, 278
  and Berryman 57, 241, 244
  and Kenney 84, 113, 126
  and MacArthur 31–2, 103, 124, 137
Blundell, Cpl Harold 184
Boana 12, 52, 60, 66–70, 73, 211, 242–3, 265–7
Bogadjim 69, 76, 78–9, 141
Bomura, Sgt Maj Akira 91–2
Booth, Sgt Bob 21–3, 25
Boram airfield 82, 92, 96–8
Bottrell, Chaplain Arthur 230
Bourke, Cpl Patrick 115, 122, 147–9
Boxall, Pte Jack 20, 24, 26, 30
Brazenor, FO Bob 37
Brooks, Lt John 199
Buang Ranges 5, 149
Buhem River 188
Buiem River 188
Bulldog Road 123–5
Bulldog Track 10, 14, 59
Bulolo 2, 5, 20–1, 85, 127, 181
Bulolo Valley 9–11, 32, 59, 123, 225
Bulu Plantation 118–19, 148
Bulwa 5, 14, 20
Buna 30–2, 103, 114, 203–4, 207
  port 116–17, 144–6, 158, 162, 225
Bunga River 188, 190
Bungalumba 60, 66–8, 235, 238, 268
Burep River 157, 192–4, 204–5
Burns, Lt Geoff 214
Bunbury, Capt Clyde 182
Burton, Sgt Stan 5, 7, 12, 18
Buso River 119, 154, 156
Busu River 48, 60–1, 118, 242–3, 256
  Australian crossing 193–202, 230–3
  Japanese crossing 230, 238, 249–53
But airfield 82, 94, 96
Butibum River 14, 203, 239, 241–3
Butler, Capt William 217
Byrne, Lt Ted 78–9

Cairns 45, 108–10, 113–15, 130
Caldwell, Fred 175
Cape Bushing 39, 41, 52
Cape Cretin 52, 158

316

Index

Cape Gloucester 42, 142, 157, 273
Carpender, Vice Adm Arthur 103, 121
Carter, FO Sydney 190
Cartwheel plan 101-2, 104
Carty, William 146, 152
Chaffey, Sgt Bill 29
Chamberlin, Brig Gen Stephen 104, 110, 124, 126, 140-1, 244, 272
Chapman, Maj Gen John 102
Childs, Lt Fred 182-5
Chivasing 52, 58-9, 67, 75-6, 91
Christensen, Sgt George 186
Clark, L Cpl John 17
Clayton, Lt Alan 168
Clothier, Cpl Les 149, 152
Cochrane, Rfn George 16
Colvin, Lt Col George 148
Condon, Pte Ambrose 'Jim' 176
Cotton, Lt Col Tom 173, 177, 213, 221
Cox, Lt William 'Sam' 229-30, 232
Coyne, L Sgt Ralph 160-1, 229
Crooks, Sgt Bill 173, 175-7
Crouchley, Sgt John 198
Cullen, Capt Harry 220

Dagua airfield 82, 96-8
Dampier Strait 41, 62
Davies, Pte Harry 175
Davies, Capt John 206
Dawat 64
Dawes, Allan 153, 156
DeLacy, Pte Russell 185
Dennis, Pte Edgar 'Mick' 24
Deschamps, Capt Paul 144
Dexter, Capt David 79-80
Dickson, FO Ron 154
Diddy camp 12, 15-22, 27, 167
Doberer, Lt Frederick Bill 20-7
Dobodura 135, 140, 203, 207, 241
    airbase 43, 84, 97, 130, 137, 226
    supply to 115, 125-6, 225
Doney, Pte William 93-4
Dougherty, Brig Ivan 128, 177, 224, 243, 273
Duchatel, Maj Charles 85
Duckham, Cpl Jack 214-15
Dudley, Capt Joe 189

Duell, Capt Arthur 182, 185-6
Dumpu 57, 142, 244, 273
Duncan, Sgt Cyril 268
Dunshea, Lt Pat 78-9
Durand airfield 173-4, 177

Eather, Brig Ken 130, 209, 212, 219-20, 226-8
Edwards, Maj Bill 12, 15
Edwards' Plantation 212, 220-2, 226, 249-50
Eisenhower, Gen Dwight D. 106, 277
Ellis, Pte Frederick 174
Emery, S Sgt Bob 14-17, 20, 267-8
Emery, Rfn John 17
Emery's Plantation 12, 226
Endo, Lt Col Torahei 38
Erap River 60, 67, 167
Esau, Capt Ken 114-15, 143, 147, 152
Evans, Brig Bernard 192-4, 198-202

Fagan, L Cpl Harry 170
Fairlie, Cpl Dave 188-9
Fewings, Pte Ernest Ray 175
Fielder, PO Fay 153, 161-2
Finisterre Range 57, 69, 76-7, 233
Finschhafen 37-43, 102, 121, 141-2
    Australian landing at 262-4, 272-3
Fleay, Lt Col Norman 28, 31
Fletcher, Cpl Dick 219
Ford, S Sgt Ernest 33-4, 93
Foster, Cpl Tom 80
Frazier, Lt Everette 85-6
Fujita, Rear Adm Ruitaro 35, 180

Gabensis 4, 11
Gabmatzung 28, 133, 166
Gabsonkek 11, 133, 166
Gasmata 6, 46, 157, 163, 276
Gawan 60, 66-7, 238, 247
Gilan 64, 262
Giles, Pte Tom 80
Gillespie, Lt Col Andrew 201
Gona 32, 216
Goodenough Island 126, 164
Gordon, Cpl Jim 222
Gow, Capt Gilbert 214-17, 227

Index

Graham, Burton 36
Gray, Sgt Alan 99
Gray, Cpl Henry 184
Green, Cpl Dave 221
Gregson, Pte Jack 29
Guadalcanal 28, 122
Guard, Harold 153

Hall, Maj Ken 221-2
Halsey, Adm William 102, 111-12
Haly, L Cpl Alan 231-2
Hamersley, Pte Andrew 233
Hamilton, Lt Horace 221-2
Hamilton, Pte Jim 22, 25-6
Hamilton, Pte Rob 22-3, 25
Hammer, Brig Heathcote 114
Hampel, Pte Ian 254
Handley, Capt Edwin 144
Hanisch, Cpl Keith 159
Hanlon, Pte Bill 232
Hannah, Lt James 196-7
Hansa Bay 99, 142
Harrison, Pte William 189
Hart, Lt Gordon 229-31, 248, 269
Hawker, Lt Bill 78, 80
Hayes, Capt Horace 221-2
Heath, Bertie 2, 21
Heath's Plantation 12, 17, 52, 133
   battle for 211-14, 217-19, 223-4
   commando raid on 21-9
Heavey, Brig Gen William 108-9, 120
Hellens, Pte Bill 185
Hemery, Peter 145-9, 151, 271
Henderson, Pte Allan 195, 199-200
Henebry, Capt John 43-4, 95
Herring, Lt Gen Edmund 224, 241
   as I Corps CO 115, 140, 244, 269
   role in Lae plan 102, 126-8, 141
   and US forces 84, 87-9, 124-8
Hill, Sgt Bernie 215
Hillberg, Pte Max 93
Hollandia 50, 273-5
Holmes, Pte John 143, 148
Hopkins, Brig Ron 31
Hopoi 48, 52, 149, 154, 188, 190
Howard, Lt Roy 14, 16-17
Howe, Pte Fred 26

Howes, Capt James 214
Howlett, Capt Les 67-9, 73-5
Hulcup, Cpl Wally 25
Hunter, Pte Bill 232
Huon Gulf 5, 8-12, 46, 121, 147, 276
Hutchins, Seaman John 159-60
Hutchinson, Col David 129, 244

Imperial Japanese Army
   18th Army 43, 50-1, 58, 98, 150, 164, 169, 234, 253, 262-4
   20th Div 41, 51, 57, 66, 69
   41st Div 41, 51, 57, 66, 179
   51st Div 36, 50-2, 164, 245
   air units 49, 83, 91, 94, 98
   engineers 62, 69, 210, 249
   regiments
   21st Regt 48, 58
   66th Regt 41, 218
   78th Regt 245, 276
   80th Regt 51, 245, 256, 276
   102nd Regt 36, 48
   115th Regt 36, 39, 48
   238th Regt 42, 51, 182, 266
Imperial Japanese Navy 6-8
   2nd Maizuru SNLP 18, 35
   3rd Kure SNLP 7
   5th Sasebo SNLP 28, 35, 218, 238
   5th Yokosuka SNLP 35
   82nd Naval Garrison 18, 35, 164, 188, 250
   air units 9-10, 49, 159
   destroyers 7, 37, 39, 41
   submarines 43-6, 48, 180
Iwata, Kamesatu 164, 235-7

Jackson, Maj James 223
Jackson, Sqn Ldr John 9-11
Jackson's airfield 136, 173-5, 209
Jacobsen's Plantation 12, 14, 17, 29, 212, 221, 226
Jaggar, Pte Brian 159, 231-2
Jensen's Plantation 209, 212
Jones, Lt Col George 130, 133

Kagayama, Sgt Shogo 249-50, 256
Kaiapit 57, 69-72, 244-6, 273

Index

Kalamsei 78–9
Kankityo 69, 245
Kasenobe 60, 65, 68
Kelliher, Pte Richard 215–16
Kelly, L Cpl Peter 221
Kemen 60, 238, 242, 253–5, 264–7
Kennedy, Capt Ted 182
Kenney, Lt Gen George 30–3, 56–7, 81–2, 89–90, 95–9, 203
  and Blamey 32, 84–6, 113
  and Herring 84, 126–7, 128
  and MacArthur 30–1, 87, 128, 167
Kesawai 70, 77
Kiari 62, 70, 235, 250, 256, 261–4
King, Maj Gordon 244–6
Kinsler, Col Ken 130–1, 242
Kiriwina Island 101, 111, 126
Kirkland's camp 75–6, 169–70
Kitamoto, Lt Masamichi 62–73
  in Lae retreat 233–8, 242, 255–63
Kneen, Maj Paul 20–7
Kunda bridge 66, 230–1, 238–9, 247–9, 253–4, 263–4, 267–9

Labu 12, 182–3
Lackey, Capt John 33–4
Lae
  air attacks 8–11, 43–4, 81–2, 163
  Allied capture of 226–8
  Allied landing at 143–57
  Japanese airbase at 38, 51
  Japanese capture of 6–7
  Japanese retreat 233–43, 247–64
  Japanese strength at 35, 39, 52–3
Laidlaw, FO Tom 190
Laing, Cpl James 176
Lakekamu River 14, 123–4
landing craft, Allied 106, 120
landing craft, Japanese 40–3
Lane's bridge 218–19
Langford, Sgt Donald 85
Lawrie, Sgt John 188, 190
Lea, Maj Howard 117
Leggett, Dudley 81
Leron River 141, 244–5, 275–6
Loh, Pte William 197
Lord, Sgt Walter Bernard 134

Lovell, Lt Frank Ken 206
Lumb, WO Harry 72–4
Lumbaip 253, 265–7
Lyon, Capt Hugh 4, 16, 18, 20
Lyon, Capt Leo 195, 197

MacAdie, Lt Col Fergus 54, 56, 79
MacArthur, Gen Douglas 21, 30, 104
  and Blamey 19, 31–2, 103, 124, 137
  and Kenney 30–1, 87, 128, 167
  role in Lae plan 109, 128, 130, 242
  strategy 101–2, 105, 141–2, 273–5
McBarron, Sig Len 16
McCallum, WO Bill 201
McDonald, Cpl Ken 'Alf' 253
MacDougal, Capt Dave 177–8, 219–21
MacGregor, Sgt Alex 199
MacIlwain, Sgt Robert 268
Mackay, Lt Gen Iven 84, 102
McLay, Capt Andrew 240–1
McLeod, Lt John 60
Macrae, Lt Don 215, 239
McRae, Maj Eric 152, 188–90
Madang 41, 58–9, 69, 102, 233, 273
  airfield 4, 15, 49, 83, 97, 150
Malahang 12, 202–3
Maley, Cpl John 80
Maloney, Cpl Pat 221
Mannion, Pte Frank 233
Marien, Bill 224
Marilinan 52, 56, 85–91, 125, 165
Markham, Pte Ken 231
Markham Point 18, 48, 53, 167, 275
  attack on 180–6, 223–4
Markham River 11, 123–4, 140
  crossing of 20, 67, 75–6, 169–71
Markham Valley 4, 57–60, 65–70, 74–6, 233–4, 244–5, 264, 272
Marshall, Cpl Doug 173–4
Marshall, Capt Eric 175
Marson, Lt Col Richard 209, 212, 214, 226, 239–40
Marston, Lt Col Robert 87–8, 90, 93
Matthews, Pte Les 26
May, Cpl Neville 197
Mayne, Sgt Robert 16
Melanpipi 235, 262

Index

Merire, Cpl 77–80
Milbourne, Sgt James 138, 243
Miles, Pte Norm 230–1
Milford, Maj Gen Edward 180
Miller-Randle, FO Alex 168, 240–1
Mills, Rfn Bernard 18
Milne Bay 28, 31, 103–4, 109–16, 121–2, 142–5, 203, 206
Mindjim River 76–7
Mollard, Maj Keith 195, 197–8, 228
Monfries, L Cpl Robert 15
Monk, L Cpl Ken 79
Morey, Lt Stan 189
Mori, Rear Adm Kunizo 180, 238, 242
Morobe 41–3, 104, 109–10, 120–1, 150, 158, 161–2, 207
Morris, Maj Gen Basil 14
Morshead, Maj Gen Leslie 113–14
Moten, Brig Murray 31–2
Mount Lunamun 14, 140, 227–8
Mount Bangeta 64–5, 267
Mukai, Maj Masatake 179–80
Munum 15–16, 27, 211
Murphy, Capt John 58–9
Murray-Smith, Pte Stephen 20–8
Murtagh, Rfn Rae 'Bill' 16
Musgrave, Pte Bill 175–6
Musom 239, 247–8, 270

Nadzab 11, 15, 27–9, 52, 209–11
 airfield build 171–2, 178–80, 226
 landing at 165–70
 plan to capture 30–3, 115, 123–42
Nakai, Maj Gen Masutaro 245–6
Nakano, Lt Gen Hidemitsu 39, 66
 and Lae retreat 233–4, 250, 257
 Lae strategy 48, 50–1, 112, 164
Narakapor 22, 29, 211
Nassau Bay 109, 150, 154, 275
New Britain 6, 38–42, 45–6, 102, 273
Ngasawapum 15–16, 29, 73, 211
Noblett, Lt Keith 17
Norman, Lt Col Colin Hugh 194–200

Ofofragen 70, 72
Operation Chronicle 111–12, 120, 139

Operation Postern 102–3, 112–15, 123, 126–8, 165, 180, 268–9
Oro Bay 104, 109, 115, 125, 207, 225

Palmer, Pte James 217
Pato 68, 73
Pearson, Lt John 134–5, 168–9
Pepper, Sgt Norman 222
Phillips, Lt Bob 14–17, 22, 25, 27
Phillips, Pte Robert 159–60
Pike, Capt Philip 144
Pitos, Cpl James 232
Port Moresby 4–5, 9–11, 97, 123–37, 172, 178, 240–4
Purcell, Cpl Frank 15–16
Pursehouse, Capt Lloyd 1–2

Rabaul 5–10, 36, 40–9, 62, 83, 141, 158, 173, 276
Rae, Pte Jim 160
Ramsden, Pte Tom 216
Ramu Valley 54, 57–9, 69–72, 76–9, 244–6, 264, 273
Riccalton, Pte James 217
Richards, Cpl Billy 214–17
Robertson, Lt Col Bill 128–9, 271
Robertson, Maj Campbell 219
Robinson, Lt Edward 85
Robinson, Padre John 223
Robson, Lt Col Ewan 212, 221–2
Rogers, Brig John 112
Rolf, Lt Robert 152
Rooke, Lt Peter 195
Rouse, Rfn John 16
Rowe, Pte Lisle 222
Royal Australian Air Force 4, 7, 36
 No. 4 Sqn 99, 127, 154
 No. 22 Sqn 163
 No. 75 Sqn 9–10
 No. 100 Sqn 163
Royal Australian Navy 103–4
Rutherford, Sgt John 178–9
Ryan, WO Peter 59–61, 65–9, 73–6, 85
Ryland, Capt Chris 221

Saidor 142, 273
Salamaua
 Allied plans for 84, 112–13

Index

Japanese strategy 48-52, 164
Japanese strength 18, 35, 39, 53
Samanzing 60, 68, 268
Sanananda 32-3, 114, 203
Sanem River 238, 257, 260, 266-8
Sangan 58, 72, 245
Sankwep River 60, 229, 233
Saruwaged Range 60-70, 73-5, 233-5, 254-9, 262, 273
Sato, Hiromasu 252, 254-5, 261-2
Savage, Rfn James 17
Savige, Maj Gen Stan 88-9
Sawers, Cpl Stuart 214-15
Sawyer, Lt Sidney 221
Schram, Cpl Alan 188-9
Scott, Pte Alfred 222
Scott, Lt Jack 223
Searle, Lt Col Bertram 156
Seddon, Capt Reg 172-5
Shattock, Lt Edmond 193
Shaw, Lt John 219
Sheldrick, Cpl Dudley 231
Shepherd, Capt Eric 27-8
Shields, Flt Lt Percy 45
Sidney, L Cpl Doug 231
Singaua Plantation 118, 188-92
Sio 41, 142, 235, 247-8, 263, 273
Smith, Cpl Frank 175
Smith, Lt Col George 181-2
Solin, Pte Edwin 23-4
Solomon Islands 83, 102, 112
Staley, Flt Lt Eric 241
Staples, Lt Walter 231
Stewart, Lt Alistair 118
Stokes, Lt Bill 211
Strickland, Pte Walter 23-4
Stringfellow, Lt Keith 20-1, 27
Sullivan, Pte John 184
Sunshine 9, 11, 20, 140
Sutherland, Lt Gen Richard 30
Swift, Pte Bill 198
Swing, Maj Gen Joseph 277

Talbot, Lt Leslie 87
Tanabe, Capt Yahachi 43-4
Taylor, Cpl Ray 93
Thirlwell, Capt George 'Max' 189

Thomas, Lt Jeffrey 265
Threnoworth, Pte John 198
Timmins, Pte Bob 232
Tolson, Lt Col John 133, 167, 241-2
Townsville 34, 89, 95, 108, 111, 120
Trevaldwyn, Lt David 231
Tsili Tsili 52, 86-100, 125-30, 135-40, 172-3, 178, 240-1, 275
Tuckerman, Capt Vic 149
Tuckey, Lt Phil 12
Tuluvu 38-43, 62, 150, 163
Turner, Sgt Claude 226
Tuskin, Spr Vernon 90

Ulap 64, 235, 262
Underwood, Pte David William 29
United States Army
  2nd ESB 108-10, 114, 117
  503rd PIR 130-3, 165-8, 224, 239, 241, 276-7
  532nd EBSR 108-9, 144, 155-6, 207
  871st Air Eng Bn 88-93, 172, 178
United States Army Air Force 91, 96-8, 126, 173
  troop carriers 33-4, 93, 99, 131, 165
United States Navy 6, 103-7, 205
  7th Amph Force 105, 109, 116, 278

Vasey, Maj Gen George 31, 127-9, 141, 167, 209, 224, 240-6, 273
Veitch, Pte Bruce 231
Vernon, L Cpl Richard 15, 24, 29
Vitiaz Strait 39, 43, 64, 273

Wackett, FO Wilbur 10-11
Wada, Seaman Kiichi 48-9, 151-2
  retreat from Lae 250, 253, 256-61
Walker, Pte James 184-5
Wall, Lt Col Reg 152
Wampit 4, 32, 74, 182
Wampit Valley 59, 140
Wanigela 30-1
Watanabe, Lt Col Sukenobu 254-7
Watson, Lt Derrick 246
Watut River 76, 129, 140, 169-70
Watut Valley 85-6, 100, 139
Watute 60, 68, 73

Index

Wau 2, 5, 20, 30-3, 59, 123-7, 275
  Japanese attack on 36, 54, 61, 88
Weitemeyer, Lt Henry 218-19
Wells, Pte Harry 114-15, 147-51, 192
Wesa 57, 78-9
Weston, Merv 156, 168, 191, 218, 222
Wewak 38, 40, 42, 69, 142, 273, 276
  airfields at 49-51, 82-4, 91-2, 150
  air attacks on 95-100
Wharton, Rfn George 12
Whitehead, Brig David 114, 191-4, 201-2, 206-7
Whitehead, Maj Gen Ennis 30, 56, 78, 87, 127-9, 138, 141
Whitelaw, Capt Sydney 265
Whittaker, Capt George 29
Whittaker's Plantation 17, 212-18
Whittle, Pte Ivan 173-4
Wills, Col Ken 241
Wilsher, Cpl Fred 24, 26
Wilson, Pte Alec 198

Wilson, Gunner David 168
Wilson, Pte Herbert 185
Windeyer, Brig William J. Victor 149, 157, 191, 272
Winning, Capt Norm 22
Woodbury, Lt Col Harry 88-9, 172
Woodlark Island 101, 111, 120
Woollacott, Flt Lt Roy 163
Wootten, Maj Gen George 113-19, 141, 146, 149, 194, 203-8, 272
Wurtsmith, Brig Gen Paul 56, 86
Wylie, Lt Mal 20-8

Yalu 15, 66, 133, 209-12, 239, 269
Yamamura, Cpl Mokato 217-18
Yanagawa, Maj Gen Shinichi 69-70
Yaula 69, 76, 78
Yokopi 69, 76-7
Yonekura, Maj Tsuneo 245-6
Yoshihara, Lt Gen Kane 41-3, 83, 150, 169, 179, 210, 234-7, 256, 262
Young, Lt Maurie 183, 185-6